ESTEEM BUILDERS
COMPLETE PROGRAM

HOME ESTEEM BUILDERS

- **Activities Designed to Strengthen the Partnership Between the Home and School**

Dr. Michele Borba

J

JALMAR PRESS

HOME ESTEEM BUILDERS

• Activities Designed to Strengthen the Partnership
Between the Home and School

Published by Jalmar Press

HOME ESTEEM BUILDERS

• Activities Designed to Strengthen the Partnership
Between the Home and School

Author: Michele Borba
Editor: Marie Conte
Project Director: Jeanne Iler
Production and Design: Matthew Lopez and Julia Tempel Olsen
Illustrator: Bob Burchett
Cover Illustration: Luis R. Caughman
Cover Design: Mario A. Artavia II
Typography: Matthew Lopez and Julia Tempel Olsen
Manufactured in the United States of America
First edition printing: 10 9 8 7 6 5 4 3 2 1
ISBN: 1-880390-65-6

> *A comprehensive K-8 program for educators, students, and parents to improve achievement, behavior, and school climate.*

The African proverb, "It takes a whole village to raise a child," is the perfect statement for the setting of my new program — *The Esteem Builders' Complete Program*. Yes, it takes all of us to create this "cycle of success"!

As an educator and parent, I know that there needs to be a program in the schools that reaches out to everyone. Thus the *Esteem Builders' Complete Program* was born. It now consists of **10 components** and over **1,200 activities** all cross-correlated to each grade level and subject area. It took 10 years of research and field testing esteem-building strategies before I was able to have all this information validated.

Another feature of this program is that it is **based on the Five Building Blocks of Self-Esteem: security, selfhood, affiliation, mission and competence.** Research has validated that self-esteem is a KEY factor in improving student behavior and academic achievement. Educators recognize the urgency of these findings and are asking themselves,

> "How do we enhance the self-esteem of students?"

Well, the *Esteem Builders' Complete Program* provides the answer to this question. Now that you have read why we need the program, please turn to the next page and read the description of each component and then see the model flowchart which shows how each component fits into the school and home.

It's an honor to be a member of this profession with you. Together we can make a difference! Let's start, we haven't a moment to lose!

Michele Borba

Michele Borba

ESTEEM BUILDERS' COMPLETE PROGRAM COMPONENTS

The components for this complete program consist of the following materials.

- **Teacher's Guide: ESTEEM BUILDERS: A K-8 Self-Esteem Curriculum for Improving Student Achievement, Behavior, and School Climate**
The program began in 1989 with the publication of *Esteem Builders*. Educators report that this manual has become the self-esteem curriculum of choice for hundreds of districts and thousands of schools in North America. It is being used in pre-schools through middle schools, in public and private settings, in multicultural as well as in special education, and with gifted as well as "at-risk" students. It contains over 250 theory-based and field-tested esteem-building activities **cross-correlated to all subject areas and grade levels.** Hence, with *Esteem Builders* it is possible to include self-esteem activities in the current curriculum.

- **AN OVERVIEW OF THE ESTEEM BUILDERS' COMPLETE PROGRAM**
This book has been prepared to make your job easier. This book contains a comprehensive description of the major elements and their roles in the *Esteem Builders' Complete Program*, as well as Esteem Builder Teams and how they function. The book is designed to assist you in the esteem-building implementation process. Within this book, you'll find invaluable charts, guidelines, and indexes to cross-reference scores of activities and techniques. Unique features of *An Overview of the Esteem Builders' Complete Program* include:

  - **A listing of all icons and abbreviations** used in the program.
  - A **summary of all major program components** of the *Esteem Builders' Complete Program*.
  - A description of the **Esteem Builder Team** including: membership, getting started, functions.
  - A complete **table of contents of all staff development** trainings in esteem enhancement.
  - A listing of all **informal assessments** such as checklists, guideline questions and surveys for your staff, administrators and parents to assess your esteem-building climate, a student-self-esteem assessment chart for each feeling, and a checklist of educator behaviors that promote each feeling, as well as suggested sources for the best formal self-esteem assessments to measure student self-esteem.
  - An **extensive index cross-referencing** over 1,000 esteem-building activities by esteem component as well as targeted audience.
  - Assessment tools for evaluating student, administrator, and staff growth in the five building blocks of self-esteem.
  - A comprehensive **description of the major elements and their roles** in the *Esteem Builders' Complete Program* including: the trainer and staff development in esteem enhancement, staff esteem, home esteem building, student esteem building, school-wide esteem enhancement, staff team building, and the esteem builder teams.
  - The **definitions of all major terms** found within the program.

- **ESTEEM BUILDERS RESOURCES**
  - A **bibliography of self-esteem resources** for students, parents, and staff.
  - An extensive list of **current self-esteem research** and statistics validating the need for self-esteem enhancement.
  - A comprehensive **list of agencies, organizations, and resources** available to the school site to aid in the esteem-building process. A summary of each listing, as well as an address, is also included.
  - A **description of school structures** actively being implemented at various sites to enhance self-esteem.

- **TRAINER'S MANUAL**
The key to establishing an ongoing and enthusiastic self-esteem program is having a trainer within the district or school. Using *Esteem Builders* as the text, the *Trainer's Manual* details the esteem-building premises in "ready-to-present" units. The manual provides the trainer with materials and 18 hours of scripts for training the staff in esteem-building development. Everything is provided for the trainer to ensure a successful program—all that is needed is the audience.

- **Audiocassette Program: THE FIVE BUILDING BLOCKS OF SELF-ESTEEM**
Consists of six tapes each 30+ minutes. Dr. Borba begins with her live keynote address *"You Are the*

ESTEEM BUILDERS' COMPLETE PROGRAM COMPONENTS

Door-Opener to a Child's Self-Esteem: Five Critical Keys." She then continues to lead the trainer and educator into an understanding of the five building blocks of self-esteem. A specially designed workbook that builds and reinforces the material is included. The tapes are delightfully narrated with special music created for your easy listening!

- **STAFF ESTEEM BUILDERS**
Research substantiates that the most neglected area of educational reform is improving the esteem and relationships of the very individuals who can be the most powerful sources of students' lives—the staff. This is the administrator's bible for enhancing staff esteem. Dozens of theory-based activities are presented to build staff self-esteem, affiliation, and cohesiveness. Surveys are available to assess current staff strengths and weaknesses. A complete guide as well as scores of activities are provided for team building, staff, and shared decision-making. In addition, a complete guide to successful team building is provided along with scores of activities and administrator ideas to improve the process. Finally, "the how-to's" toward improving staff relationships, collegiateness, communication, and shared decision-making are offered.

- **HOME ESTEEM BUILDERS**
Educators are provided with a variety of activities designed to strengthen the partnership between home and school, and to help parents in their home esteem-building endeavors. Included in this manual are 40 home esteem-building activities, 13 parent newsletters, a complete script for a parent in-service, and plans for school-wide events for parents. In addition, the manual contains dozens of techniques to enhance communication between the home and school, and handouts with esteem-building tips for educators to provide parents with during conferences.

- **ESTEEM BUILDER POSTERS**
Eight posters featuring important esteem-building principles can be hung in the classroom, faculty room, training session room, or home to serve as visual reminders to everyone involved in the esteem-building process.

    1. *Teachers Make Differences!*
    2. *Five Building Blocks*
    3. *Esteem Builders' Implementation Model*
    4. *Brainstorming Rules*
    5. *Goal-Setting Steps*
    6. *Sparkle Statements*
    7. *Esteem Builder Thoughts*
    8. *Conflict Solving*

- **SPARKY BUILDERS' KIT***
Sparky the Puppet, a hand puppet for primary-aged children, provides another means of reinforcing the use of positive statements through storytelling and drama. Scripted activity cards (30) provided on 5 ¹/₂"x 8 ¹/₂" cards are bound together for easy teacher use. Each card features a puppet script or a student activity to increase classroom positivism and climate. Included in the kit is the Sparkle poster filled with positive statements they can say to each other.

- Videocassette: **ESTEEM BUILDERS IN ACTION***
This video demonstrates how schools across North America have incorporated the activities and principles of Esteem Builders at their unique sites. By visiting esteem-building schools, viewers can see the impact of the program on children as well as its ease of implementation. This video is meant to be used with school board members and district administrators to help them select self-esteem as a key priority for their schools.

* Not part of the School Kit — sold separately.

ESTEEM BUILDERS' IMPLEMENTATION MODEL ©

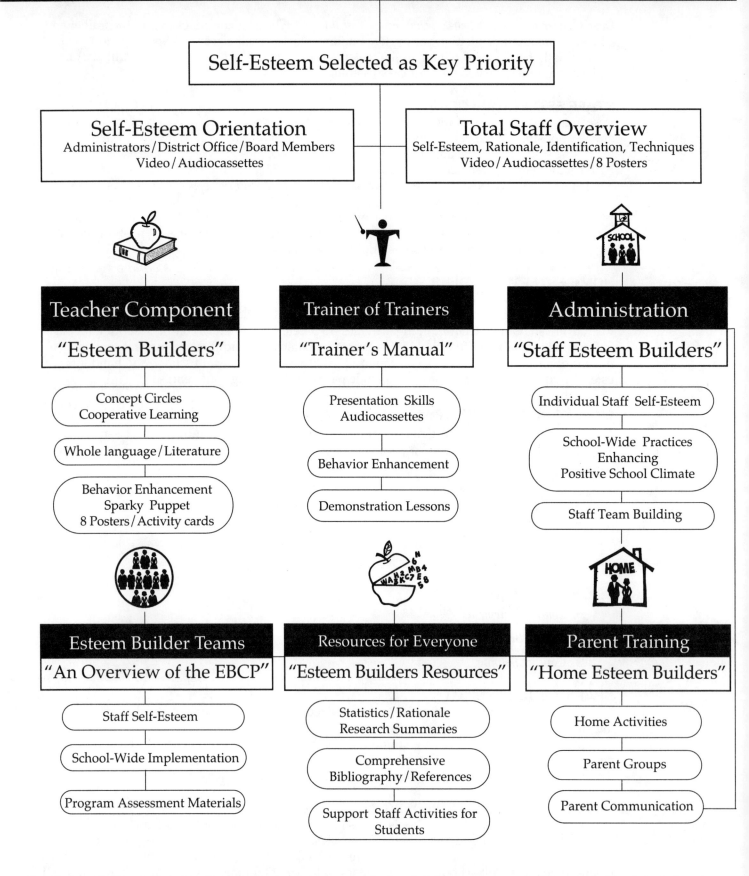

Self-Esteem Selected as Key Priority

Self-Esteem Orientation
Administrators / District Office / Board Members
Video / Audiocassettes

Total Staff Overview
Self-Esteem, Rationale, Identification, Techniques
Video / Audiocassettes / 8 Posters

Teacher Component
"Esteem Builders"

- Concept Circles
  Cooperative Learning
- Whole language / Literature
- Behavior Enhancement
  Sparky Puppet
  8 Posters / Activity cards

Trainer of Trainers
"Trainer's Manual"

- Presentation Skills
  Audiocassettes
- Behavior Enhancement
- Demonstration Lessons

Administration
"Staff Esteem Builders"

- Individual Staff Self-Esteem
- School-Wide Practices
  Enhancing
  Positive School Climate
- Staff Team Building

Esteem Builder Teams
"An Overview of the EBCP"

- Staff Self-Esteem
- School-Wide Implementation
- Program Assessment Materials

Resources for Everyone
"Esteem Builders Resources"

- Statistics / Rationale
  Research Summaries
- Comprehensive
  Bibliography / References
- Support Staff Activities for
  Students

Parent Training
"Home Esteem Builders"

- Home Activities
- Parent Groups
- Parent Communication

The **Esteem Builders' Complete Program** is founded on **researched and field-tested** esteem-building strategies. It is designed to include all aspects of the school, home, and community, with special attention to the "at-risk" student. It is based on the recognition that everyone who touches the life of a child must be involved in the enhancement process.

ESTEEM BUILDERS' COMPLETE PROGRAM ©

What Educators Say About Dr. Borba

"We have seen many changes—all positive—as a result of using Dr. Borba's materials, including higher test scores and fewer discipline problems. Students are taking responsibility for their actions and are problem-solving on their own. Children are beginning to parent their parents."

— Nancy Kong, Self-Esteem Coordinator
San Jose, California

"Our teachers are trained in understanding the components of self-esteem and use any activities from [Borba's] Esteem Builders that fit into the curriculum. The parent program is the next step in our self-esteem plan. Home Esteem Builders will enable us to tie our existing parenting programs into the self-esteem model."

— Cliff Gordon, Director Psychological Services
Tulare, California

"Children are better able to express their feelings and needs; they have become more verbal in the classroom setting as a result of taking part in the [Borba] self-esteem activities. In addition, the activities have raised my (teacher) self-esteem as well as helped me to be a better parent to my children."

— Beatriz Jordan, Program Specialist
Miami, Florida

"Parent workshops on [Borba's] esteem-building techniques are offered in each of our fifty schools. Also, many schools are sending home esteem-building activities to be done as a family. There appears to be a much clearer belief in and focus on kids."

— Dave Schlei, Consultant
Kitchener, Ontario, Canada

"If it's true—and I believe it is—that self-esteem in children is most influenced by their parent(s), then the adult we need to focus on first is the parent. Home Esteem Builders by Dr. Borba does what all self-esteem programs should do: it focuses on the adults that have the most influence on a child's life. Children are the obvious recipients."

— Bill Holley, Social Worker
Orland Park, Illinois

"Dr. Michele Borba's visit to our community was so exciting and informative. I feel I could put into action many ideas for our family. She is very dynamic, with so much to give!"

— Ann Parker, Parent
Gunnison, Colorado

HOME ESTEEM BUILDERS

- **Activities Designed to Strengthen the Partnership Between the Home and School**

Dr. Michele Borba

JALMAR PRESS
ROLLING HILLS ESTATES
C A L I F O R N I A

Dedication

This book is dedicated with gratitude, respect, and love to my parents, Dan and Treva Ungaro. As my first esteem builders, they've always been my greatest cheerleaders, teaching me to believe in myself. And now that I'm a parent, they've become my best models of esteem building for my own children. They just instinctively knew how to do it all along.

Table of Contents

Chapter 5: Home Esteem-Builder Activities

Chapter 6: Prescriptive Home-Esteem Building **243**

Chapter 6: Prescriptive Home-Esteem Building

Home Esteem Builders was developed on the premise that a home and school partnership is an integral element of effective esteem building. The material in this book provides educators with the resources to help parents enhance their children's self-esteem. Before distributing any of these materials to the students' homes, please make sure that they have been translated into the primary language of the parents.

Preface

My strong feelings toward parenting evolved slowly from my own experiences as a special education teacher. Though trained by some of the best teaching instructors in the country, I found I was rarely able to use my instructional skills with the students. Instead of teaching, I found myself more often being caught up in two quite different kinds of roles: either behavior management technician or counselor—or both. If I wasn't interrupting my lesson plans to intervene in a behavior dispute, I was wearing the hat of "amateur counselor" and trying to persuade students that they could indeed do an activity if they'd just give it a try.

While brewing over my dilemma in the faculty room one afternoon, I came upon an article in an educational journal that described the correlation between how students feel about themselves (their self-esteem), and their academic performance and behavior. I can still hear myself saying, "Aha, that's it!" From that moment on, my goal was to improve the self-esteem of my students so that, in the process, their learning and behavior would improve. I began to develop techniques and materials for enhancing students' self-esteem, many of which went on to be published. I recognized that the esteem-building techniques I was using had a definite impact on my students' self-images...they were improving...and along with an enhancement of their self-esteem came improvements in their academic progress.

I also recognized that I had those students only five hours a day. Everything I did during those five hours to improve their self-esteem was working while they were with me. What I had to come to grips with was the unmistakable fact that when they left me they went on to other significant persons in their lives, who were also impacting their self-esteem. More often than not the impact was negative. That was the first moment I realized that, to have the greatest positive impact on my students' self-esteem, I had to involve the parents in the process. The key question was, "But how?"

I began by calling each parent personally and asking one question: "If I could teach you something that would help your child, what would you like to learn?" The results were fascinating. All different topics emerged from math to printing to study skills. Despite these seeming differences, parents all had one notion in common: they wanted to help their children succeed. I knew they would be interested in self-esteem enhancement as a way to achieve this result. The next question I had to ask myself was, "How do I best reach them with the concepts?" I promised myself I wouldn't be tied into the traditional 7 to 8 o'clock evening in-service session. Instead, I would seek more non-traditional alternatives. One month I tried a "Make-and-Take" Session on a Saturday morning where parents and children together could create activities to enhance their children's self-esteem. They loved it. The next month I tried after-school sessions focusing on a different topic every other week. I found that only a few parents could attend, but those few that did appreciated the information.

The following month I again asked the question, "How can I help?" and received an interesting answer from a large group of parents. "Can you please talk to the children's siblings? They don't understand why their brother or sister is acting so differently and it's causing a lot of family problems." That month the session was for all the brothers and sisters of my students. The youngest sibling was five and the oldest participant was eighteen. The parents all reported that marked changes happened in their families once the brothers and sisters knew what they could do to help their troubled sibling.

One session was particularly interesting. I realized that every parenting session I had had so far was held at the school site. Though the parents were coming, I often noticed that they were unable to relax during the session. It was always as though they were on guard and a bit tense. That was when I decided to find a parent who would be willing to hold a session at his or her home. I found such a parent and we had the most successful parenting meeting ever. Parents were much more relaxed and open with one another, as well as with me, during the time we spent together. From then on, each succeeding meeting was held at a nearby parent's home.

I learned a lot from those parents. They reaffirmed my feeling that they did indeed want to help their children learn. They helped me learn that I had to extend my thinking beyond the "let's hold an evening in-service to help you learn to help your child" concept. If I wanted parents to attend parent sessions, I had to first identify their needs and concerns and then find specific ways to meet them. I learned that just because parents don't show up at one parent gathering does not mean they aren't interested. I learned not to give up but to try different alternatives to parent education.

And, finally, I learned probably the most important premise that's guided the development of *Home Esteem Builders,* that is: that educators can help parents in improving and enhancing the self-esteem of their students. Not only did the esteem-building activities help the parents but they helped me in the classroom with my students. Working together we *did* make a difference! This manual is devoted to that joint teacher-parent effort to continue making a difference.

Michele Borba
Palm Springs, California

The Case for Home Esteem Building

From the vantage of recent studies in building self-esteem it seems that a partnership between parents and schools is not only desirable but also necessary if the child's self-esteem is to be maintained at a positive level.

—DR. STANLEY COOPERSMITH

The first day of kindergarten is a milestone in the lives of children. It's a day when they begin to look ahead toward independence in a new environment. Their lives will be touched by a myriad of people of varying roles and ages who, by their very existence, will help them form an answer to the famous "Who am I?" question. Teachers, counselors, coaches, principals, custodians, peers, secretaries, cafeteria workers, bus drivers, aides, and yard duty workers (to name just a few) will assume new positions with varying levels of influence in the student's mind. Parents and family will no longer be the only primary persons in the child's life. If these new significant others consider and treat the child as a worthwhile and important human being, and are in turn seen as worthwhile by the child, they will help him/her develop a more positive sense of self-esteem.

Though new sources of self-esteem enhancement (or deterioration) emerge for the student the moment he/she steps off the school bus, the most important esteem builders for the student remain unchanged. As soon as the bus returns the child to his/her home, the first esteem builders of his/her life (the parents) once again become primary.

Though research conclusively demonstrates that teachers can create opportunities for life-changing experiences for their students, parents clearly are their children's first esteem builders. Their impact on the development of their child's self-esteem is unquestionably far-reaching and long-lasting. It is therefore almost pointless to discuss strategies for fostering the self-esteem of students unless the continuing impact of the parents on their child's development in this regard is also addressed.

PARENTAL CONCERN

Most educators instinctively recognize the premise that the home cannot be separated from the students' learning process. However, they become frustrated when attempting to include the parents. More often than not, though the school has gone to elaborate efforts to offer a parent in-service in esteem building or other topics, the parent turnout for such events is generally low. All too often the response to holding another event is, "Why try? Parents just aren't interested in their children's learning these days, or they just don't have the time." Stop if you ever hear yourself saying those words; this assumption could never be further from the truth. I strongly believe that now, more than ever, parents desperately want to know what to do to help their children. The enormous increase in the sale of "how to help your child" books should be justification enough. Parents are buying them in record numbers. Every other article in home-oriented magazines focuses on some kind of "parenting tip" concept "to help your child succeed." It's a very rare parent who doesn't want to give his/her heart and soul to help his/her child.

Perhaps what educators need to do is stop and analyze why the parents didn't come to the in-service they worked so hard to present. One of the biggest reasons revolves around a four-letter word that plagues everyone: T-I-M-E. Educators need to stop and ask themselves some very serious and pertinent questions, starting with, "Is what we are offering relevant to parents?" and another golden question, "Are we offering the program at a time when parents can attend?"

Think for a moment about how the family has changed. All the statistics tell us that the June Cleaver era of the two parent/two children "all living under the same roof" family is definitely passed. June is just not there today with the milk and cookies when Beaver comes home from school. In the majority of cases, June is now an active member of the workforce. Beaver, in most cases, is coming home from school with a key around his neck to a house that will be empty for the next few hours. Dad, according to the latest census statistics, is probably not living in the home because he and June are divorced.

When June does come home, she's exhausted. But she's still expected, after working eight to ten hours, to instantly put a meal on the table, help Beaver with his homework, and then freshen up with new makeup to hurry to the evening parent meeting. If Dad is a member-in-residence, the same scenario applies to him. He must quickly run off to pick up the babysitter so that Beaver has child care during the two hours Mom and Dad are gone for "parent education." Never before has there been a time when the school needs to do so much creative planning around the theme, "How do we increase parent involvement?" I contend that the interest is there. Maybe the concepts have just been presented to the parents in an inappropriate and inconvenient manner.

My own work is based on the following three premises:

1. That parents do desperately care about their children and do want to be an integral part of the entire learning process that takes place at school, including the building of self-esteem.

2. That the most effective enhancement of students' self-esteem takes place when the parents are actively involved with the school in the process. Together the home and school can make significant differences in esteem building for students.

3. That most parents want to become active partners with the school in the enhancement of their children's esteem:

   • Do they clearly understand how building self-esteem can directly help their children's school achievement, behavior, and chances for success in life (no one should ever *buy into* a program unless he/she understands the rationale behind the program)?

   • Are specific, practical strategies for esteem enhancement offered that parents can use at home?

   • Are the programs for parent education offered at a more convenient and accessible time? As educators we must begin reeducating ourselves on not only the value of parent education but also why parents have stopped coming to the schools. Too often, we've simply blamed the parents.

   • Do they understand that they *can* make a difference in the self-esteem of their children (and they can since that self-esteem is learned and changeable)?

The above notions are an important place for us to begin our further discussions.

EDUCATING PARENTS

Parent education in a student esteem-building program is both desirable and effective. When parents are taught practical strategies to improve their children's self-images, the impact is felt not only in the home but also in the classroom.

Educators' efforts to build the self-esteem of students in their classrooms become even more effective when parents are reinforcing the same strategies with their children at home. Working together as partners in esteem building, parents and teachers can make a difference on the students' self-esteem.

Too many students arrive at school doors devoid of the experience in the building blocks needed to develop self-esteem. Research confirms that these building blocks are **Security, Selfhood, Affiliation, Mission** and **Competence**. In all too many cases, the absence of these crucial self-esteem building blocks creates a downward spiral of low self-worth. The student with poor self-esteem then becomes another tragic social statistic. The good news, however, is that this cycle need not continue its downward plunge, for the following reasons:

- **Self-esteem can be changed, regardless of age.**

- **Self-esteem is learned; therefore, it can be taught.**

- **Parents can become an integral part of the esteem-building process if the school uses innovative planning to increase parent involvement.**

The Case for Home Esteem Building

There are at least ten good reasons why schools should commit wholeheartedly to involving parents in home esteem building:

1. **There is a clear and urgent need.** Statistics blatantly tell us of the plight of American students. Suicide, pregnancy, substance abuse, dropping out and underachievement are all trends that continue to plague our youth. All indicators project that this trend is not temporary nor is it expected to reverse. The tragic news is that research clearly points to the continued emotional destruction of our greatest resource: our children.

2. **Prevention is better than intervention.** There is an old proverb that says, "An ounce of prevention is worth a pound of cure." The idea has a great deal of validity in regard to home esteem building. Waiting to begin self-esteem programs at the high school level is ludicrous. The sooner educators begin an intervention program, the more successful the results will be. How much more powerful an esteem-building program would be if we didn't have to intervene at all! The most effective technique for curtailing any problem is to prevent it from happening at all. A home esteem-building program is not only effective for students but at the same time teaches parents life skills they can use with their children who are not yet of school age (or even born!).

3. **There is broad-based growing support for parent involvement in the school setting.** Throughout *Home Esteem Builders,* I have continuously cited educational studies clearly supporting parent involvement. The latest Gallup polls surveying both parents and educators point out the shared interest that exists in more ongoing, active parent involvement. The desire is there.

4. **Self-esteem can be taught and changed.** Research verifies that students are not born with high and healthy self-esteem. Self-perceptions are instead acquired and learned. This premise is the basis for esteem building and why parents must be involved in the process. Students are constantly learning new information about themselves that they store to form self-evaluations. Teachers and parents can be trained to learn how to best enhance student self-esteem and create the conditions that most effectively build it.

5. **Parents' attitudes influence self-esteem.** The significance of parents' attitudes toward their children can never be underestimated. Coopersmith's work has shown that while children's self-esteem is not related to family wealth, education, social class, parents' occupations, geographic living area, or

always having mother at home, what is significant is the quality of the relationship that exists between children and the significant adults in their lives.[1] While educators do not have control over parental attitudes, they can be instrumental in helping parents recognize how critical their attitude is to the level of their children's self-esteem.

6. **Working together is more effective than working alone.** Reframing students' self-images is not an overnight process. It takes both time and consistency on the part of esteem builders to help children see themselves in a more positive light. It is obvious that the esteem-building process would be so much more effective if teachers and parents worked collaboratively to reinforce the same techniques at home and at school.

7. **Parents can be valuable resources for teachers.** Taking the time and energy to enhance the home and school connection is beneficial to both parties. Parents are much more likely to feel positive and support school issues when they perceive they are being treated respectfully by the school. Relationships based on frequent contact are more solid. Both parties are more likely to feel comfortable contacting one another regarding students' negative behavior or achievement. Both parties are more likely to pull together and work together to jointly benefit the students.

8. **Parents want to know how to help their children.** A premise that accompanies the role of parenthood is that parents almost universally want their children to be successful and happy. The greatest obstacle standing in the way of parents' effectiveness in esteem building is that they've never been taught the skills to enhance their children's self-esteem. Repeated surveys of parents as cited in this book verify that parents do want educators to help them in their quest.

9. **Educators can teach parents esteem-building principles.** There is probably no agency better equipped to teach parents esteem-building principles than the school. The school has the facilities to hold parenting education classes, all the needed supplies and materials are at beck and call, the esteem-building techniques are available, and most importantly, the clients are known. The twenty-first century will bring about a revolution in education. A key change in this revolution will be the development of ongoing programs for parents such as day care and parenting education.

10. **By using appropriate esteem-building premises, parents can enhance their children's self-esteem.** The final point is probably the most important point in the case for a home esteem-building program: educators can teach parents esteem-building principles that will directly enhance their children's self-esteem. The case for schools to create a home esteem-building program is too strong to ignore. Perhaps the most important point for home esteem building is the most obvious: the program will directly impact the lives of students by creating opportunities for the development of more positive and healthier self-esteem.

Does Home Esteem Building Make A Difference?

The development of a parent-teacher partnership is certainly attracting the interest of educators. Asking if such a partnership will aid teachers in similar esteem-building efforts in the classrooms is a valid question. One of the most significant studies directed at helping parents improve their children's self-esteem was conducted over two decades ago by Brookover and his associates. Working with approximately fifty low-achieving ninth-graders, these researchers developed three types of experimental programs to impact students' self-concept and achievement. They wanted

---

1. Coopersmith, Stanley. *The Antecedents of Self-Esteem.* San Francisco, CA: W.H. Freeman & Co., 1967.

to find out which technique would have the greatest impact on students' self-images.

One method involved working with parents as a group for a one-year period to raise parents' academic expectations and evaluations of their children. During group meetings, researchers discussed a variety of topics with the parents in order to assist them in helping their children to develop more effectively. The parents were specifically told not to regard or reinforce any negative statements their children might make about their academic ability. Instead the parents were asked to constantly remind their children that they were capable as students and ought to be better in school. Parents were also told to reward students with commendatory remarks and support any positive statements they made about their school ability. The second method involved having students work with counselors. The third method paired students with university "experts." In the second and third methods, counselors and university experts attempted to convey information on self-esteem and achievement enhancement directly to the students.

Brookover and his colleagues found that parents who participated in the group sessions were able to induce significant positive changes in their children's self-perceptions and perceptions of ability to achieve academically. At the end of a year, the study reported that the parent strategy was the only one of the three methods which was successful in increasing the academic self-concept and achievement of the students. Brookover suggests "a key to the success of the strategy may have been telling parents in the beginning that they were, in part, responsible for their children's low academic self-concepts and that they could be instrumental in changing them. Whatever the key may be, this study demonstrates that parents and teachers can form a partnership which will effectively lead to improved student self-concept. Consequently, these findings should prompt us to begin developing other partnership strategies for working with students."[2]

Research on Parent Partnerships

Considerable research in the past decade confirms the fact that parent partnerships with the school to maximize student learning are an essential element of effective education. This fact can no longer be ignored. A recent NEA poll found that more than ninety percent of teachers, in all parts of the country and at all grade levels, stated that more home-school interaction would be desirable. A nationwide Gallup poll of public attitudes toward education reflects a similar interest. When asked what more the public schools should be doing, a suggestion frequently cited was "closer teacher-parent relationships." Interestingly enough, parents shared the same position. Eighty percent of parents with school-age children agreed with the idea of parents attending school one evening a month to learn how to improve children's behavior and interest in school work.[3] In reviewing the survey findings taken from over a ten-year period, Gallup concluded:

"A careful examination of survey findings for the past 10-year period leads to this conclusion: Many of the problems of the schools can be solved only if parents become more involved than they presently are in the educational process. Parents must, in fact, be regarded as part of the teaching team. A joint effort by parents and teachers is essential to deal more successfully with problems of discipline, motivation, and the development of good work habits at home and in school." The Gallup findings further stated, *"For little added expense (which the public is willing to pay) the public schools can, by working with parents, meet educational standards impossible to reach without such cooperation."*

The Gallup poll is just one of many studies reaching the conclusion that a parent-school partnership is not only plausible but essential. A host of research, in fact, validates the rationale for forming active home-school partnerships. Consider the following findings:

2. Brookover, W.D., T. Sailor, and A. Paterson. "Self-Concept of Ability and School Achievement." *Sociology of Education,* 1964, 37: 271-278.

3. Gallup, G.H. *The 10th Annual Gallup Poll of the Public's Attitudes Toward the Public Schools.* Phi Delta Kappan, 1978: 33-45.

- An extensive and rigorous review of forty-eight studies of educational programs with parent involvement found that the fuller the participation of parents, the more effective were the results obtained.[4]

- Bronfenbrenner, in a review of a variety of early intervention programs, concluded that the active involvement of the family is critical to program success. Family-school involvement reinforces and helps sustain the effects of school programs.[5]

- A Phi Delta Kappa review of a number of studies pointed to the benefits of parent involvement.[6]

- In a review of parent involvement studies, Henderson stated, "Taken together, what is most interesting about the research is that it all points in the same direction. The form of parent involvement does not seem to be critical, so long as it is reasonably well-planned, comprehensive, and long-lasting."[7]

Several studies have investigated the feasibility of educators training parents in skills of self-enhancement. One study analyzed several different designs and found that the one having the most significant impact on increasing student self-esteem was the one which involved working with parents over a one-year period.[8] In weekly meetings conducted by an educator, parents participated in group discussions presenting various topics related to self-esteem. Strikingly significant results followed. Brookover's work demonstrated that the school can enhance not only achievement gains in low-achieving students but also improve their self-esteem by conducting

structured, consistent, and planned parent-education programs.

ON TO SOLUTIONS

The evidence supports the following conclusions: that parents are concerned about the level of their children's self-esteem, that parent education in a student esteem-building program is both desirable and effective, and that parent partnerships work. So the real question is, "How do we get parents to participate in implementing esteem-building principles?"

Just consider how much more powerful the school esteem-enhancing program would be if the parents would use the same principles with their children at home! Thus was born *Home Esteem Builders* for those schools seeking to achieve the strongest esteem-enhancement program possible through a solid parent-school partnership. The book contains dozens of techniques, all designed to help educators teach parents how to enhance the self-esteem of their children.

Educators are provided with forty weekly take-home activities designed to enhance the five building blocks of self-esteem and with preprinted newsletters that teach parents the essentials of the esteem-building process. Other features include a complete script for a parent in-service. Dozens of specific ways to enhance communication between home and school are provided. Directions are also provided for a Make-and-Take Session in which parents create esteem-building activities for use at home.

As one principal, Percy W. Jenkins, aptly stated,

---

4. Leler, Hazel. "Parent Education and Involvement in Relation to the Schools and to Parents of School-Aged Children." Ron Haskins and Diane Addams (eds.), *Parent Education and Public Policy,* ABLEX Publishing Co., Norwood, NJ, 1983.

5. Bronfenbrenner, Urie. *Is Early Intervention Effective? A Report on Longitudinal Evaluations of Preschool Programs,* Vol. II. Department of Health, Education and Welfare, Washington D.C., 1974.

6. Phi Delta Kappa. Why Do some Schools Succeed? *The Phi Delta Kappa Study of Exceptional Urban Elementary Schools.* Phi Delta Kappa, Bloomington, IN, 1980.

7. Henderson, A. *Parent Participation—Student Achievement: The Evidence Grows.* National Committee for Citizens in Education, Columbia, MD, 1981.

8. Brookover, W.B., et al. *Self-Concept of Ability and School Achievement II: Improving Academic Achievement Through Students' Self-Concept Enhancement.* U.S. Office of Education, Cooperative Research Project No. 1636. Michigan State University, Office of Research and Publications, Lansing, MI, 1965.

"The role of the parent in the development of the child's self-concept and motivation is vital. The school, through parent-education programs, can make parents aware of their roles in these areas and can assist them in developing techniques for the improvement of self-concept."[9] This is the very premise that *Home Esteem Builders* is built upon. Together parents and teachers can make noticeable differences in children's self-esteem.

Home Esteem Builders was developed on the premise that a home and school partnership is an integral element of effective esteem building. The material in this book provides educators with the resources to help parents enhance their children's self-esteem. Before distributing any of these materials to the students' homes, please make sure that they have been translated into the primary language of the parents.

9. Jenkins, Percy W. "Building Parent Participation in Urban Schools." *Principal Magazine,* November 1981, 22.

1

Home Esteem-Building Climate

HOME ESTEEM BUILDERS

- The Self-Esteem Tryangle
- The Five Components of Self-Esteem
- Characteristics of Effective Home
  Esteem-Building Schools
- The Home Esteem Builders Program
  –Parent Education
  –Home-School Communication
  –Home Esteem-Building Activities
  –Prescriptive Home Esteem Building

1

The Home Esteem-Building Climate

The greatest barrier to achievement and success is not the lack of talent or ability but, rather, the fact that achievement and success, above a certain level, are outside our self-concept, our image of who we are and what is appropriate to us.

—NATHANIEL BRANDEN

THE SELF-ESTEEM TRYANGLE

Within the past decade a revolution in self-esteem has taken place. Schools are seriously viewing self-esteem as important to the educational process in the face of a predominance of research that has reached the same conclusion: the level of a student's self-esteem has a direct impact on his/her level of academic performance. The higher the student's self-esteem, the greater the likelihood that the student will achieve academically. The lower the self-esteem, the less likely the student will aspire to achieve and the less likely he/she will in fact achieve. The promise of enhancing achievement by increasing self-esteem is based on the fact that a student's inner view of self drives his/her outer actions and behaviors. Since there are three elements contributing to an individual's performance, this concept can be described by a triangle.

Selfhood

The first element, Selfhood, consists of all the facts the student has acquired internally about himself/herself. Selfhood can also be called identity or self-concept. These facts include

information about his/her roles, interests, physical characteristics and values. All of these facts make up a student's identity. They help form a student's answer to the all-important "Who am I?" question. Shown here are two different students. Both students have formed certain facts about who they are.

Notice that the students have described merely facts. No evaluation of themselves was involved. This personal identity is called "selfhood." Selfhood may be accurate or inaccurate, clear or confused, but not positive or negative. Selfhood, or self-concept, is all the descriptions a student has formed of himself/herself. The facts the student has acquired may or may not be true in actuality. The critical point is that the facts are perceived by the student to be true and therefore they have become part of his/her sense of Selfhood.

Self-Esteem

These facts form the basis for the second element of the performance triangle: Self-Esteem. From these facts, the student begins to form an opinion of himself/herself and places a value judgment on the selfhood description based largely on how valuable or worthy the individual perceives himself/herself to be.

For example, the student may have attached a description to his/her identity which reads, "I am a student." The degree to which the student is satisfied or dissatisfied in that role is an indication of his/her self-esteem. One student may perceive himself/herself in the role of student as, "I am capable. I try my hardest. I am a good student." Another student may have attached the same descriptive label ("I am a student") but formed quite a different judgment: "I am stupid. I never know the answers. I can't do anything right." Self-esteem is a value judgment. It may be either a positive self-esteem, or a neutral or negative interpretation, but it is always evaluative. As Nathaniel Branden states, "[Self-esteem is] the experience of being competent to cope with the basic challenges of life and being worthy of happiness." The extent to which the individual perceives himself/herself as being capable and worthy determines the extent of his self-esteem. (The overall evaluation of all the descriptions the student has placed on himself/herself is his/her level of self-esteem.) The following graphic shows how two students with similar kinds of self-descriptions can form two very different levels of self-esteem. Here are the same two students who have formed quite different value judgments about themselves based on the overall judgments they've placed on their roles.

OVERALL JUDGEMENT: POSITIVE SELF-ESTEEM

OVERALL JUDGEMENT: NEGATIVE SELF-ESTEEM

These two students have similar kinds of self-descriptive labels but both students have formed markedly different interpretations of who they are. One student has an overall feeling that concludes, "I am mostly happy with who I am," while the second student has formed an overall opinion that cries out, "I don't like myself. For the most part I am not a worthwhile and capable person."

Actions

Though parents and educators may recognize the wonderful strengths, talents, and capabilities students possess, students may have concepts of themselves that do not recognize these assets. All too often a tragedy occurs for our youth: students' self-concepts get in the way of their self-esteem. The inescapable fact is that individuals act according to how they think about themselves. Students with low self-esteem are more likely to act in ways that perpetuate their feelings of unworthiness and incapableness. Their external behaviors and actions are motivated by their inner experiences and self-evaluations. The level and quality of motivation, achievement, and behavior students display are a reflection of the way they view themselves. Henry Ford described this principle when he stated, "Whether you think you can or whether you think you can't, you're right!" Our students' actions are in direct relationship to their feelings about themselves. All three elements of the performance triangle, Self-Concept, Self-Esteem, and Actions, are crucial in improving student achievement and behavior, and must be recognized in helping students to change the view they have of themselves. Together, the elements create what I call a "TRYangle"© because so much of our students' performance is based on the single premise of "whether I think I can."

CHARACTERISTICS OF HIGH ACHIEVERS

What differentiates students with high self-esteem from those with low self-esteem? This is a question so many parents and educators ask themselves. To begin with, these high self-esteem students have an "I can" attitude, and that feeling propels them through life. When high self-esteem students are asked, "What are you good at?" they inevitably are able to tell you their strengths, skills, and assets. They are individuals who have quite an accurate assessment of their capabilities.

High self-esteem students are also able to accept their weaknesses. They just plain admit them: "And here are some things I'm not so good at." What separates these children from low self-esteem students is that they don't devalue themselves for their weaknesses; instead, they just acknowledge them. They recognize their shortcomings and their mistakes but don't dwell on them. They don't spend time in undue self-devaluation because they are able to compensate for

their "down moments" from the reserve of all the positive experiences and strengths they know they have in their lives. As a result, they don't quit or blame others when they do have failing moments. Instead, they stand up, brush off their knees, and try again.

High self-esteem students are "self-starters" and internally motivated. They set goals for themselves, and they don't depend on others to do the work for them or solve any problems they encounter on the way toward their goals. In the end, when they achieve their goals (and generally they do because they don't give up; instead they tailor the strategy toward accomplishing their goals even if something is standing in the way), they acknowledge themselves for their successes. These children don't need the "scratch and sniff sticker" as a reward for reaching their goal. High self-esteem students say to themselves, "I did it!" or "I did a great job!"

There is enormous value in enhancing the self-esteem of students. The benefits of esteem building efforts appear not only in higher student achievement and improved behavior but also in a positive change in classroom climate, as witnessed by countless educators who have seen the results. "The classroom is just a nicer place to be!" they remark. The reasons why the enhancement of students' self-esteem is of value are numerous:

- The higher the students' self-esteem, the better able they are to concentrate on learning. All of their energy and attention can be focused on the task at hand. Low self-esteem students, on the other hand, cannot put their full attention on learning because they are distracted by how badly they feel about themselves.

- The higher the students' self-esteem, the better equipped they are to deal with life's adversities and traumas. Setbacks and mistakes don't cause them to quit and give up. High self-esteem students pick themselves up and start again. They manage life's challenges more effectively.

- The higher the students' self-esteem, the more compassionate and caring they are toward other individuals. In their dealings with others, these children think in more sociocentric patterns and display fewer egocentric behaviors because they're not "caught up in themselves." They are more empathetic toward others.

- The higher the students' self-esteem, the more their behavior is in line with their true feelings of self. The old axiom, "We act how we feel about ourselves," has never been more valid!

- The higher the students' self-esteem, the better able they are to attempt new tasks and take risks. Such students usually learn more easily because they are willing to try new material presented to them. They feel more comfortable and secure with themselves. They are also more trusting of others.

- The higher the students' self-esteem, the more inclined they are to keep trying rather than quit and give up. Obstacles and mistakes don't derail these children; instead, they become more active problem solvers, trying to figure out what else they can do. These children generally learn from their mistakes. They seldom devalue themselves for a setback or mistake. Instead, they say, "So what can I do differently next time?"

- The higher the students' self-esteem, the more relaxed and content they are with life. Because they generally are more secure and comfortable with themselves, their daily lives are not cluttered with feelings of insecurities or tensions about, "What will people think about me?" Instead, they meet life with openness and trust.

- The higher the students' self-esteem, the better able they are to enjoy the company of others. Relationships with peers are more open and natural. These students are able to cooperate with and respond positively to others. One reason they are able to do so is because they have positive feelings about themselves.

- The higher the students' self-esteem, the more control they have over their own lives. Students with lower self-esteem do not trust themselves and their decision-making capabilities. As a result, they continually seek out others for encouragement, direction, and support. Students with higher self-esteem trust themselves. They recognize they have power and control over their own lives. These students have developed a greater sense of responsibility for the direction and course of their lives.

- The higher the students' self-esteem, the more motivated and productive they are. So much of their choice to "continue" and "try again" is guided by their past experiences, which have validated an "I can do it" approach to life. These students are willing to keep on trying because they know what it feels like to succeed. Along the way to their goals, these students constantly self-acknowledge their efforts, giving themselves feedback and support. They don't depend on others because they recognize in the end that true self-esteem cannot be given to them by others—it must be created internally.

- The higher the students' self-esteem, the more comfortable they feel with themselves. They don't need to be constantly patted on the back because they've developed a deep belief in their own value. These students are "self-empowered."

ENHANCING STUDENTS' SELF-ESTEEM

Most educators agree that self-esteem is critical to health and happiness. Hundreds of staffs across the country have written the "enhancement of student self-esteem" as a major school goal. The dream of educators is to have more "internally motivated," "achievement-oriented," and "caring and compassionate" students on their roll sheets.

The key question I'm always asked at parent and educator in-services is, "So how do we get them to be this way?" In other words, "Can we improve student self-esteem?" and if we can, "How do we do it?" My answer to these questions is always the same. Three premises are involved:

- **Self-esteem is learned.**

- **Self-esteem is changeable.**

- **Educators and parents do have enormous control in home and school environments to create the conditions that enhance such change.**

Let's analyze each one of these premises. It is important to understand each one in order to enhance students' self-esteem.

Self-esteem is learned. To the best of my scientific knowledge there are no genes for self-esteem. There are no children born with high or low self-esteem. Instead, our children have acquired their self-esteem through repeated experiences in their pasts. How children choose to interpret those events will largely determine the level of their self-esteem. Events can be perceived as positive, negative, or neutral. The more positive perceptions students have about their lives, the greater chance they have to create self-beliefs that read, "I'm acceptable, capable, and worthwhile." Negative events may be interpreted as the opposite: "I'm stupid, unacceptable, and unworthy." Remember, self-esteem is not something educators can give to their students. It's a feeling built from within.

Self-esteem is changeable. From the premise that self-esteem is learned, a second principle arises naturally and unavoidably: "If self-esteem is learned, we can teach it and change it." Self-esteem is changeable. It is essential to keep this concept in mind because it means that parents and educators do have esteem-building power. How individuals feel about themselves is changeable at any age, regardless of their specific situations. Some of the most discouraging words I hear adults say are statements beginning with "If only." "If only the students weren't so old, then I could help." "If only I had this student sooner." "If only the student didn't have to go home to

such a negative family." "If only's" are deadly because they inhibit us from trying to help improve the students' self-esteem. These two words can lead educators to the erroneous conclusion, "I can't make a difference for this student, so why should I try?" Squelch the "If only's" because self-esteem is changeable.

True, it will be more difficult to see changes in self-esteem with some students, particularly those who are older or dealing with a lot of trauma in their lives. A general rule regarding self-esteem improvement is, "The lower the first esteem components are (particularly Security and Selfhood), the slower the change." Often these students will need more extensive support in esteem enhancement with an outside therapist or counselor. These cases, though, are atypical. In most cases, self-esteem is changeable. You can make differences.

Educators and parents do have enormous control in home and school environments to create the conditions that enhance such change. If self-esteem is learned and changeable, then it is possible for educators and parents to acquire the skills to create those changes. The desire to help students is usually already there. What is needed

THE BUILDING BLOCKS OF SELF-ESTEEM

is the knowledge of how to create the conditions to enhance the change. That's why Home Esteem Builders was written, to provide practical and specific ways to increase students' self-esteem. This manual is based on the premises that self-esteem is learned and changeable, and that educators and parents can create the conditions to enhance the change.

The degree to which children feel worthwhile and capable is based on how well they are developing in five specific components. These components make up the building blocks of self-esteem.

The Five Building Blocks of Self-Esteem

- **Security:** The essential feeling of physical safety, trust, and emotional security.

- **Selfhood:** The feeling of individuality, self-knowledge, or personal identity; the question of "Who am I?"

- **Affiliation:** The feeling of belonging and connectedness.

- **Mission:** A sense of purpose and aim in life; the "where we are headed" issue.

- **Competence:** The feeling of capableness; self-empowerment.

The feeling of security. Students who feel secure are free from the fear of being intimidated or harmed. Because they have developed the capacity to trust their environment and the people around them, they can be open to risk new experiences. They also can handle change or spontaneity without undue personal discomfort. They move with a readily apparent feeling of self-assuredness. Their posture is direct and projects confidence instead of stress, anxiety, and fear. These children feel safe knowing there are people they can count on. Feeling emotionally safe, these children can open up to others and share their ideas and feelings. Students high in the feeling of security might say, "The rules in my school are necessary and fair" or "I can count on my teacher."

The feeling of selfhood. These are students with healthy feelings of individuality. They have attached descriptions to themselves that are accurate and clear. Here are children who know who they are and what they believe in. These students feel adequate and worthy of praise. They can also handle constructive criticism because they recognize their unique qualities and special contributions. The security that comes from a sense of selfhood allows them to praise and compliment others. Students high in the feeling of selfhood might say, "I am a lot of things...a boy, a soccer player, a son, a grandson, a nephew, an artist, and a brother" or "I'm not as good-looking as a movie star, but when I smile I know I'm beautiful."

The feeling of affiliation. Students with a strong sense of affiliation feel appreciated and accepted by people who are important to them. They feel good about their social experiences and generally feel connected to others. Past successes with others allow them to seek out new relationships and maintain present friendships. They are able to cooperate and share as well as show compassion toward others. Because they possess these qualities of affiliation, they are generally sought out by others in return. Students high in the feeling of affiliation might say, "I like being with my family," "I sure have a lot of good friends," or "Most people like me."

The feeling of mission. Students with a sense of mission have a feeling of purpose in their lives. They know where they are headed. There is an aim and direction to their existence. These students not only set realistic and achievable goals but are able to follow through on them. Problems and obstacles don't get these children down. They meet them head-on knowing there are choices in life. They seek alternatives and plan options so that problems can be minimized and the goal can still be reached. Students high in the feeling of mission might say, "Yesterday I got fifteen spelling words right. Tomorrow I'm going to try for seventeen," or "I may not be good at soccer right now, but I know what I can do to change it."

The feeling of competence. Students with a feeling of competence are not only aware of their strengths but are able to accept their weaknesses. Failure is rarely an issue for these children. In fact, highly competent individuals perceive mistakes as valuable learning tools. The feeling of competence allows students to validate themselves as "a success." Each experience of success results in these students perceiving themselves as more capable. These students are more willing to take risks and share their ideas and opinions. Here are students with an "I can do it!" kind of an attitude. These students know that they have power and control over their own lives. They have acquired a sense of self-empowerment or self-efficacy. Students high in the feeling of competence might say, "I learn fast," "Sure, I'll try," or "When I messed up that time, I really discovered what I needed to know."

- *The sense of security:* This child feels safe, knowing there are people he/she can count on.

- *The sense of selfhood*: This child has a strong sense of individuality, and feels adequate and worthy of praise.

- *The sense of affiliation:* This child is able to cooperate and share as well as show compassion toward others.

- *The sense of mission:* This child takes initiative, feels responsible for his/her actions, seeks alternatives to problems, and evaluates his/her past performance.

- *The sense of competence:* A child who feels competent is not only aware of his/her strengths but is also able to accept his/her weaknesses.

HOME ESTEEM BUILDERS AND ESTEEM BUILDERS

These five vital feelings, which constitute the components of high self-esteem, serve as the basis for the Esteem Builders' Complete Program. This process for building students' self-esteem is based on the premise that parents and educators do have enormous control over creating the conditions that develop students' feelings in these five specific areas. In the past ten years, literally dozens of self-esteem manuals aimed at increasing students' self-esteem have been published. Whereas student self-esteem activities are abundant, the one area that continues to be overlooked is the involvement of parents in the enhancement of their children's self-esteem. As a society, we have been remiss in teaching parents how to parent. Children's first teachers, their parents, have never been taught how to help their children become happy, successful, and confident human beings. A central belief of the Esteem Builders' Complete Program is that the greatest differences for students in self-esteem enhancement will come when the school and home work together as partners in this process.

Home Esteem Builders is a unique manual aimed at providing educators with the tools to teach parents how to help their children feel good about themselves. The activities and strategies presented in this manual are designed to enhance the feelings of Security, Selfhood, Affiliation, Mission and Competence. This framework was first described in my publication, *Esteem Builders: A K-8 Self-Esteem Curriculum for Improving Student Achievement, Behavior and School Climate*, now used in more than 60,000 classrooms in North America. Both volumes are designed to complement one another and to be used simultaneously to enhance students' self-esteem, and both have been developed for use by educators. The main difference between the two volumes is the intended audience. A brief description of each volume follows:

- *Esteem Builders.* Based on the five components of self-esteem, this manual provides educators with more than 250 esteem-building activities for use in the classroom with students. Field-tested activities are cross-cor-related to all subject areas and grade levels.

- *Home Esteem Builders.* With this manual, educators can provide parents with activities they can use at home with their children to enhance the five components of self-esteem. Thus, the same esteem-building principles teachers are implementing in classrooms can be reinforced in the home. The book offers a myriad of home esteem-building strategies to teach parents how to build their children's self-esteem. It is based on the premise that parents play a crucial (if not the most criti-cal) role in developing the five feelings of self-esteem in their children.

ENHANCING THE COMPONENTS

Though positive self-esteem can be acquired with less than all five of the feelings intact, in general, the higher the number of feelings possessed, the higher the overall level of self-esteem. Thus, the esteem builder must deliberately plan and address all five of the components of self-esteem.

Esteem enhancement is a slow, deliberate process. Here are a few points educators should keep in mind as they begin:

1. The feelings are generally acquired sequen-tially. Home Esteem Builders addresses this issue by deliberately placing all the activi-ties, strategies, and correspondences to the parents in a specific order. For maximum effectiveness, it is strongly recommended that educators maintain the order of the activities. Security is the prerequisite to the other components; therefore, it is always the first building block addressed. Selfhood, Affiliation, Mission, and Competence follow sequentially.

2. Reframing self-esteem will take place slow-ly but it will take place. Both parents and staff must constantly be reminded not to expect dramatic results overnight. Remember, students have had many years to form their self-perceptions. Be patient!

3. Consistency in using esteem-building strate-gies is crucial. The esteem builder must be willing to make a conscious effort each day to help students develop more positive feel-ings about themselves. An abundance of Home Esteem Builder Activities are provid-ed in this manual so that parents can contin-ually be reminded of the strategies.

4. Consistency on the part of both parents and educators in implementing the strategies is also very important. The esteem-building strategies will be much more successful if parents are reinforcing the same techniques at home that educators are using with students in the classroom. Keep in contact with parents to assess how the activity is going. Do the par-ents have questions? Are the parents feeling successful? Are their children receptive to the strategies? Are parents seeing the same results at home that educators are seeing in the classroom? These are the kinds of ques-tions that should be continually addressed.

5. The attitude of the esteem builder (teacher or parent) plays a significant role in helping students form a more positive self-picture. In the end, remember the most powerful esteem-building strategy may not be the paper and pencil activity but the way esteem builders present the task to the students. Educators must constantly recognize that children are monitoring them not just by their words but by their actions. Conveying respect and acceptance of their students as human beings may be the educators' most powerful tool in the formation of many stu-dents' self-perceptions.

Characteristics of Effective Home Esteem-Building Schools

Research on parent involvement arrives at one strik-ingly similar conclusion: a home-school partner-ship is not only desirable but in many cases essen-tial for the best results in student success. While the research findings are conclusive on this one point, they are far from reaching a consensus on the best way to go about encouraging widespread parent participation in school esteem-building programs. There appears to be no blueprint for the ideal home-school partnership. There is no one model that can be singled out above others as the most effective approach, and no one set of practices that every school should adopt in sealing the partnership. However, schools engaged in effective home esteem-building efforts do share a fundamental set of principles. These include:

1. The staff is committed to the concept of student and staff self-esteem enhancement. Most schools have, in fact, chosen self-esteem as a major focus or schoolwide mission. The staff share a strong belief that self-esteem is a critical element in the educational process.

2. The school environment is a warm, positive, caring place where students feel cared about. Staff members work hard to create a nurturing atmosphere.

3. Parent-school communication is frequent and open. Communication techniques vary widely from school to school. Methods such as principal home newsletters, home visits, weekly student progress reports, frequent phone calls, and parent education classes are a few options such schools employ. While the methods vary, in every case home-school communication is practiced as essential to the home esteem-building process. Staff members recognize that effective home-school communication must be ongoing and planned.

4. Parent education in student esteem enhancement is recognized as essential. Home esteem-building schools believe that parents can and should work as a team with the school in the enhancement of student self-esteem. Staff members continually plan ways to teach parents how to help their children. They recognize that they must work frequently with each family.

5. Parent involvement is encouraged. In many cases, extensive efforts are made to involve the parents in their children's education. Creative options to involve reticent parents are constantly analyzed and tried. These schools attempt to correct areas which might hinder parent involvement, such as language barriers, transportation, child care, and working hours.

6. A partnership is built between family and school. Home esteem-building schools consider the home and school as natural extensions of one another.

7. Staff members believe that by working closely with the home and creating a strong home-school partnership the outcome will be powerful differences in students' achievement and behavior.

8. Finally, staff members recognize that such an esteem-building school does not happen over night. The school, instead, sets realistic, specific and measurable goals each year aimed at enhancing students and staff self-esteem, and home esteem building. Ongoing records are kept of the esteem-building techniques that have been employed, such as the increased number of contacts made with parents, parent education classes offered, parent newsletters sent home, and parent responses. By means of a careful evaluation, the school will have data to show how far it has come and what new steps should be taken to further enhance the home-school partnership the following year.

THE HOME ESTEEM BUILDERS PROGRAM

For the past decade, I have conducted self-esteem seminars for hundreds of parents across North America. A key component to my seminars has always been to give parents not only the "why self-esteem is important and what it can do for your child" part, but also the "and this is what you can do at home to start enhancing your child's self-esteem." That second element—what parents can do to help their children feel better about themselves—is always the part parents thank me for. Weeks after leaving the site, I receive letters from parents expressing the idea,

"Thank you for telling me what I could do to improve my child's self-esteem." Each time I speak, my experience reaffirms my belief: parents desperately want to know what to do to maximize their children's academic success and chances for happiness, and educators can teach parents these skills.

A comprehensive assortment of activities, techniques, and procedures is offered in this manual so that schools can help parents in home esteem building. All the activities are aimed at the same objective: to strengthen the home-school partnership and thereby increase the chances for the enhancement of students' self-esteem. The many techniques presented are categorized in the following four main approaches:

1. **Parent Education**…ways to educate parents in esteem enhancement.

2. **Home-School Communication**…ideas to strengthen home-school communication.

3. **Home Esteem-Building Activities**…practical, fun activities parents can do at home with their children to build self-esteem.

4. **Prescriptive Esteem Building**…ways for the staff to assist individual parents seeking additional help in enhancing their children's self-perceptions.

SPECIAL COMPONENTS OF HOME ESTEEM BUILDERS

Home Esteem Builders is a unique manual aimed at helping parents help their children feel good about themselves. The book offers a comprehensive assortment of activities, techniques and procedures with one objective in mind: to strengthen the home-school partnership and thereby increase the chances for the enhancement of students' self-esteem. The manual includes the following special features.

1. Parent Education

In nearly all cases, parents want to help their children succeed; they just need to know what to do.

One of the keys to a successful parent involvement program is for educators to provide parents with concrete "how to's" on an ongoing basis. Parent education in esteem building also should be offered in a wide variety of forms so that parents can choose the form most appropriate to their needs. The following parent education menus are provided in *Home Esteem Builders*.

- **Parent In-Service.** A complete one-hour parent in-service script entitled *Self-Esteem: The Key to Your Child's Success* is provided on page 73. In addition to the script, the component includes handouts, blackline masters for transparencies, parent invitation, room setup chart, presenter time line, and ideas to maximize parent involvement.

- **Parent University Day.** Guidelines are included for setting up a once-a-year, comprehensive parent program called Parent University Day. The day is one in which parents can attend a variety of mini-workshops featuring ways parents can help their children.

- **Lending Library.** Another form of parent education is to offer parents a smorgasbord of videotapes, books, and cassettes on the topic of home esteem building. An extensive bibliography of outstanding sources for parents is included, as well as guidelines for setting up the lending program.

- **Make-and-Take Session.** Parents are invited to this school-sponsored event where they make esteem-enhancing activities they can take home to use with their children. A sample is provided on page 69.

2. Home-School Communication

Ongoing communication between home and school is a major factor in generating increased parent involvement. The communication should be open, honest, and two-way. To aid in the enhancement of these principles, this manual offers the following:

- **Phone Communication Techniques.** An assortment of ideas and activities to enhance home-school communication are offered, including Phone Trees, Sunshine Calls, principal phone logs, and school hotlines.

- **Esteem Builder Grams.** This is a complete package of newsletters to send home on a regular basis to students' parents. Each news gram features a short article concerning a topic essential to esteem enhancement. All newsletters are ready-to-duplicate so that educators can instantly incorporate them into their own school newsletter or home communication. Simple ideas and activities for family esteem building are described in each Esteem Builder Gram, along with pertinent rationale for doing the activity. Esteem Builder Grams can be found on pages 143 to 168.

- **Home-School Grams and Messages.** A variety of forms providing parents with vital information on the progress of esteem enhancement in the classroom are ready-to-duplicate and send home with students.

3. Home Esteem-Building Activities

The third component of a solid home-school esteem-building program is to provide parents with ideas they can use at home to enhance their children's self-esteem. Home Esteem Builders offers three complete programs:

- **Home Esteem Builder Activities.** Forty ready-to-duplicate activities are provided for parents to use in home esteem enhancement. Each activity is based on current research on self-esteem and is designed to build one of the five feelings of self-esteem.

- **Home Esteem Building Calendar*.** This calendar contains twelve months of esteem building activities—one activity for each day of the year. Each day features a short, theory-based activity parents can easily do with their children to enhance self-esteem.

- **Esteem Builders Reading Program*.** In this complete program, educators will find reading cards, extensive book lists, certificates of accomplishment, teacher reading progress forms, and letters inviting parents to read at home with their children. Each selection of quality children's literature specifically addresses at least one of the five building blocks of self-esteem.

4. Prescriptive Home Esteem Building

The final component offers staff members ways they can help individual parents use esteem enhancement practices:

- **Conferences.** Special forms with suggested esteem-enhancement practices are provided (see pages 251 to 270) for educators to use in the parent-school conference process. Ideas or tips to enhance the five building blocks are provided as well as prescriptive conference sheets to recognize individual students' self-esteem strengths and weaknesses.

Home Esteem Builders purposely provides a variety of methods for encouraging parent participation in school esteem-building programs. Not all methods will work with all parents. In the end, each school must determine which methods best meet the needs of its parents. The flowchart found on page 23 is a visual guide to the wide variety of approaches to strengthen the home-school partnership that are found in this manual.

EVALUATING THE PROGRAM

The most effective home-school partnerships to not happen at once; they are always well-planned by the school. Such a program begins with the staff committing themselves to helping parents learn to enhance the esteem of their children. Generally, the staff then writes a mission statement summarizing their belief and commitment to family esteem building. It is important for the staff to always keep in mind that change takes place slowly. Home-school collaboration in student esteem enhancement will not happen overnight. The staff must continually set specific, measurable goals as to their yearly plans for home esteem building.

A detailed record of school-initiated strategies for home esteem building should be kept. A record-keeping form has been included on page 24 for charting your school's plans for a home-school partnership. The Home Esteem Building Record form is organized according to the four special components of home esteem building found in this manual: Parent Education, Home-School Communication, Home Esteem-Building Activities, and Prescriptive Home Esteem Building. Only by evaluating a program carefully can a school assess how far it has come and where it needs to go to further improve the home-school esteem-building partnership.

Unreachable Parents

One of the biggest questions educators commonly ask me is, "What about the parents we can't reach?" This is certainly an issue that needs to be addressed. If your staff has attempted to create a stronger parent-school partnership and is feeling unsuccessful because parents are resisting or seem to be "uninterested," it may be time for the staff to ask themselves a few questions:

1. Did we survey the parents to make sure our activities meet their needs?

2. Are parents not attending functions due to problems obtaining child care? Has the school offered to provide child care at a minimal charge or at no cost at all? Is a service group such as the Girl Scouts able to provide such services?

3. Is the language or limited educational background of the parents an issue? Are parents aware that translators will be available to translate the information for them?

4. Is parental transportation an issue? Have we tried to remedy this problem by providing transportation to and from the parent activity?

5. Is the time of the activity causing parents any difficulty? Have we surveyed the parents to determine what is the best day and time for them? Has the school attempted to be flexible in the time the activities are offered?

6. Have we attempted to establish a trusting relationship with parents who are resistant? Very often parents feel threatened by the educator's background or manner. Past experiences between the school and parents may have been negative. Has the school attempted to bridge this relationship?

These are a few of the issues each school seriously needs to address. If the staff can honestly say, "Yes, we have done our best to remedy any major problems that may be impeding a home-school partnership," then it is time to look at the reality of the issue. Ideally, teachers would like every parent to give one hundred percent to helping their children succeed. The flip side of the coin may be coming up instead: the parent may not be showing the kind of support the school desires, and, in some cases, there may be no support at all.

At this point it's time to say, "We've done our best to reach parents; they just weren't willing to grab on at this time." We need to create opportunities for parents to help their children; we need to invite parents to learn how to enhance their children's self-esteem — but, in the end, it is their decision as to whether they choose to R.S.V.P. Yes, we'll lose a few of our parents as well as our youth. They will drift on downstream. The school, though, can serve in a critical role as life-saver to other parents who are willing to be helped. In the meantime, always remember to continue to keep your invitations open. Such a process may be lengthy and frustrating but in the end may have an unexpected and welcome outcome...one day you may just find the reluctant parent knocking on the door.

HOME-SCHOOL ESTEEM-BUILDING PARTNERSHIP

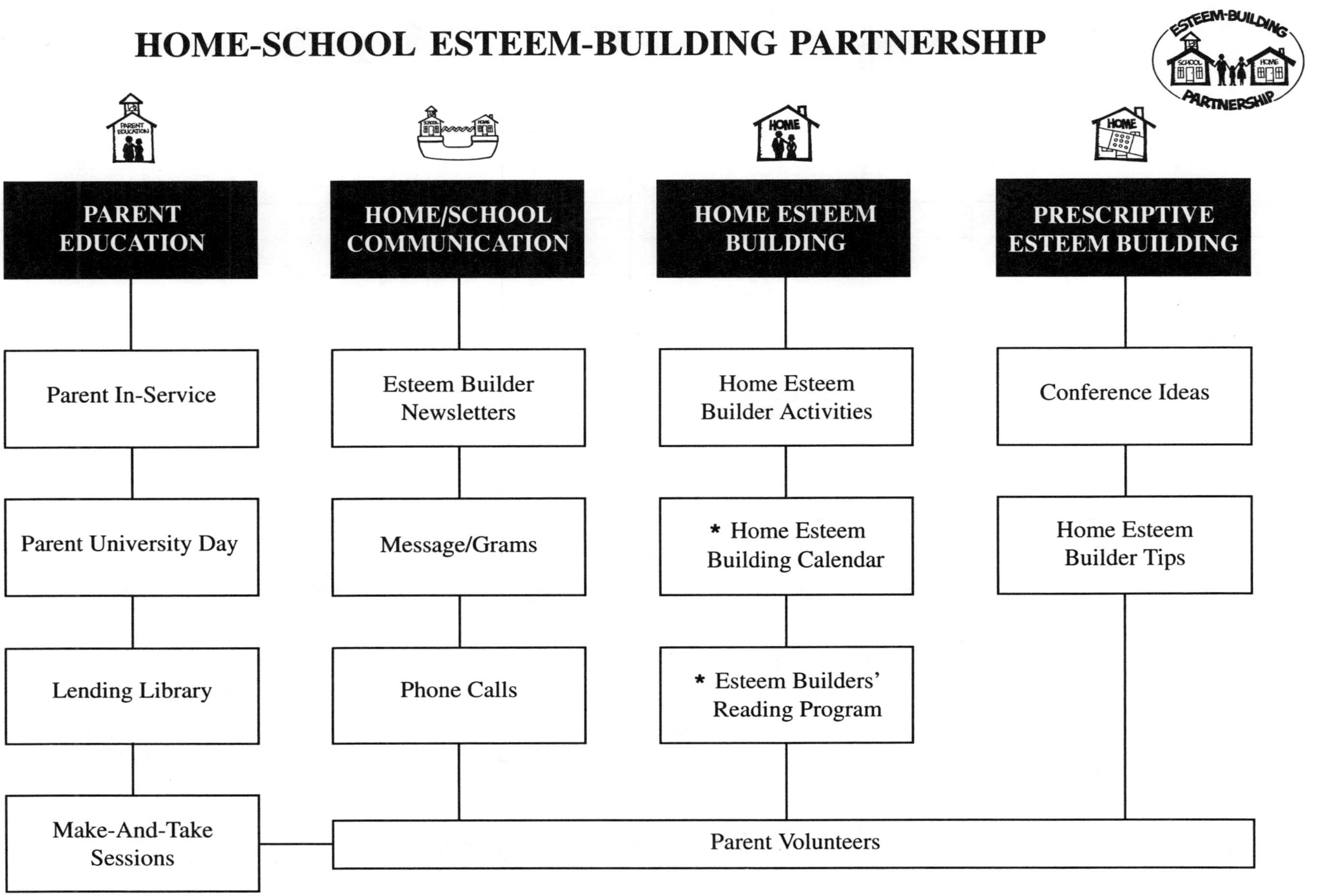

PARENT EDUCATION

- Parent In-Service
- Parent University Day
- Lending Library
- Make-And-Take Sessions

HOME/SCHOOL COMMUNICATION

- Esteem Builder Newsletters
- Message/Grams
- Phone Calls

HOME ESTEEM BUILDING

- Home Esteem Builder Activities
- * Home Esteem Building Calendar
- * Esteem Builders' Reading Program

PRESCRIPTIVE ESTEEM BUILDING

- Conference Ideas
- Home Esteem Builder Tips

Parent Volunteers

* Separate programs available through B.L. Winch & Associates/Jalmar Press

Esteem Builders' Complete Program
Jalmar Press, Rolling Hills Estates, CA

HOME ESTEEM BUILDERS

HOME ESTEEM-BUILDING RECORD

PARENT EDUCATION	HOME-SCHOOL COMMUNICATION	HOME ESTEEM-BUILDING ACTIVITIES	PRESCRIPTIVE HOME ESTEEM BUILDING

Esteem Builders' Complete Program
Jalmar Press, Rolling Hills Estates, CA

Notes

2

Developing a Home and School Esteem-Building Partnership

HOME ESTEEM BUILDERS

- Surveying the Climate
- Setting the Stage for Open Communication
- Inviting Parent Participation
- Recognizing Parent Involvement

ACTIVITIES LIST

Parent Participation

Home Esteem Builders was developed on the premise that a home and school partnership is an integral element of effective esteem building. The material in this book provides educators with the resources to help parents enhance their children's self-esteem. Before distributing any of these materials to the students' homes, please make sure that they have been translated into the primary language of the parents.

2

Developing a Home and School Esteem-Building Partnership

*School life should grow gradually out of the home life....It
should take up and continue the activities with which the
child is already familiar in the home.*

—JOHN DEWEY

PARENT INVOLVEMENT

American demographics reveal that parents today are a lot different than those of a generation ago. In 1955, almost sixty percent of American families fit the "Leave It To Beaver" family image consisting of a working father, a housewife mother, and two children. In those days, a principal or teacher could dial a child's home number during the day and find a parent at home. Those were also the days when parents could be counted on to show up for cookie sales, support school fundraisers, attend back-to-school nights and parent meetings, and help teachers by working in the classroom. Today only seven percent of American families fit that description. For the majority, time is precious. A recent survey revealed that on an average day an American mother spends 27 minutes talking or reading to her children; fathers spend less than 10 minutes.[1] (These statistics are high; other sources point to even more dismal figures—13 1/2 minutes per day for mother, and 11 minutes per week for father.)

The fact that more than half of today's American mothers work certainly explains these figures. As for the involvement of parents with their children in the school, Joyce L. Epstein, a principal research scientist with the Center for Research on Elementary and Middle Schools, estimates that more than seventy percent of all parents have never been involved in a volunteer activity. While most parents cannot be called on to actively work at the school, there are still a number of parents who can be counted on to do hours of beneficial volunteer work. Parents can participate in a wide range of volunteer opportunities. With the restructuring of the American family unit, it is vital for the staff to take into account the limited hours most parents have and to create innovative strategies. For instance, not all volunteering need be done during school hours. The school should indeed encourage volunteer participation from parents. As Percy Jenkins, principal of Ocean Hill Intermediate School in New York, aptly stated, "When parents become involved in the instructional process, they are most likely to make school a priority for their children."[2]

SURVEYING THE CLIMATE

Creating a climate for an effective home-school partnership in which parents and school work together in a shared commitment for student esteem enhancement is never accidental. Such a partnership evolves slowly as educators deliberately take action until the vision of "parents and school working together" becomes a reality.

---

1. Heymann, Tom. *On An Average Day.* Survey Research Center, University of Maryland, Fawcett Columbine Press, NY, 1988.

2. Jenkins, Percy W. *Building Parent Participation in Urban Schools.* National Association of Elementary School Principals, Association for Supervision and Curriculum Development, November 1981, 23.

Before beginning extensive planning of strategies to involve parents in the home esteem-building process, a strong suggestion is to first assess how parents and staff perceive the existing parent involvement program. Too often, schools spend long hours and lots of energy planning activities for parent involvement only to discover that parents really desire an entirely different emphasis. To begin, educators should ask themselves a few questions:

• **Have we taken the time to ask parents how we as a school can best help them help their children in the learning process?**

• **If we've tried parent education programs that were poorly attended, do we know why?**

• **Do we know what specific times parents would be most able to come to school for parenting classes?**

• **Is what we are offering what parents want to take?**

Do not assume that because parents did not show up to an in-service or conference that they didn't want to come. In fact, there may be a number of reasons why parents could not make the session. Is the session offered in the parents' native language? Is the program held at a time when parents can come? Do parents have transportation to the session? Can parents afford child care? Can parents find child care? Is the topic one parents are interested in? These are just a few questions schools must seriously consider before concluding that "the parents are just not interested."

Questionnaires

Begin the "parent survey" by creating a list of key questions to ask parents regarding parent education. The answers to these questions will help in setting up more effective parenting programs since planning can be based on this specific information. Don't obtain this information through questionnaires sent home to parents via students because the return rate is usually quite low. Furthermore, the parents who do respond are generally the same ones. The key is to try and reach all parents to determine how the school can best meet their needs. Personal individual contact with each parent is the most effective technique to ensure that the school obtains every parent's opinion. Consider setting up a telephone tree for each homeroom class that calls only the oldest siblings in the school. Parent volunteers could be responsible for surveying the parents. Parent conferences at which classroom teachers solicit answers from each parent attending is another option. In the few cases when parents are not accessible by phone, a home visit may be necessary.

It is best for individual schools to create their own questions to ask parents, since the staff will be aware of special circumstances and issues pertinent to the parents at that school site. The following questions are provided as suggestions only. Keep a record of each call and the response of each parent. The records will help in future parent education planning sessions.

Surveys

In addition to the questionnaires, two surveys are provided to help assess the existing parent-school partnership climate.

Parent Checklist of a Home-School Partnership. This survey is designed to be sent to the home of each oldest sibling. Duplicate a copy for each student who is the oldest sibling at the school and address it to the parent.

Checklist of School Behaviors That Promote a Home-School Partnership. This survey, a duplicate of the Parent Checklist of a Home-School Partnership, is designed for the staff to complete. It is important to survey not only the perceptions parents have concerning the existing home-school partnership but also the staff's perceptions. Compare the results of the staff survey with the parents' responses to assess the extent to which the home and school agree on their partnership in student esteem enhancement. Very often difficulties in creating a strong working relationship have resulted from marked differences in perception between the staff and parents. Total the results of the staff and parent surveys and report them to the faculty.

SETTING THE STAGE FOR OPEN COMMUNICATION

In too many cases, parents hear from the school only when their children are in trouble. Educational researchers confirm the fact that school personnel communicate far too infrequently with parents. One study found that more than one-third of the parents surveyed had never had a teacher conference. Fifty-nine percent of the parents had never received a phone call from the school and ninety-six percent had never received a home visit.[3] When characteristics of the most effective business practices are examined, ongoing communication between the organization and its clients is always cited as a critical element.[4] The practice of effective listening and ongoing open communication between the school and the home is a behavior that must be established.

Establish Open Communication Early

There are a number of techniques that schools can employ to enhance a home and school rapport. When the initial interaction with parents is positive, both parents and educators are more likely to feel comfortable contacting one another in the future when issues regarding students arise. Relationships based on infrequent communication are rarely as open and warm as those in which contacts are more frequent. The best approach is to start the communication flowing from the very beginning of school. Parents then recognize from the first day of school that the staff is committed to developing a collaborative relationship with them.

Get-Acquainted Reception

For younger students in particular, the beginning of school is often a scary experience. Anything the school can do to ease that uncertainty is greatly appreciated. One way to meet students in a non-threatening manner and to establish a friendly, caring relationship is to invite parents and children to a "get-acquainted reception."

Obtain the principal's permission to have a reception on a weekday before school begins. Then send a letter of introduction to the children, inviting them to attend a get-acquainted reception in their new classroom and giving parents the date and time. (Hold the reception to an hour or less.)

Keep the event simple. Push two desks together and cover them with a paper tablecloth or with butcher paper. Arrange a simple centerpiece of fresh-cut flowers and provide treats and a beverage. Perhaps a room mother could help you by bringing in cookies and a punch.

Warmly greet each child as he or she arrives. Solicit help from parents with making name tags. (Have small pieces of paper, felt-tip pens, and safety pins available for this purpose.) Parents and children can work together at a table set up with the necessary supplies to create their own name tags. Perhaps suggest that children not only include their name but also a few hand-drawn pictures depicting personal interests or hobbies.

After everyone has had a snack, call the children together, make introductions, and tell them a story. During the story time, parents could be invited to fill out any necessary school forms or index cards with personal information such as their address, phone number, occupation, emergency numbers, and a sentence or two describing their children's interests or strengths. Before the children leave, thank them for coming and express an anticipation of happy times to come.[5]

Before School "Drop-In"

Students, regardless of their age, have "pre-school jitters." In the few days before school begins, while teachers are setting up their class-

---

3. Epstein, Joyce, Henry L. Becker et al. *Study of Teacher Practices of Parent Involvement: Results from Surveys of Teachers and Parents.* Summary paper prepared by Center for Social Organization of Schools. Baltimore, MD: Johns Hopkins University, 1983, 5-6.

4. Peters, Thomas, and Robert H. Waterman. *In Search of Excellence: Lessons from America's Best Run Companies.* New York: Harper & Row, 1982.

5. Borba, Michele and Craig Borba. *Self-Esteem: A Classroom Affair.* Harper Collier, 1978, 10.

rooms, why not designate a day for parents and students to drop by the classroom and say hello? The visit need be no more than a few minutes (this can be stated specifically in the invitation) but in those minutes, the basis could be established for a year-long rapport.

In a letter or card sent to parents and children two weeks before school starts, educators could introduce themselves and, as their new teachers, briefly welcome the children to their classrooms. Then teachers could state that they will be available to briefly meet with anyone who wishes to come by and see their classrooms on the following times and dates. If desired, teachers could request that anyone who wishes to come by during a certain week call the office first to state the time and date of their visit.

First-Week Phone Call

During the first weeks of school, educators should take a few moments to personally phone each parent to introduce themselves. The conversation need not take any more than a few minutes but it will set a powerful and positive tone for the remainder of the year. During the conversation, teachers could briefly describe their expectations for the year and invite parents to keep an open dialogue with them regarding their children. Teachers should also tell parents how to reach them if there are problems or questions (i.e. by leaving messages with the school or by asking students to deliver notes).

Student Welcome Letter

Teachers can lay the groundwork for home and school communication by mailing welcome letters before the school year begins to the students who will be in their classrooms. In the letter, teachers could describe themselves and perhaps a few special projects and events that are planned for the year. The letter will create in children the expectation of a personalized and friendly classroom atmosphere. The letter evokes in parents' minds the image of a caring teacher who has taken the time to personally connect with their children.[6]

Introductory Letter to Parents

Another way to begin establishing communication with the students' parents is in an introductory letter. Teachers could write a letter to parents introducing themselves and their program. In the correspondence, they could specifically state their interest in creating a positive teacher-parent relationship. This would also be a good time to invite parents to attend the first back-to-school night or to personally drop by their children's classrooms to meet and discuss with teachers what they have planned for the school year. Send the letter so that it arrives either a few days prior to the opening of school or within the first days of the school year.

INVITING PARENT PARTICIPATION

In this decade of hurried schedules, the school, more than ever before, must think of creative alternatives to invite parent involvement. The time constraints of parents must always be considered. Very often parents do not attend school events because "it's one more hour away from home." Several of the ideas suggested below allow parents to remain at home. There are numerous ways to involve parents in the school system, including:

- **Curriculum Participation.** Parents can listen to their children for ten minutes each evening, sign their children's homework on a daily basis, or help their children with a term project.

- **Room Parents.** One or two parents are assigned to each classroom teacher to help facilitate home-school communication, class outings, and parties. The room parent calls other parents to delegate responsibilities such as driving or donating food or party favors.

- **Parent Hosts.** The primary purpose of these parents is to try and get other parents involved. They can greet other parents as they enter the school, act as hosts for general

6. Borba, Michele and Craig Borba. *Self-Esteem: A Classroom Affair.* Harper Collier, 1978, 11.

parent activities such as family nights and open school days, or call home to welcome a parent new to the school.

- **Phone Trees.** Here is a task working parents can do during the evenings. Certain parents are designated as "telephone tree" operators. Their task is to reach other parents in each grade/class to remind them about upcoming events or to find out who can provide rides for field trips, find needed materials, or provide help for a particular family.

- **Talent Bank.** Capitalize on the talents, skills, and hobbies of parents. Ask parents to volunteer information about a special talent or skill they possess or an occupation they are experienced in. Throughout the year, parents could be called upon to provide a mini-lesson or lecture to a class or assembly concerning their skill or occupation.

- **Assignment Correction.** Another possibility for parent volunteerism is to send home special art projects that need cutting out or prearranging, or student papers that need correcting. (Provide parents with an answer key.)

- **Tutoring.** Parents with free time during school hours can volunteer to tutor students one-on-one with supervision from the teacher.

- **Referral Service.** A group of parents can organize an information and referral service for other parents who need assistance in such areas as child care, carpooling, recreational activities, etc.

- **Physical Education Activities.** Parents with free time during the school recess or lunch hours can provide valuable service by working with a few children to teach them outdoor games or athletic skills.

- **Make-and-Take Projects.** Capitalize on the artistic talents of a few parents. Ask them when they have any spare time to help with special art projects for school events (plays, bulletin boards, newsletters, etc.)

- **Materials and Supplies.** Always let parents know the kinds of materials and supplies needed for school projects. Too often resources are destroyed that could be reused.

Here are more glimpses of creative ideas educators are successfully using to promote a home-school partnership aimed at enhancing the esteem and achievement of their youth:

- **Homework Hotlines.** Los Angeles School District wanted to increase the involvement of parents in their children's homework. Through surveying parents, educators discovered one of the biggest stumbling blocks to homework supervision was that parents were unsure about what their children had been assigned to do, so the school district began a homework hotline. Parents call a designated number and listen to a message teachers record each night giving a brief description of class assignments. Educators have noticed greater involvement by parents in their children's homework since the district initiated the assignment recordings.

- **Homework Materials.** In the Capistrano Unified School District in California, teachers were given release time or paid over the summer to develop K-6 materials in the areas of language, science, and social studies. All the home learning materials were specifically designed to be easy to use. As part of the development of materials, parents were encouraged to provide educators with feedback to ascertain the ease of the materials as well as the difficulty. Preliminary evidence of student achievement gains suggests that involving parents in their children's home learning activities could result in improvement payoffs for students.

- **Observation Week.** Saratoga Unified Elementary School District recognized that parents rarely observe their children's classrooms in action, even though such an experience can be an effective way for parents to learn about the instructional program. In Saratoga, one week during the school year is set aside as Observation Week, in which parents may visit the school and observe any classroom.

- **Shadow Your Child Day**. A variation of Observation Week is the Shadow Your Child Day. Parents are invited to sit in on regular classrooms with their children. Students are given incentives to have adults attend. They are free to leave after sharing a lunch together with their parents or guardians.[7]

- **Parent Educational TV Program.** The San Diego County Office of Education uses its educational television network as an instructional avenue for parents. Educators set up a weekly parent education program called "The Parent Hour." The program features local psychologists, teachers, administrators, and other specialists who share parenting information. Parents are invited to call in to the station with questions which are answered by the educational panel. Each school is encouraged to tape the shows and use them at parent education programs or lend them to parents to view at home.

- **Parent Luncheon.** Katherine Finchy School in the Palm Springs Unified School District in California holds a special parent luncheon in which each child is invited to bring a parent or guardian to eat lunch with. The cafeteria is colorfully decorated by teachers and children. Parents eat lunch with their children at tables set up specially for each class.

- **Family Picnic.** Sally Songy, also of the Palm Springs Unified School District, holds an end-of-the-year family picnic at a nearby park. Each child's family is invited to bring a picnic lunch or dinner for their own family as well as one dessert to share with everyone else. The teacher arranges events and fun family games.

- **Parent Education Night.** Gilroy Unified School District holds a once-a-year parent education night. Teachers, administrators, and psychologists hold thirty-minute classes. Topics are determined by a survey sent out to parents several weeks prior to the event. Parents then choose two or three classes (such as building esteem, disciplining with consequences, helping with homework, selecting great read-aloud books) to attend during the evening.

- **Parent Room.** Many schools set aside a room at the site for parents. Here parents can meet informally for many different reasons, including gatherings for parent support groups.

- **Parents' Library Corner.** A small section in the school's library is designated specially for materials and displays that are of concern to parents.

- **Parent Peer Groups.** A K-12 school in Washington, D.C. has formed parent peer groups. The groups meet once a month rotating meetings at the school and parents' homes. A teacher or principal always participates in each group. The parents discuss different topics at each session related to the issue of "how to effectively exercise parental authority."[8]

Parent Helpers

Children respond positively to the interest, love, and concern of parent helpers. With minimal training, parent helpers can supervise some activities and free teachers to spend more time helping children with special needs, conducting student conferences, and initiating new projects.

Before inviting parents to become classroom helpers, the staff could generate a list of activities another adult might do in the classroom, including tutoring, cooking, making art projects, reading with a child, or practicing motor skills. This list could then be incorporated in a letter requesting helpers for these activities; the letter is then sent home with students. To facilitate parental

7. Chrispeels, Janet A. *"The Family as an Educational Resource."* Community Educational Journal, April 1987, 15.

8. Harter, N. and R. Lodish. *"Parent Peer Groups as School Friends."* Independent School, May 1985, 21-22.

cooperation, clearly state the time and date of the work sessions in the letter.

If you prefer not to have parents work in their children's classroom, consider bringing in parent helpers from another class or volunteer aides from the PTA or a nearby college (particularly from psychology, child development, and sociology classes). Often high school students in psychology classes can arrange an hour once a week for practicum experiences.

It is helpful to arrange an after-school meeting to welcome prospective parent helpers and introduce them to the teachers. This is also a good time to acquaint parent helpers with the classroom and its facilities, including the location of supplies. Explain the goals of the classroom and/or school and tell parents how their assistance will meet needs the staff cannot cope with alone. During this time, also explain discipline policies and discuss the kinds of problems that might arise.

Then, ask the parents to write down their names and phone numbers, the activities in which they have a particular interest, their special qualifications, and times convenient for them to assist in the classroom. Point out that it is vital to the school's program that parent helpers be dependable.

Room Preparations

To prepare the classroom for the daily presence of parent helpers, designate a place where the helpers can find the project materials they will need for assisting that day. (Be sure to put the materials out ahead of time!) Also place a loose-leaf notebook in the helper area. In the binder write special instructions for parent helpers to direct them in working with the students.

A special *Aide Instructional Log* is provided in this section. Duplicate a few copies, punch them with a three-hole punch, and insert the pages in the binder. The Aide Instructional Log can be used to plan aide tasks ahead of time. On the form, staff members can list which aide they would like to have work with which child. Describe the task briefly and simply (i.e. "page 53, math book"). Encourage parent helpers to write on this form any questions they have, observations they've made about a child, and statements regarding their availability for future sessions. Written comments from aides regarding a student work session (i.e. "Sarah had difficulty on the math page" or "Assignment was very easy; Bill could do it on his own") can prove to be an invaluable communication device between teachers and parent helpers. Emphasize that teachers will not be able to talk with the helpers during class time since "time on task" with the students is so valuable.

Parent aides can also be an invaluable help to teachers in preparing materials. Clerical tasks, such as running off dittos, mending games, or laminating projects, can be put in a large box marked "Clerical Aide Tasks." Be sure to include all supplies needed to complete the task and attach a note providing any special instructions.

Suggest to students that they periodically show their appreciation to parent aides by giving them handmade cards or original drawings in addition to saying "thank you." At the end of the year consider having a special "Aide Appreciation Reception" in which all helpers are invited and presented with homemade thank-you cards and a carnation, and served cookies and punch.

Recognizing Parent Involvement

Parent involvement should always be recognized. The Super Parent Award is designed to show the school's appreciation for parents who give of their time and effort. Duplicate the forms on bright-colored paper and always have a few copies on hand to send home when appropriate occasions arise.

Notes

Chapter 2 Activities

HOME ESTEEM BUILDERS

Date_____   Surveyor _____

Parent(s) Names _____
Student's Name _____ Teacher _____
Student's Name _____ Teacher _____
Student's Name _____ Teacher _____

• Would you be interested in learning how to help your child?

• What specific kinds of things would you be interested in learning? (If the parent cannot think of specific topics, provide a few suggestions—e.g. helping your child with homework, disciplining, reading aloud, helping your child be more organized, etc. Create a list and keep adding to it.)

• If we offered parenting classes, would you be interested in attending?_____ What time and day would be most convenient for you to attend the parenting class? _____

• Is there anything that might hinder you from coming to a session? _____ What is it and how can we help? _____

• Have you attended past parent programs? If so, what was the title/topic of the program?
_____

• Did you consider the program to be valuable to you? If so, why? If not, please tell me why it was not helpful and how it might have been changed to make it more helpful.
_____

• Other questions to ask: _____
_____
_____
_____
_____

• Comments from parents: _____
_____
_____
_____
_____

Esteem Builders' Complete Program
Jalmar Press, Rolling Hills Estates, CA

PARENT CHECKLIST OF A HOME-SCHOOL PARTNERSHIP

Dear Parent:

We need your help. As you may know, our school is committed to the concept of the esteem enhancement of your child. We recognize that one of the critical elements of an effective esteem-building program is a strong home-school partnership. Could you please take a moment to complete the following survey? Return it as soon as possible to your child's teacher. Your ideas are important to us and will help us in our efforts as a school to enhance our partnership in esteem building with you. Thank you!

As a parent do you feel your child's school...	Never 1	Sometimes 2	Frequently 3	Always 4
1. Encourages parents to serve in the role of classroom or school volunteers?	___	___	___	___
2. Makes special efforts such as newsletters, home visits, phone calls, to keep home and school communication open?	___	___	___	___
3. Believes that parents should work as a team with the school in the enhancement of student self-esteem?	___	___	___	___
4. Employs frequent and varied methods to educate parents in esteem building?	___	___	___	___
5. Provides parents with specific ways to help enhance their children's self-esteem?	___	___	___	___
6. Helps parents understand their children's specific esteem strengths?	___	___	___	___
7. Makes ongoing efforts to help parents keep abreast of their children's school progress?	___	___	___	___
8. Makes strong efforts to correct possible areas which might hinder parent involvement such as language barriers, child care and parental working hours?	___	___	___	___
9. Continually analyzes options to involve more reticent parents in their children's school progress?	___	___	___	___
10. Takes the time to survey parents' needs in esteem enhancement and find out specifically what the school can do to meet those needs?	___	___	___	___

Please tell us one way we as a school could help you best enhance the self-esteem of your child.

_____

_____

_____

_____

HOME ESTEEM BUILDERS

(Checklist Continued)

Do you feel our school has effective home-school communication regarding your child's work, school activities and behavior?

Yes _____ No _____

If no, please tell us one idea we could try to improve this communication.

_____

_____

_____

_____

_____

_____

_____

Any other comments?

_____

_____

_____

_____

_____

_____

_____

Thank you for helping us!

Child's Grade _____

Esteem Builders' Complete Program
Jalmar Press, Rolling Hills Estates, CA

CHECKLIST OF SCHOOL BEHAVIORS THAT PROMOTE A HOME-SCHOOL PARTNERSHIP

Directions: For a quick survey of your school's effectiveness in creating a home-school partnership, complete the following items:

As a school:	Never 1	Sometimes 2	Frequently 3	Always 4
1. Do we encourage parents to serve in the role of classroom or school volunteers?	____	____	____	____
2. Do we make special efforts such as newsletters, home visits, phone calls, to keep home and school communication open?	____	____	____	____
3. Do we believe that parents should work as a team with the school in the enhancement of student self-esteem?	____	____	____	____
4. Do we employ frequent and varied methods to educate parents in esteem building?	____	____	____	____
5. Do we provide parents with specific ways to help enhance their children's self-esteem?	____	____	____	____
6. Do we help parents understand their children's specific esteem strengths?	____	____	____	____
7. Are ongoing efforts made to help parents keep abreast of their children's school progress?	____	____	____	____
8. Are strong efforts made to correct possible areas which might hinder parent involvement such as language barriers, child care and parental working hours?	____	____	____	____
9. Do we continually analyze options to involve more reticent parents in their children's school progress?	____	____	____	____
10. Do we take the time to survey parents' needs in esteem enhancement and find out specifically what the school can do to meet those needs?	____	____	____	____

Areas we could improve in to enhance the home-school partnership in esteem building:

_____

_____

_____

_____

_____

_____

_____

_____

_____

Esteem Builders' Complete Program
Jalmar Press, Rolling Hills Estates, CA

(Checklist Continued)

Do you feel our school has effective home-school communication regarding your child's work, school activities and behavior?

Yes _____   No _____

If no, please tell us one idea we could try to improve this communication.

_____
_____
_____
_____
_____
_____
_____
_____

Any other comments?

_____
_____
_____
_____
_____
_____
_____
_____

Thank you for helping us!

Child's Grade _____

Esteem Builders' Complete Program
Jalmar Press, Rolling Hills Estates, CA

"Esteem Building…the key to school and personal success.…We can make a difference."

Dear _____

    Hello! My name is _____. I am going to be your new teacher. I'm really looking forward to the beginning of school and to meeting you. During the summer, I've been busy making lots of fun games and activities for our classroom.

    We're going to learn so many exciting things this year. A few of the projects we have planned are_____ . I'm especially excited because we're going to learn about you.

    I hope that you're having a fun summer. I can't wait to hear about what you've been doing! See you on the first day of school.

                       Fondly,

Esteem Builders' Complete Program
Jalmar Press, Rolling Hills Estates, CA

HOME ESTEEM BUILDERS

"Esteem Building…the key to school and personal success.…We can make a difference."

Dear Parents,

Hello! My name is Bob Smith and I will be your child's math teacher for this school year. I wanted to take a moment of your time to introduce myself and to welcome you and your child to my classroom. I have taught in the Saratoga School District for the past seven years. Prior to working in Saratoga, I taught for five years in the Gilroy Unified School District. I completed my undergraduate work at San Jose State University and received my Master's degree from Santa Clara University.

I am very committed to making this school year successful and positive for both you and your child. To help ensure that it will be a beneficial year for your child, I want to stress to you how important I feel it is to keep the communication between us open. If at any time during the year, you'd like to discuss your child's progress, please feel free to call me. I am available at the school until 4:00 p.m. every day. You could call the school office at 867-2274 and leave a message with the secretary asking that I get back to you.

Our first back-to-school night is scheduled this year on October 5 at 7:00 p.m. I hope you plan to attend the event. It is during this time that I will be discussing in detail your child's academic program for the year. I will describe my expectations and special projects that your child will be assigned. I also will be covering my homework and grading policy as well as displaying the school materials we will use during the year.

I look forward to meeting you and working with your child. I know that by working together we can create the best possible learning conditions for your child's school success.

Sincerely,

Esteem Builders' Complete Program
Jalmar Press, Rolling Hills Estates, CA

"Esteem Building…the key to school and personal success….We can make a difference."

Dear Parent:

Can you please help us? We're off to such a great start toward having an outstanding learning year. We have many activities and projects planned. We could certainly use your help if at all possible! You can be an important part of your child's learning process. We'd love to have you participate. If you can help us in any of the ways listed below, please check the item(s) and return the checklist with your child tomorrow. Feel free to add other ways you'd like to help with the students.

_____ assist in the classroom (or school) an hour each week
_____ make activity items at home
_____ run off dittos at school
_____ correct student work at home
_____ help prepare art projects at school
_____ help laminate materials at school
_____ listen to children read at school
_____ provide transportation for field trips
_____ make treats for class parties
_____ relay parent messages by phone
_____ share special knowledge with students in school; for example: present a science experi-
ment, read poetry, show slides of a foreign country or another state, exhibit and talk
about a hobby

A skill I could share is _____
Another way I could help is _____
_____
The days that I could help are _____
The times of day I could help are _____
Comments: _____
_____
Parent's Signature: _____

Thank you for your interest! If you have any comments or concerns please stop by or call.

Sincerely,

Esteem Builders' Complete Program
Jalmar Press, Rolling Hills Estates, CA

HOME ESTEEM BUILDERS

AIDE INSTRUCTIONAL LOG

Date _____

STUDENT	AIDE	ASSIGNMENT	AIDE COMMENTS

Esteem Builders' Complete Program
Jalmar Press, Rolling Hills Estates, CA

Super Parent Award

This award is given to

_____

for _____

_____

Thank you for your interest and support. It is appreciated!

Signed: _____

Date: _____

Super Parent Award

This award is given to

_____

for _____

_____

Thank you for your interest and support. It is appreciated!

Signed: _____

Date: _____

Esteem Builders' Complete Program
Jalmar Press, Rolling Hills Estates, CA

RESOURCES LIST

The following sources are recommended for helping parents learn the skills of self-esteem enhancement. Though there are many "how-to" books available for parents, these were chosen because of their simplicity or research-based approach to home-esteem enhancement. A few resources that are particularly valuable are annotated. These sources might be ones schools could consider purchasing for a School Resource Lending Library on self-esteem.

Bagin, Don; Grazian, Frank; and Harrison, Charles H. *School Communications: Ideas That Work.* Woodstown, NJ: Communicaid Incorporated, 1980.

Baron, Bruce; Baron, Christina; and McDonald, Bonnie. *What Did You Learn in School Today?*: New York, NY: Warner Books, Inc., 1983.

Becker, Henry Jay and Epstein, Joyce L. "Parent Involvement: A Survey of Teacher Practices." *Elementary School Journal*, November 1982, 85-102.

Bennis, Warren and Nanus, Burt. *Leaders.* New York, NY: Harper & Row, 1985.

Brandt, Ronald S. (ed.) *Parents: Partners & Schools.* Alexandria, VA: Association for Supervision and Curriculum Development, 1979.

Brown, Patricia R. and Haylock, Kati. *Excellence for Whom?* Oakland, CA: The Achievement Council, 1984.

Cattermole, Juleen and Robinson, Norman. "Effective Home/School Communication from the Parents' Perspective." *Phi Delta Kappan.* September 1985, 48-50.

Chrispeels, Janet A. "The Family as an Educational Resource." *Community Educational Journal,* April 1987, 10-17.

Clark, Reginald M. *Family Life and School Achievement: Why Poor Black Children Succeed or Fail.* Chicago, IL: University of Chicago Press, 1983.

Comer, James P. "New Haven's School-Community Connection." *Educational Leadership,* March 1987, 13-16.

Seeley, David S. "Education, Dependence, and Poverty." *The Education Digest,* January 1987, 6-9.

Seeley, David S. "Partnership's Time Has Come." *Educational Leadership,* September 1986, 82-85.

Sikula, Roberta. "A Crucial Issue, School-Community Relations: A Systematic Approach." *NASSP Bulletin*, February 1981, 55-62.

Walberg, Herbert J. "Families As Partners in Educational Productivity." *Kappan*, February 1984, 397-400.

Notes

3

Parent Education

HOME ESTEEM BUILDERS

- Parent In-Service
- Parent University Day
- Parent Lending Library
- Make-and-Take Sessions

ACTIVITIES LIST

SECURITY

SELFHOOD

AFFILIATION

MISSION

COMPETENCE

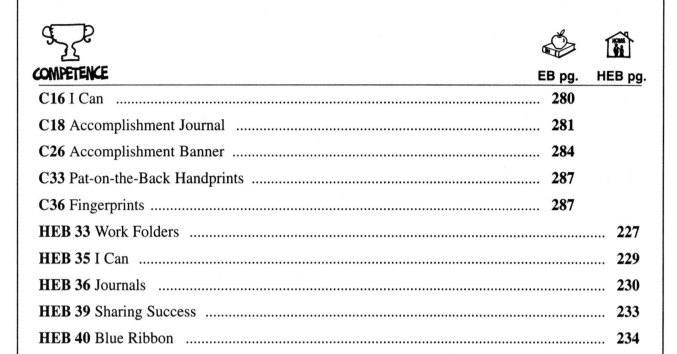

COMPETENCE

Home Esteem Builders was developed on the premise that a home and school partnership is an integral element of effective esteem building. The material in this book provides educators with the resources to help parents enhance their children's self-esteem. Before distributing any of these materials to the students' homes, please make sure that they have been translated into the primary language of the parents.

3

Parent Education

The relation between parents and children is
essentially based on teaching.

—GILBERT HIGHET

There is one premise in regard to parenting that is almost universal: parents want their children to succeed in school and in life. The parenting section shelves in any local bookstore verify the concerns parents have about their children. All of them are stocked with books dealing with the same general theme: "How to help your child." Parents want to know how to improve their children's school achievement, behavior, and self-esteem. The sad fact in our society is that in all too many cases no one has told them what they can do to enhance their children's potential. Schools can help fill in the gap by providing parents with information and strategies on effective parenting techniques. *Home Esteem Builders* was developed as one way to help educators teach parents critical skills in esteem enhancement.

"How do we best teach parents the skills of esteem enhancement?" is a critical question the staff must ask themselves as they begin to involve the home as a major component of the schoolwide esteem-building plan. *Home Esteem Builders* provides a number of guidelines to help educators answer this question as well as specific and practical strategies and activities to accomplish this goal. One of the most traditional ways the school has for educating parents is the delivery of a one-hour in-service presentation. It remains as one of the easiest ways to present information since all parents are generally invited to attend at the same time. This is a time when the essential questions of a self-esteem program

can be addressed. The most important questions parents need answers for include the following:

- **What is esteem building?**

- **How does self-esteem impact achievement and behavior?**

- **Can I really improve my child's self-esteem?**

- **What is the school doing to improve student self-esteem?**

- **What can I do at home to help enhance my child's self-esteem?**

PARENT IN-SERVICE

What follows is a complete one-hour parent in-service that may be conducted on the school site at a time and date most convenient for the majority of attendees. The staff presenter is provided with a complete script designed to help parents recognize that not only is self-esteem critical to their children's happiness and success but also that it is learned. The script is presented only as a suggested format and can be adapted to fit any school's unique program. The presenter needs to remember, though, to balance the rationale for the program with specific and simple activities to do at home. At the conclusion of the in-service, parents want to walk away with two things.

1. **Why is my child's school committed to self-esteem and what impact will enhancement have on his/her performance?**

2. **What concrete techniques can I do to enhance my child's self-esteem?**

The in-service may also be an opportunity to describe the school's year-long plans in home esteem building. Here is an ideal time to describe student esteem-building activities the school plans to implement that will require the support and collaboration of parents. These activities could include:

• **Parent Lending Library**

• **Esteem Builder Grams**

• **Home Esteem Builder Activities**

• **Home Esteem Builder Tips**

• **Home Esteem Building Calendar***

• **Esteem Builders' Reading Program***

Plans for activities such as these could be described or demonstrated. If the school has already actively implemented school and classroom self-esteem activities, why not share these with the parents? Student projects can be displayed on walls and bulletin boards and photographs of esteem-building classroom activities can be arranged on walls or in scrapbooks. Teacher materials and resources currently being used in classrooms could be set up on tables for display. A video presentation showing students actually involved in self-esteem activities could even be arranged. There are endless possibilities for educating parents in esteem enhancement. At the same time, the school can accomplish a major goal of the session: to acquaint parents with its self-esteem program.

Educators recognize that, ideally, a solid school-wide esteem-building program should involve the parents in the process. Unfortunately, the general scenario these days is the fact that not all parents (or in some cases, very few parents) attend the event. There are ways, however, the staff can improve parent attendance. Many of these ideas

are offered in this section. Increasing attendance at the in-service must always be deliberately planned for by the staff. It is strongly suggested that the staff vigorously engage in an all-out campaign to have as many parents as possible in attendance at the in-service. Remember to document the various methods used to encourage parents to come to the function. The list can prove helpful to assess what was successful (as well as what was ineffective) as the staff prepares for future school-sponsored parenting functions. Whether the activity was well attended or not, the staff must recognize that in the end the most important point was that a concerted effort was made to invite the home to learn esteem-building premises.

In-Service Components

• A complete one-hour presentation script entitled "Self-Esteem: The Key to Your Child's Success."

• An invitation for parents to attend the presentation, to be sent home by the school.

• A list of suggested activities for enhancing family esteem. Activities to display or demonstrate at the presentation are described in detail in either *Esteem Builders* or *Home Esteem Builders*.

• OH2 Building Blocks of Self-Esteem (found on page 88) to make into an overhead transparency for use at the presentation.

• A Presenter Check-Off List specifying all materials and equipment the trainer needs for a successful presentation.

• A list of techniques for the school to use in maximizing parent participation at the in-service.

• A Presentation Time Line of items for the staff or in-service presenter to attend to before the presentation.

• A list of suggested background readings to familiarize the presenter with the material prior to the presentation.

- Blackline masters to duplicate as participant handouts (found in *Trainer's Manual*).

- Chart with suggested room setup for the presentation.

MAXIMIZING PARENT PARTICIPATION

Because parent involvement is an essential component of strong self-esteem programs, it is important that parents be in-serviced in the five feelings of self-esteem and their impact on student achievement and behavior. The school-sponsored evening parent in-service is one of the most common and effective vehicles to disseminate this information. Educators, though, frequently ask, "How do we increase parent participation at the event?" Deliberate planning is the most important method of increasing parent involvement. For instance, spend time as a faculty thinking about all the possibilities that could prevent parents from attending the event (i.e. transportation, babysitting, an inability to read the notices, need for translation, etc.), then troubleshoot ways these situations could be remedied. Many schools that have gone to rather elaborate means to ensure parent participation have been successful in achieving a large turnout simply because they had anticipated possible problems and arranged alternatives.

The following suggestions are methods schools have used to maximize parent participation:

News Releases. Contact the local newspaper well in advance of the in-service. In many cases, the school is responsible for supplying the text. Call again to confirm that the article will appear. Invite a reporter to cover the actual event if desired.

District/School Bulletins. Feature the event in all school and district bulletins. Begin highlighting the event at least one month prior to the scheduled date. Plan to have a minimum of three notice reminders.

Babysitting Services. Parents frequently avoid evening meetings due to babysitting conflicts. Offer to babysit their children! Frequently publicize

that you will be doing so. Enlist the help of a community agency, such as the Girl Scouts, to furnish the services. Set aside one or two classrooms furnished with a television and VCR. A G-rated movie could then be shown. Be sure to also have a few adults supervise the classrooms.

Class Competition. Many schools set up a competition between classes to see which class has the largest parent turnout. Students in the winning class receive "prizes" such as popsicles, ice cream cones, or a popcorn party.

Room Mother Phone Tree. Ask one or two mothers from each classroom to phone each student's home on the day of the event (or the day before) to remind parents of the event.

Student Invitations. Have students write a personal invitation/reminder about the event to take home to their parents (or duplicate the Parent Invitation form provided in this section and have students fill in the appropriate information).

Engraved Invitations. A few schools mail engraved invitations for the event to each student's home. Older students can address their own invitations as well as those of younger students. These professionally printed invitations may be an added expense, but can be quite effective.

Teacher Letter. A personal letter to each parent from the student's teacher can be very valuable. To save time, the letter could be photocopied. The letter should state why the teacher feels the event would be valuable for parents and why he or she hopes they will attend.

Teacher Phone Calls. Though calling parents to remind them of the activity is very time-consuming, there is no denying that this procedure produces the best results. A teacher's personal recommendation to a parent to attend the function is a powerful incentive to attend. Keep in mind that not every parent may need to be contacted, but how about the parents of at-risk students? This method may be well worth the time.

Home Visits. In a few cases, visiting homes to personally invite parents may be in order.

Final Reminder. Don't overlook a final reminder on the day of the event. A note can be printed on colored ditto paper, perhaps with a colored border. Ask each student to add a personal note.

FINAL POINTS BEFORE THE IN-SERVICE

Finally, before arranging the presentation, think carefully about the needs of your audience. Here are a few key questions to ask regarding parents to determine if any final points have been overlooked.

- Does the date of the activity conflict with any other community or school events (or television specials)?

- Are some parents unable to attend due to transportation needs? Could a carpool be arranged?

- Can the parent read the notices? If not, can an interpreter call or visit some homes to personally deliver the message?

- Is the meeting arranged at a time conducive to parental attendance? A survey can be taken to find out which time would be most convenient for parents. Many schools offer in-servicing at a variety of times to meet the needs of working parents.

- Is the school meeting the needs of a local population that is culturally and linguistically diverse? Will translators be available and are parents aware that translators will be available at the presentation?

- Is the in-service being taped or videotaped for parents who cannot attend but would still like to receive the information? The tape could be shown again at other times or checked out of a school lending library.

- Are the school's facilities and communication systems conducive to serving handicapped parents?

- Would parents feel that this topic really is appropriate to their needs and relevant to their child?

PARENT UNIVERSITY DAY

A unique parent in-service concept is called Parent University Day. Once a year the district (or school) arranges a half-day program on a Saturday to present parents with ways they can help their children at home. The University Day is held at a local school so that classrooms can be used for each training session. The program features various mini-workshops on parenting. Topics for the mini-workshops are endless but all have the central theme of parent education. A few ideas include:

- Homework Tips
- Problem Solving
- Positive Discipline
- Reading Aloud
- Math
- Communication Ideas
- Conflict Management
- Arts and Crafts
- Self-Esteem Tips
- Alternatives to Television
- Implementing the Home Esteem Builder Program

Mentor teachers and local school personnel provide the training. Workshop leaders choose topics that reflect their specialties. Each workshop runs around fifty minutes in length.

Many schools choose to begin the University Day with one large session at which all participants gather to hear an opening speech on self-esteem enhancement, usually given by an outside consultant. Local businesses could sponsor this keynote speaker. Parents are then free to choose the workshops that interest them the most. School bells let participants know when each mini-session is over and it is time to locate the next "class." Babysitting could be provided by local Girl Scouts in one or two available classrooms on site. School personnel, including the superintendent, central office staff, principals, teachers and board members, are available throughout the day to share their support and expertise.

Generally, schools that have tried this approach notice that the first time University Day is held, parent enrollment is low; however, recommendations from the previous years' enthused attendees and newspaper coverage usually doubles the number of participants the following year. Each year the enrollment grows as parents discover how worthwhile the sessions are for home application. *(Idea suggested by Cupertino School District, Cupertino, California, and Gilroy Unified School District, Gilroy, California.)*

PARENT LENDING LIBRARY

Aiding parents in the enhancement of their children's self-esteem is a major element of a strong esteem-building program. Many schools find that one of the easiest ways to achieve this goal is to create a lending library of self-esteem resources for parents. These resources could include parenting videos, audiotapes, games, and books. The price of such a venture can be reduced by networking with other schools. Resources could then be rotated among schools so that new materials are made available to parents. Two keys to the success of such a program are awareness and accessibility.

Awareness

Though the school may have stocked the most elaborate supply of esteem-building materials, the resources often remain untouched simply because parents are unaware of their existence. The availability of such resources must be publicized to the parents. A few ways to let parents know about an esteem-building Parent Lending Library are:

- **Newsletters.** Any school publication sent home could include a quick synopsis of one or two items available for checkout by parents. Many principal newsletters include a small section in each edition alerting parents to the newest parenting resources available. A heading on the column such as "Parenting Resource: What's New" alerts parents to browse through the section. It also serves as a reminder that materials are available to

> ### PARENTING RESOURCE: WHAT'S NEW
>
> A wonderful new book has just been added to our Parent Lending Library that I thought you'd like to know about. It's called *I Think I Can, I Know I Can!* The book is written by Susan Isaacs and Wendy Ritchey and deals with a powerful subject: how to help children use positive self-talk. We know that what we say to ourselves internally and aloud can have a profound effect on our emotional and physical well-being. This book helps parents focus on helping their children use the self-talk method to become more confident and emotionally secure. It deals with a simple, five-step program that has proven effective in clinical and school settings. If you're interested, please drop by our school's Parent Lending Library located right outside our front office. Feel free to check it out and read it at home.

borrow. Always remind parents where the lending library is located. Above is a sample of the column entitled "Parenting Resource: What's New."

- **Parent Conferences.** Encourage staff members to take time at parent conferences to suggest esteem-enhancing books parents can read to their children at home. Remind staff members that it is often more effective to recommend one or two items rather than hand out an entire booklist. A few items from the Parent Lending Library could be made available at the conference for immediate checkout if desired.

- **Bulletin Boards.** A self-esteem bulletin board permanently hung in a central, visible location at the school can prove very helpful for parents. The board could contain information on self-esteem materials, conferences, parenting tips, and ideas and could be continually updated. Also consider displaying photographs of school and classroom esteem-building activities.

- **Parent Meetings.** Any parent meeting is an opportunity to mention parenting materials and their availability. A table could also be easily set up at the meeting to display a few items.

Accessibility

In order to be fully utilized, self-esteem materials must also be accessible to parents. Not only should parents be aware of titles and contents, but the resources must be in visible, easy-to-reach areas for checkout. A few suggestions to make materials more accessible include:

- **Idea Exchange Table.** A table in a central school location could be permanently set up for parents. All types of self-esteem materials for parents to browse through could be displayed. Materials could include student self-esteem samples, games, suggested reading lists, parent-made esteem-building activities as well as books and tapes. Encourage staff members to continually restock the table with new ideas.

- **Checkout System.** A checkout system similar to a library lending system could be developed at the school. Attach a manila envelope library pocket to each item and create a corresponding index card with the item's title. Insert each card into the corresponding library pocket. Display the materials on a table along with a small box to store checkout resources. Encourage parents (and staff!) to check out items by simply filling out their name, phone number, and checkout date on the library card and leave the card in the box. Many schools set the table in a visible location such as inside the school office. Checkout materials could include books, games, audiocassettes, and videocassettes. Because such resources are expensive, protect the materials by placing the library in a safe location. Some schools list materials on the office bulletin board, keeping the actual library either behind the secretary's counter or in the children's library.

Note: A list of suggested resources for parents is provided. While this is by no means meant as a complete list of available products, it is a beginning referral to some of the more viable resources.

Resources for Parents

The sources found on pages 97 to 99 are recommended for helping parents learn the skills of self-esteem enhancement. Though there are many "how-to" books available for parents, these were chosen because of their simplicity or research-based approach to home esteem enhancement. A few resources that are particularly valuable are annotated. These sources might be ones schools could consider purchasing for a School Resource Lending Library on self-esteem.

MAKE-AND-TAKE SESSIONS

Many schools have discovered that an effective way to educate parents in esteem enhancement is holding a school Make-and-Take Session. Sessions are usually held on a Saturday or after school, though any other convenient time is a possibility, and last about one-and-a-half to two hours. At the session, a wide variety of simple esteem-building samples are displayed. All of the items are activities parents can do at home with their children to enhance self-esteem. Parents are free to choose from this assortment and create samples for themselves. All of the materials needed to create the patterns are available. Teachers are also available during the session not only to help parents make the samples but to discuss how the activity may be used in the home.

Including children in the activity is optional. Schools that choose not to include children provide on-site child care services. Local scouting groups could be called upon to help out. The session usually ends with a group of parents enthused about now having in their hands a few concrete esteem-building activities to try with their children. In addition, teachers find that the session's informal setting invites parents to respond in a more open way with questions and concerns about their children. Valuable discussions between parents and teachers transpire because the opportunity for a home-school partnership has been created.

Planning the Session

To ensure an effective session, a number of items need to be considered beforehand. Here are a few areas that must be planned for prior to the Make-and-Take Session.

- **Room.** The room where you have the session should be one that is large enough to hold all the materials as well as the people. The space should have large tables (as well as chairs!) for people to create the materials and extra long tables to display the samples. Several big garbage cans also need to be in the room.

- **Time.** There are many options to determine what time the session is held. The most important consideration is the needs of your parents. If the majority of them work, consider an evening or Saturday session. A home-survey that could be quickly filled out and returned might ask, "If you were to come to a Make-and-Take Session, what would be the best time for you?"

- **Date.** Choose a date that conflicts the least with parents' schedules. Check for any outside community engagements. Saturdays often are difficult because children's athletic games are usually scheduled on this day. Some investigative work may be required to come up with the ideal date.

- **Materials.** Materials such as tagboard may need to be ordered in large quantity prior to the event in order to reduce the cost; therefore, it is essential to have a rough estimate of the number of parents estimated to come. A Telephone Tree in which parents call other parents could provide this information. A flyer with a place to respond "yes" or "no" is another way to determine an approximate attendance number.

- **Sample Materials.** The most time-consuming part of the program is creating the activity patterns. At least one-and-a-half patterns per participant should be available. This is another reason why it is important to know how many parents plan to attend. Consider having parent

aides or older students cut out the sample patterns. Patterns should be durable. Ideally, they should all be made out of heavyweight tagboard and laminated. Over the years, many people may be tracing around the same pattern.

Make-and-Take Patterns

The list of activities parents could do at a Make-and-Take Session is endless. It is important to consider the following criteria in selecting patterns for parents to make at the session:

1. They should be **simple** to make. Parents want to be able to quickly make a number of samples and bring them home. Any activity that is too time-consuming is not appropriate for this session. The main idea is for parents to be able to make the materials created at the session again with their own children at home.

2. Materials needed for the pattern should be **inexpensive** and **readily accessible** to the parent. The best activities to present are ones that are not only quick and easy to make but inexpensive to create. Since the school will be providing the materials for parents to use at the session, it is important to keep the cost of the materials in mind. Consider selecting patterns that only require materials such as construction paper, tagboard, marking pens and crayons, scissors, paste, and yarn or string. These materials are also generally available to parents around the house or can be purchased at a minimal cost.

The activities found on the following page are suggested for the Make-and-Take Session because they meet the "simple and inexpensive" criteria. All the activities may be found in *Esteem Builders* by Dr. Michele Borba.

Choose seven to twelve different activities, depending on the number of participants expected. Create the completed pattern for each activity and laminate the sample for durability.

Pattern Station. Set up a table for each activity. On the table place a completed sample that has been laminated. In addition, place all the materials parents need to make a sample to take home. For example, if SH18: My Identity Shield was chosen by the faculty as one of the suggested Make-and-Take activities, the pattern should contain the following materials:

- A completed identity shield that has been laminated. It is always fun to have an actual student sample of the completed activity available. If the samples are to be returned to the student, you may wish to pin all the samples up on one bulletin board.

- A tagboard shield for parents to trace around (enlarge the pattern on page 132 of *Esteem Builders* to 18" by 22"). If a larger number of participants are anticipated, a few tagboard patterns should be provided. These patterns are merely the shape of the shield. Ideally, they should be made on heavier tagboard-weight paper so they can be traced a number of times.

- Scissors.

- Marking pens or crayons.

- The directions for making the identity shield. Run off a number of copies from page 109 of *Esteem Builders*. Parents can then glue the directions to the activity on the back of their completed samples.

Material Table. In addition to the "pattern station" set up for each activity, set up on a "material table" several of the following items:

- scissors (it's always a good idea to ask parents to bring a pair from home)
- glue or rubber cement
- one paper cutter
- laminating machine (only if available)
- extra marking pens and crayons
- poster board or tagboard
- rulers
- pencils
- hole punches
- staplers
- garbage cans
- construction paper
- yarn or string

Code	Title	Page
S31/32	Sparkle Line	66
S36	Sparkle Greeting Bags	67
SH1	My Physical Self	101
SH2	Me Riddle	102
SH6	Me Doll	103
SH9	Walking Me Puppet	104
SH12	Paper Bag Face Puppet	104
SH18	My Identity Shield	109
SH21	Wanted Poster	110
SH33	Me Banner	141
SH34	I Collage	142
A21	Friendship Recipes	179
A22	Friendship Wheel	179
A32	Sunrays	184
A38	Compliment Hanging	186
M22	Goal Wheel	234
C10	Favorite Work Folder	278
C12	Things I Can Do	279
C14	Paper Chains	280
C26	Accomplishment Banner	284
C33	Pat-on-the-Back Handprints	287
C39	Positive Wristbands	288

MAKE-AND-TAKE INVITATION

Duplicate a copy of the following invitation on bright-colored cardstock-weight paper supplying the date, time, and location. Send home a copy to each parent. Remember to also send home additional reminders and publish the event in all the newsletters and community newspapers. A parent "Phone Tree" calling each parent personally for an R.S.V.P. is always a good idea. Having an approximate number of parent participants in mind is critical since materials must be ordered.

Your Child's School Invites You to A Unique and Special Esteem-Building "Make-And-Take" Session.

✳

Date: _____

Time: _____

Place: _____

An assortment of activities will be available for you to copy and make. All activities are easy to make and can be used at home as Family Esteem-Building activities to enhance your child's self-esteem. And all materials will be provided. PLEASE JOIN US!

PLEASE RSVP _____

Esteem Builders' Complete Program
Jalmar Press, Rolling Hills Estates, CA

Notes

Chapter 3 In-Service

SESSION 8	TIME: 1 HOUR

A Parent In-Service

Self-Esteem: The Key to Your Child's Success

OBJECTIVES

At the conclusion of this session parents will:

- Gain an awareness of the critical impact self-esteem has on their children's academic achievement and behavior.
- Identify the five building blocks of high self-esteem: Security, Selfhood, Affiliation, Mission, and Competence.
- Gain a knowledge of home esteem-building activities that can be done in the family.
- Identify characteristics of children with high self-esteem in each of the five building blocks of self-esteem.
- Understand how to implement the Home Esteem Builder Program.
- Recognize that parents and schools together can serve as partners in enhancing students' self-esteem.

MATERIALS

- Overhead projector, screen, and transparency pens.
- Microphone.
- Table (3-4') to hold the overhead projector (or overhead projector cart).
- Tape recorder (optional).
- Extension cord (optional).
- Name tags.
- Marking pens (for participants to write names on name tags).
- Several copies of *Esteem Builders* and *Home Esteem Builders.*
- Esteem Builders Activity samples to demonstrate or display.

HANDOUTS/OVERHEADS

- BL 15 Self-Esteem: The Key to Your Child's Success.
- OH 2 Building Blocks of Self-Esteem.
- Sample of first month from the Home Esteem Building Calendar*.

BACKGROUND READING

The in-service facilitator must have a thorough knowledge of the presentation material. The following pages in *Esteem Builders* are highly recommended as reading material prior to the presentation:

* Separate programs available through

1) Introduction to Self-Esteem (pages 1-11);
2) A Strong Foundation: Building Security (pages 45-51);
3) Clarifying the Inner Picture: Building Selfhood (pages 95-101);
4) A Cooperative Spirit: Building Affiliation (pages 159-167);
5) Purpose with Responsibility: Building Mission (pages 217-222);
6) "I Am A Winner!": Building Competence (pages 269-274).

ESTEEM BUILDER ACTIVITIES

Parents appreciate theory and research, but when they leave an in-service they want to have concrete activities they can immediately do with their children. Therefore, a strong component of a successful presentation is demonstrating actual techniques and activities parents can use at home to enhance self-esteem. There are dozens of activities described in *Esteem Builders* and *Home Esteem Builders* from which to choose. Samples from each book are recommended.

Prior to the presentation, choose two to four sample activities parents can do at home to enhance their children's self-esteem. Make each activity on brightly-colored construction paper or tagboard. Student-made activities are particularly well-received by parents. Sample activities should be demonstrated and/or displayed from each of the five building blocks of self-esteem. Sample activities along with complete directions are found in either *Esteem Builders* or *Home Esteem Builders*. Each activity is coded as to its location.

The following activities from *Esteem Builders: A K-8 Self-Esteem Curriculum for Improving Student Achievement, Behavior and School Climate* by Dr. Michele Borba are particularly recommended as activities parents can do at home with their children for "family esteem building." All may be easily demonstrated or displayed at the in-service.

Code	Title	Page
S13	List of People I Can Depend On	55
S24	Sparkle Statements	62
S25	Smile Book	63

 (S = Security Section in *Esteem Builders*)

Code	Title	Page
SH15	A Movie of My Life	107
SH18	My Identity Shield	109
SH21	Wanted Poster	110

 (SH = Selfhood Section in *Esteem Builders*)

FAMILY ESTEEM-BUILDING ACTIVITIES

Code	Title	Page
A21	Friendship Recipes	179
A22	Friendship Wheel	179
A38	Compliment Hanging (adapt to "family compliments")	186

 (A = Affiliation Section in *Esteem Builders*)

Code	Title	Page
M1	What I Like...What I Want to Change	223
M19	Daily Goal Setting	234
M22	Goal Wheel	234
M26	I Think I Can	236

 (M = Mission Section in *Esteem Builders*)

Code	Title	Page
C6	Class Strength Book (adapt from Child Strength Book)	276
C8	Strength Barbell	277
C10	Favorite Work Folder	278
C16	I Can	280
C18	Accomplishment Journal	281
C26	Accomplishment Banner	284

(C = Competence Section in *Esteem Builders*)

In addition to activities found in *Esteem Builders*, the Home Esteem-Building Activities found in *Home Esteem Builders* can also be easily demonstrated. In particular, consider displaying the following as fully-made samples:

Code	Title	Page
HEB 9	Family-Name Shields	204
HEB10	Time Line	205
HEB12	Me Collage	207
HEB14	Things I Like Collage	209
HEB16	The Inside Scoop	211
HEB17	My Family Shield	212
HEB18	Family Tree	213
HEB22	Compliments	217
HEB26	My Responsiblities from School	221
HEB28	Making Self Changes	223
HEB33	Work Folders	228
HEB35	"I Can..."	230
HEB36	Journals	231
HEB39	Sharing Success	234
HEB40	Blue Ribbon	235

In addition to sample activities, the parent in-service is an ideal time to describe other aspects of the school's home esteem-building program. The presenter could, for instance, have samples of any or all of the following program components and briefly describe how each will be used:

- Esteem Builder Grams
- Parent Lending Library
- Home Esteem Building Calendar *
- Esteem Builders' Reading Program *

SELECTING ACTIVITIES

The session facilitator may choose from a wide assortment of esteem-building samples to demonstrate and/or display to parents. In selecting samples to display or demonstrate at the in-service, keep in mind the following points:

- **Age Suitability.** Choose ideas suitable to the age of the participants' children. If the audience is composed of parents of K-8 children, choose two samples for each idea presented: one sample appropriate for younger students, and the other more appropriate for older students. A grade-level recommendation for each activity is found in *Esteem Builders*.

- **Size of Activity.** The larger and more colorful the display the better. Keep in mind the size of the audience and the fact that participants in the back rows may not be

- **Simplicity.** Choose activities that are both simple for parents to do and simple for the presenter to explain. Parents are receptive to ideas that are quick and easy to do. An important in-service goal is to present parents with a number of activities they can do with their children. More complicated activities take too much in-service time to present.

- **Variety.** Select various types of activities. Not all participants appreciate "arts and crafts" projects. For each component, consider demonstrating the following:

  - Two arts and crafts ideas (one for younger students; one for older).
  - One "quick" esteem-building technique.
  - One or two selections of children's literature as reading suggestions.

During preparation time, it is recommended that the facilitator create a chart such as the one on page 94. Several weeks prior to the in-service, begin to choose the activities that will be demonstrated. While many of them are ready to duplicate from *Esteem Builders'*, it will take time to make the samples needed. Better yet, borrow student samples from staff members who are using the *Esteem Builders* program with their students.

Consider also displaying student samples of completed esteem-building activities on bulletin boards and walls inside the room where the presentation will be held. Photographs hung on walls and posters of students doing the activities in the classrooms always create an attractive and pleasing display. Many schools also set up in a corner of the room a screen showing videotaped images of esteem-building student activities.

PROCEDURE

1. In-Service Introduction

Note: The in-service introduction should be brief (no more than five minutes). Your goal is to make the group feel welcome and to let them know a little bit about you and the purpose for the in-service. The introduction should be memorized so that it flows quickly and smoothly.

Welcome the group to the workshop. Thank everyone for taking the time to come despite their busy schedules. Briefly introduce yourself and your position at the school. If you are a parent, mention the fact. You may wish to give a short summary of who you are to establish your credibility (i.e. your role, your involvement with the school esteem-building process, your primary motivation for doing what you're doing).

Briefly state the purpose of the in-service: to help parents gain an awareness of how self-esteem impacts their child's achievement and behavior. Explain that self-esteem also plays a critical role in our health and happiness.

Stress the commitment of the school toward the enhancement of self-esteem. Emphasize how strongly the staff feels about the concept of self-esteem and student achievement and behavior. Mention that the enhancement of student self-esteem is a primary objective of the school staff.

2. Define Self-Esteem

Explain that *"self-esteem is the judgment or opinion we hold about ourselves. It's the extent to which we perceive ourselves to be worthwhile and capable human beings."* Mention that there is no judgment more important since self-esteem impacts all of our thinking and behavior.

Emphasize that self-esteem is learned. No child is born into the world with high and healthy self-esteem. Children acquire and learn self-esteem through important experiences in their lives. Mention that the best news about anything that is learned is that it is changeable. Stress that self-esteem can be changed and changed at any age.

Explain that self-esteem has a strong impact on the lives of our children. Emphasize that:

> *"we all want the best for our children (i.e. to have friends, to use their talents, to make the world work for them). We also know that all the material possessions in the world don't guarantee happiness. Researchers tell us the foundation for happiness and success is a positive judgment of self."*

3. Five Building Blocks of Self-Esteem

Explain that since self-esteem is learned, all educators need to know is how to teach it. Ask participants to reflect upon a time when they felt really good about themselves. Ask the group to continue thinking about the experience, trying to remember the experience in as much detail as possible. Tell them to think about what contributed to their feeling so good and to ask themselves: *"What were you doing? Who were you with?"* Briefly explain that the positive experience they encountered most likely can be described by one or more of the following feelings:

- You felt secure, safe, and trusting of your environment.

- You felt special or unique and had a sense of your own unique gifts. You felt you did something that only you could have done in that particular way. You felt worthwhile.

- You felt important and appreciated by someone who you respected and whose opinion you valued.

- You felt you were in charge and getting the things done that you set out to do. You had a goal or a purpose and you were successful in achieving what you wanted.

- You felt successful or that you had made a difference. You had a feeling of pride in yourself that said, "I did it!" You felt capable.

Mention that each of these feelings represents one of the five building blocks that comprise high self-esteem. Stress that the experience participants had probably satisfied a basic emotional need. That experience in turn helped reinforce a belief in their own value and competence as a person. Explain that each of the feelings just described has a specific name.

Display OH2 Building Blocks of Self-Esteem on the overhead projector. Using a pointer or a pencil, briefly describe each of the five feelings. Say:

"The five feelings that nurture high self-esteem are: Security, Selfhood, Affiliation, Mission, and Competence. Let me describe each feeling for you. The first nurturer of high self-esteem is a sense of Security. This is a feeling of trust or safety. It is the most critical feeling of self-esteem since all other feelings generally build from this first component. It is the foundation of self-esteem. The second feeling is a sense of Selfhood. This feeling means that the individual really knows who he or she is. The child has a strong, accurate identity. This is the 'Who am I?' question. The third feeling is Affiliation. This means that the child has a sense of connectedness or belonging. He or she feels appreciated by people who are important to him or her. The fourth feeling is Mission. Mission means 'purpose or direction.' It implies the individual knows where he or she is headed. A child with Mission generally is a goal-setter and a self-starter. The final feeling is a sense of Competence. This means the child feels a sense of accomplishment and capableness. He or she has a sense of power knowing he/she can make a difference in his/her own life."

Mention again how critical these feelings are to achievement and behavior. Stress that these feelings are universally felt needs and that the whole process of enhancing children's self-esteem stems from understanding these five feelings.

Mention also that the five feelings are generally acquired sequentially. Each feeling usually builds on the previous feeling. **Explain that the place to start rebuilding is with the first feeling. Say,** *"Let's take a look at each of these feelings a little more in-depth, examine why they are important to your child, and then talk about some things you can do at home to enhance each of the five components of high self-esteem."*

Explain that the five feelings are addressed by a self-esteem program used in the school called *Esteem Builders*, written by Dr. Michele Borba. Mention that the program is being used throughout North America by hundreds of schools and that parents and teachers who are using the techniques report positive changes in student achievement and behavior. Hold up a copy of the book.

Encourage participants to take notes on their handouts as you describe each of the five feelings.

4. Security

Describe the first feeling of self-esteem: a sense of Security. Say:

"Security is the first feeling to be acquired. By definition it means that individuals have a strong sense of trust. It involves a feeling of being comfortable and safe, knowing what is expected, being able to depend on individuals and situations, and comprehending rules and limits. Children who have strong feelings of security are self-assured. In classrooms, they feel comfortable enough to raise their hands and say: 'I don't get it. Can you help me?' That involves taking a risk. Many children are not comfortable taking even such small risks as asking a question, yet we know that risk-taking is essential to learning. Students who feel secure are kids who can

trust not only other people but also themselves. They feel emotionally and physically safe."

Briefly paraphrase the work of Dr. Stanley Coopersmith, emphasizing the impact his research findings have on family esteem-building practices. Explain that Coopersmith was a child psychologist at the University of California at Davis. Say:

"His research goal was to try and ascertain what family conditions help promote high self-esteem. His research team studied more than 1,700 boys and their families and found that children with the highest self-esteem had three critical elements common to their homes:

- *"They came from backgrounds where they experienced the kind of love that expresses respect, concern, and acceptance. As children they were accepted for their strengths and capacities as well as for their limitations and weaknesses. It was clearly 'love with no strings attached.'*

- *"Their parents were significantly less permissive than were parents of children with lower self-esteem. Within the household there were clearly defined limits, standards and expectations, and as a result, children felt secure.*

- *"The families functioned with a high degree of democracy. The children were encouraged to present their own ideas and opinions for discussion (even ones that deviated from those of their own parents)."*

Encourage parents to examine their own family parenting practices. Emphasize that the best esteem-building environments are ones in which all three of these elements are found.

Emphasize that security can be rebuilt in the home at any time, but that it takes planning and commitment. Mention the suggestions on the following page that parents can quickly begin doing at home:

- **"Do Not Disturb" Sign.** An inexpensive "Do Not Disturb" sign can be made or purchased to hang on a door. At least once a week parents invite their children individually to come with them into the "Do Not Disturb" space to talk privately and to enjoy each other alone.

- **Birthday Letters.** Parents can express their love to their children with a special birthday letter. On each child's birthday, they write a special letter recapturing the year (accomplishments, special memories, his/her growth) and reaffirm their feelings for him or her. At a private moment parent and child read the letter together and then store it in a safe deposit box. For a twenty-first birthday present, all the letters are given back to the child tied in a ribbon.

Note: In addition to these ideas, display or demonstrate to participants a few pre-selected Esteem Builder Activities of your choice to enhance the feeling of Security.

5. Selfhood

Describe the second component of self-esteem: a sense of Selfhood. Say in your own words:

"When students have a strong sense of security, the second feeling that is generally acquired is a feeling of selfhood. This feeling means that children have a strong sense of self-knowledge. They possess accurate information about themselves, and they know who they really are. These kids know their interests, their roles, their physical characteristics, their attitudes, and their attributes or strengths. We can also call this 'self-concept.' This feeling is especially important for your children these days because apparently this feeling acts as a powerful buffer to stress and trauma.

"Researchers have done extensive work with individuals who have endured incredible personal trauma, such as concentration camp victims, P.O.W.'s, and hostages. They wanted to find out which of them were now leading healthy, emotionally-intact lives despite their traumatic experiences. Again and again they determined that the one variable all these individuals possessed was a strong sense of identity. Our children desperately need more accurate pictures of self. Many of them are evaluating themselves on the basis of inaccurate information. An easy way to spot these children is to go up to them and ask: 'What are your strengths?' You usually get one of two answers back: 'Nothing,' or 'I don't know.' You can help your children develop a more accurate self-concept."

Emphasize to participants that there are many ways to enhance their children's feeling of Selfhood. Mention the following suggestions that parents can quickly begin doing at home. Whenever possible show the audience actual samples of the activities:

- **Me Collage.** On a large piece of paper parents create a Me Collage with their children. Magazine pictures or words depicting what's special or unique about their children are glued on the collage. Interests may also be included.

- **Me Mobile.** Using materials such as yarn, clothes hangers, scissors, glue, tape and construction paper, parents work with their children to create a Me Mobile which depicts their children's interests, skills, and physical characteristics. Pictures are hung from yarn attached to the hanger. Photos, magazine pictures, written descriptions, actual objects, and self-drawn pictures may also be included on the mobile.

Note: In addition to these ideas, display or demonstrate to participants a few pre-selected Esteem Builder Activities of your choice to enhance the feeling of Selfhood.

6. Affiliation

Describe the third feeling of self-esteem: a sense of Affiliation. Say:

"Children with high affiliation are children who feel connected or feel they belong to a group that's important to them. They also feel approved of, appreciated, and respected by others. We all know that friends play an enormous role in our self-esteem. The U.S. Office of Education tells us that a lack of this feeling is the second leading predictor of who will drop out of school. A number of our students are desperately trying to find a sense of affiliation and can't find it appropriately. Gang affiliation is increasing in our inner-city areas across this country.

In the classrooms, class bullies and class cutups are rampant. William James, the father of American psychology, tells us that eighty to ninety percent of our behavior is guided by the need to be recognized. Children desperately need to feel recognized and connected. The single most important way you can rebuild this feeling for your child is by creating a strong sense of belonging in your family."

Explain that the family unit is the greatest source of belonging for children. Emphasize that parents can make critical differences in enhancing the feeling of affiliation for their children. Mention that "family esteem building" should be planned and consistent. Encourage parents to find a time each week to do affiliation-building activities with their children. Encourage parents to write down a time convenient for family esteem building in the space provided on their handouts.

- **Feature One Member of the Family.** Each week one member of the family is featured as a "special person" just because he/she is part of the family. This privilege is rotated among family members. Special celebration privileges could include: being served their favorite dinner, choosing the evening read-aloud selection, having a special friend over for the night, receiving a special card under their pillow reaffirming the love felt for the individual.

- **Me Hanging.** The family creates a special Me Hanging for each member. This individual's special qualities are brainstormed as a family. One family member acting as the "recorder" writes the qualities on a piece of paper. The privilege is rotated among family members.

- **Celebrate Accomplishments.** One special dinner plate, different from the family's regular dinner plates, is used to celebrate any family member's accomplishment. For one evening, that individual is given the privilege of eating dinner on the "special plate." The plate can also be used for special family celebrations.

Note: In addition to these ideas, display/or demonstrate to participants a few preselected Esteem Builder Activities of your choice to enhance the feeling of Affiliation.

7. Mission

Describe the fourth feeling of self-esteem: a sense of Mission. The following information is suggested as a guideline for the presentation. Say:

"Children with a feeling of mission have purpose and direction in their lives. Students with a sense of mission are joys to have in families and classrooms. They don't always depend on us to make decisions for them or acknowledge their efforts. These kids know they have choices and alternatives. They are goal-setters, and they also usually reach their marks because the goals they set for themselves are realistic and achievable. They are more internally-operated individuals. When they complete a project they do something that is a fabulous life skill: they acknowledge their efforts inside their heads instead of waiting for us to pat them on the back. Children with low mission stumble often because they don't know there are alternatives, and they are constantly dependent on us for encouragement and direction. Our goal is to help children become more internally-operated so they are not so dependent on us."

Explain that an essential component of mission is a feeling of purpose, direction, and responsibility. Emphasize that parents can enhance this feeling at home. Describe a few of the following activities and other preselected projects from *Home Esteem Builders* to enhance mission:

- **Let Children Know Mistakes Are OK.** Parents should emphasize to children that mistakes are permissible. Explain that mistakes are how we learn—they help us improve.

- **Share Mistakes.** Emphasize that parents are powerful role models for children. Encourage parents to share their own mistakes with their children using the following model: (1) admit the mistake… "This is what I did wrong," and (2) state what they will do differently next time… "Next time this is what I will do."

- **Role Play Handling Failure.** Parents can role play with their children how to cope with failure. Practice what to do and say in situations such as: striking out on a baseball team, accidentally causing injury to someone, spilling something at someone's home.

Note: In addition to these ideas, display or demonstrate to participants a few preselected Esteem Builder Activities of your choice to enhance the feeling of Mission.

8. Competence

Explain the final feeling of self-esteem: a sense of Competence. Say:

"We all need to know we have succeeded. We all need to hear, as Wayne Dyer says, 'success ringing in our ears.' Competence is a feeling of success and capableness in things regarded as important or valuable to the individual. These children have a sense of self-efficacy since they know they have power and control over their lives. A feeling of incompetence is what the U.S. Office of Education has identified as the leading predictor of who will drop out of our school system. Parents and teachers together can play an instrumental role in helping children feel a sense of competence by creating opportunities for them to succeed. We also need to help children recognize their strengths and competencies. Such a process enhances their feeling of capableness and thus their self-esteem. Students' self-esteem will be enhanced because they have a sense of self-empowerment."

Explain that an essential component of competence is the feeling of accomplishment. Parents can build an awareness of their children's unique strengths and capabilities. Parents can also help their children become more aware of their individual accomplishments and strengths. Suggest a few of the following Home Esteem Builder Activities to enhance children's competence as well as other samples you may wish to display:

- **Recording Progress.** Each week children record their progress on a blank cassette tape. Parents can try this activity in a variety of areas, including auditory memory (poetry or rhymes) and oral language (reading an original story or interviewing a friend).

- **Favorite Work Folder.** Children are provided with a special folder or box to store their class work or favorite projects. Each week parents ask their children to choose one paper or project they are most proud of and to place it inside the work folder.

- **Things I Can Do.** Parents can help children keep track of their progress by encouraging them to draw, write, or glue in photographs of their accomplishments or significant milestones in a special "accomplishment journal."

- **Strength Collages.** Children can make a collage showing their strengths. They may use their own drawings or cut and paste pictures from magazines.

- **Develop Strengths.** Encourage parents to find an avenue of success for each of their children. It could be music, dance, karate, art, athletics, etc.

Note: In addition to these ideas, display or demonstrate to participants a few preselected Esteem Builder Activities of your choice to enhance the feeling of Competence.

9. Conclusion

- **Home Esteem Builder Activities.** Briefly describe some Home Esteem Builder Activities and show samples of a few completed activities. Mention that students will be bringing home the activities once a week. Encourage parents to do the activities at home with their children. Stress that the completed activity need not be sent back to school.

- **Home Esteem Builder Calendar.*** Briefly show a sample of the Home Esteem Builder Calendar. An overhead transparency of a calendar page could be displayed on the overhead project if desired. Mention that a calendar page will be sent home once a month for parents to put on the refrigerator. Stress that the activities are designed as "quick esteem builders" that the family can do together to enhance children's self-esteem.

- **Parent-School Activities.** Any other parent-school partnership ideas planned by the school (i.e. weekly newsletters, Esteem Builders' Reading Program*, Lending Library, parent conferences, etc.) could be explained to participants at this time.

Emphasize again that the staff is committed to the concept of self-esteem enhancement. Explain that the staff realizes this cannot be done alone and that the most powerful changes will happen for our children when staff and parents work together. Read the poem found on page 178 to the participants.

Notes

Notes

Chapter 3 In-Service Forms

BUILDING BLOCKS
OF SELF-ESTEEM

Esteem Builders' Complete Program
Jalmar Press, Rolling Hills Estates, CA

PRESENTATION TIME LINE

A time line of activities that need to be completed prior to the delivery of a successful presentation follows. The list is meant only as a guideline; items should be adapted to reflect the unique needs of the school site.

ONE OR TWO MONTHS PRIOR

___ Agree as a staff on the priority of holding a parent in-service on esteem building.

___ Choose a staff member to become the in-service presenter. Because the success of the presentation depends largely on the person selected to play this key role, the following characteristics should be taken into consideration when selecting the presenter:

  • Enthusiastic and committed to the enhancement of self-esteem
  • Organized
  • Knowledgeable about the subject or willing to do additional reading about the session
  • Comfortable and effective speaking in front of groups

___ The presenter is provided with a copy of the presentation script and reading materials. He/she should begin preparing for the presentation at least one month prior to the event.

___ Select a location site for the presentation. The location should comfortably accommodate a large number of participants.

___ Choose a date and time for the presentation. Check with the district office and local newspaper to make sure there are no other community or school events scheduled for the same day that could conflict with the presentation.

___ Reserve the room at the location site for the presentation.

___ Call local Girl Scout organizations (or other sources) about the possibility of their providing babysitting services for the evening. Arrange for the service.

___ Duplicate parent invitations.

___ Send out handouts to be duplicated.

___ The presenter, with input from educators, chooses esteem-building activities to demonstrate and/or display. Choose activities according to the selection process listed under "Selecting Activities to Demonstrate." Begin making sample activities for the presentation. A parent committee might be formed to assist in this process.

PRESENTATION TIME LINE

THREE WEEKS PRIOR

____ Ask staff members to begin saving student-made samples of esteem-building projects that could be displayed or demonstrated at the in-service.

____ If desired, videotape and/or photograph esteem-building activities conducted in the school and/or classroom. This can be displayed to parents before and after the presentation.

____ Place a reminder notice in the weekly school news bulletin.

____ Send home parent invitations.

____ Contact local newspapers to feature the event in an upcoming article. Arrange for the information to be sent to the news office.

____ The presenter should practice the presentation script aloud to become thoroughly familiar with the sequence.

TWO WEEKS PRIOR

____ Place a reminder notice for the presentation in a weekly school news bulletin.

____ Reserve all equipment needed for the presentation. Equipment could include the following: overhead projector, screen, extension cord, cassette tape recorder, TV monitor, videotape player, microphone.

____ The presenter should practice the script aloud, relying only on note cards. It is strongly suggested that the presenter tape record or videotape himself/herself practicing the entire presentation. The presentation should also be timed from beginning to end to ensure that it is less than one hour.

ONE WEEK PRIOR

____ Process all videotaping and photographs.

____ Recheck with the organization providing babysitting to verify all is in order.

____ Pick up the duplicated handouts.

____ Purchase name tags for parents to wear at the presentation and felt tip marking pens to write their names.

____ Convert blackline masters into overhead transparencies.

Esteem Builders' Complete Program
Jalmar Press, Rolling Hills Estates, CA

PRESENTATION TIME LINE

____ Make up a sign-in sheet for parents to sign their names as they enter the presentation.

____ Gather all Esteem Builder Activities to demonstrate and display. All should be completed at this point.

____ Make any bulletin board displays for the walls in the presentation room.

____ Send a reminder about the presentation to all parents.

____ Ask for staff volunteers to greet parents as they enter.

____ Verify again that the equipment for the presentation is arranged.

____ Meet with the custodian regarding the upcoming room arrangement. Do a walk-through of the room with the custodian to verify all is in order. Provide the custodian with a copy of the "room setup chart."

____ Arrange for refreshments for the presentation (if desired). Order cookies. Buy coffee, napkins, punch, and cups. Borrow large punch bowls and ladles. Designate a committee to be responsible for the refreshments.

____ Arrange for the newspaper to send a reporter to cover the event if desired.

____ The presenter should be familiar enough with the presentation script by now to use only a brief keyword outline. It is strongly suggested that the presenter now practice the in-service using all demonstration materials and props.

ONE DAY PRIOR

____ Arrange a Parent Phone Tree where each parent calls another parent to remind him or her of the event.

____ Send home one final reminder (at this point a strong suggestion is a student-made invitation).

____ Call the babysitting organization one last time for a final check.

____ Check with the custodian, verifying the room setup and the required number of chairs.

____ The presenter should practice the entire in-service using all equipment and display items. Ideally, a colleague should stand at the far back and sides of the room to verify that the speaker is clearly audible and overheads are visible.

Esteem Builders' Complete Program
Jalmar Press, Rolling Hills Estates, CA

PRESENTATION TIME LINE

DAY OF THE PRESENTATION

____ Set up the room as soon as possible. Arrange for extra chairs to be in a nearby location.

____ Set up the room(s) for babysitting. Remove any valuable or breakable objects. Set up the video equipment to show movies to the children during the presentation.

____ Set up the presentation equipment (display table, overhead projector, screen, microphone, tape cassette if desired for background music).

____ Test all equipment (particularly the overhead projector and microphone).

____ Set up the sign-in table (name tags, sign-in sheet, handouts, marking pens).

____ Set up the refreshment table (coffee, punch, punch bowl, ladle, cookies, cups, and napkins). Arrange for someone to plug in the coffee maker and set out the cookies and punch at the last minute.

____ If Esteem Builder Activities on videotape are to be shown, arrange for a screen and video camera to be placed in a corner of the presentation room.

____ Display esteem-building materials: copies of *Esteem Builders* and *Home Esteem Builders,* samples of Home Esteem Builder Activities and the Home Esteem Building Calendar.

____ Make a few signs (if needed) guiding parents to the location of the presentation.

ONE HOUR BEFORE

____ Presenter sets out transparency, note cards for the speech, and any activities to be demonstrated during the speech on a table.

____ Make the punch, plug in the coffee maker.

* Separate programs available through B.L. Winch & Associates/Jalmar Press

PARENT INVITATION

Duplicate a parent invitation, such as the one provided, on bright-colored paper. Fill in the pertinent information regarding the presentation (time, location, date) and send a copy home with each student.

You are cordially invited to attend a seminar for parents. The seminar title is: "Self-Esteem: The Key to Your Child's Success."

Your child's teachers feel this is a topic of critical impact since the feeling of self-esteem is essential to your child's achievement and behavior. The many practical ideas that will be shared are ones parents can use immediately to help their children feel good about themselves and achieve their highest potential.

Date: _____

Time: _____

Location: _____

Free child care will be provided.
We hope you will be in attendance!
Please RSVP _____

Esteem Builders' Complete Program
Jalmar Press, Rolling Hills Estates, CA

HOME ESTEEM BUILDERS

ACTIVITIES TO DEMONSTRATE/DISPLAY AT IN-SERVICE

COMPONENT	ACTIVITY TITLE	LOCATION/SOURCE	STATUS

Esteem Builders' Complete Program
Jalmar Press, Rolling Hills Estates, CA

PRESENTER CHECKLIST

Personally check and recheck the room hours prior to the in-service. In particular check all equipment to ensure it is in working order:

OVERHEAD PROJECTOR
- ○ - Clear from a distance
- ○ - Visible to all seats in the room
- ○ - Spare bulb or extra projector available just in case
- ○ - Cord taped down to prevent tripping
- ○ - Cart or table for projector placed appropriately
- ○ - Screen

MICROPHONE
- ○ - Hooked up
- ○ - Clearly audible from all parts of the room
- ○ - Feedback problems (Walk under and in front of any speakers.)
- ○ - Cord long enough (It is best to be able to move and not be in front of a podium.)

DISPLAY TABLES
- ○ - Table near the entrance for name tags, sign-in sheet, and handouts
- ○ - Name tags
- ○ - Pens
- ○ - Sign-in sheet
- ○ - Extra tables to display samples of student activities

REFRESHMENT TABLE (Optional)
- ○ - Napkins
- ○ - Coffee Maker
- ○ - Coffee
- ○ - Cream and Sugar for Coffee
- ○ - Cups
- ○ - Punch
- ○ - Cookies

PARTICIPANT CHAIRS
- ○ - Appropriate number (Remove extra chairs and have them available in the back instead…people tend to sit in the back first.)
- ○ - Extra chairs (If needed.)

HANDOUTS
- ○ - Home Esteem Builder Activity sample
- ○ - In-service handouts
- ○ - Other handouts

ESTEEM-BUILDING DISPLAYS
- ○ - Photographs, Student Samples, etc.

BABYSITTING FACILITY
- ○ - Personnel ready
- ○ - Videotape, TV Monitor, and VCR

PRESENTER MATERIALS
- ○ - Speech note cards
- ○ - Home Esteem Building Calendar * Sample
- ○ - Home Esteem Builder Activity samples
- ○ - Transparency: The Building Blocks of Self-Esteem
- ○ - Activities to demonstrate or show during the in-service
- ○ - Glass of water and pitcher (if desired)
- ○ - Copy of *Esteem Builders*
- ○ - Copy of *Home Esteem Builders*

IMMEDIATELY PRIOR TO THE IN-SERVICE
- ○ - Greet participants at the door along with other staff members. Staff members can personally give each participant a handout as they come in.
- ○ - Invite participants to sign their names (optional) on a sign-in sheet and fill out a name tag. A table could be placed by the door to hold name tags, pens, sign-in sheets, and extra handouts.
- ○ - A few staff members could stand at the back of the room helping to seat participants. They could also find additional seating for participants if necessary.

* Separate programs available through B.L. Winch & Associates/Jalmar Press

Esteem Builders' Complete Program
Jalmar Press, Rolling Hills Estates, CA

SELF-ESTEEM: THE KEY
TO YOUR CHILD'S SUCCESS
A Parent In-Service

KEY POINTS OR IDEAS I WANT TO REMEMBER

_____

_____

_____

_____

_____

_____

_____

A time of the week we could commit to "Family Esteem Enhancement" is...

_____

_____

Awareness of individual strengths is a critical component of esteem building.
Identify a strength of your child. How will you help your child experience the strength?

CHILD	STRENGTH(S)	AREAS TO ENHANCE

FIVE FEELINGS OF SELF-ESTEEM:

 Security: A strong sense of assuredness; feeling emotionally and physically comfortable and safe.

 Selfhood: A feeling of individuality; accurate self-knowledge and understanding.

 Affiliation: A feeling of belonging and connectedness; feeling accepted, approved of.

 Mission: A feeling of purpose and motivation; goal-setting; taking responsibility.

 Competence: A feeling of success and accomplishment; awareness of strengths; a sense of efficacy.

Esteem Builders' Complete Program
Jalmar Press, Rolling Hills Estates, CA

RESOURCES LIST

The following sources are recommended for helping parents learn the skills of self-esteem enhancement. Though there are many "how-to" books available for parents, these were chosen because of their simplicity or research-based approach to home-esteem enhancement. A few resources that are particularly valuable are annotated. These sources might be ones schools could consider purchasing for a School Resource Lending Library on self-esteem.

Briggs, Dorothy. *Your Child's Self-Esteem: The Key to His Life.* New York: Doubleday, 1970. A self-esteem classic; a readable and invaluable source describing how self-esteem is literally the key to a child's life.

Clarke, Jean I. *Self-Esteem: A Family Affair.* San Francisco: Harper & Row, 1978. Creative ways to help self-esteem flourish using theory and techniques based on Transactional Analysis.

Clabby, John F. and Maurice J. Elias. *Teach Your Child Decision Making.* New York: Kensington Publishing, 1981. Practical approaches to teaching children the critical skills of decision-making.

Clemes, Harris and Reynold Bean. *How to Raise Children's Self-Esteem.* Sunnyvale, CA: Enrich Publishers, 1980. A unique book offering parents practical advice to help foster high self-esteem in children through four conditions of self-esteem. Other books in this series include *How to Raise Teenagers' Self-Esteem, How to Discipline Children Without Feeling Guilty, and How to Teach Children Responsibility.*

Coloroso, Barbara. *Winning at Parenting...Without Beating Your Kids.* Littleton, CO: Kids Are Worth It! 1989. A two-tape cassette program to help children become responsible, caring, and loving individuals. An entertaining and powerful message for positive family problem solving.

Dobson, James. *Hide or Seek.* Old Tappan, NJ: Revell, 1974. A very readable book about self-esteem and its relevance to today's youth.

Dyer, Wayne. *What Do You Really Want for Your Children?* New York: Avon, 1985. Straightforward advice about raising children and increasing their self-esteem.

Elkind, David. *The Hurried Child: Growing Up Too Fast Too Soon.* MA: Addison Wesley, 1981. An outstanding source for parents and teachers describing the dilemma of today's stressed-out youth and the impact it creates on the development of identity. Highly appropriate even a decade later.

Eyre, Linda and Richard Eyre. *Teaching Children Responsibility.* New York: Ballantine, 1986. A guide to help children learn self-responsibility.

Faber, Adele and Elaine Mazlish. *How to Talk So Kids Will Listen and Listen So Kids Will Talk.* New York: Avon, 1980. A helpful guide presented in an appealing format dealing with effective techniques to increase communication between parents and children.

Ginott, Haim. *Between Parent and Child.* New York: Macmillan, 1965. Published over thirty years ago, but still a very pertinent book.

Glenn, H. Stephen and Jane Nelsen. *Raising Self-Reliant Children In a Self-Indulgent World.* Rocklin, CA: Prima Publishing & Communications, 1988. Seven building blocks for developing capable young people.

Gordon, Thomas. *Parent Effectiveness Training: The Tested Way to Raise Responsible Children.* New York: McKay, 1970. Proven communication techniques packed with examples and exercises to enhance parent-child relations. A classic communication text.

Greene, Lawrence J. *Smarter Kids.* New York: Ballantine, 1987. A sourcebook to increase students' organizational, coping, and decision-making skills.

Hart, Louise. *The Winning Family: Increasing Self-Esteem in Your Children and Yourself.* Oakland, CA: LifeSkills Press, 1990. This supportive book focuses on the personal development of parents along with the development of their children. It is a guide to healing the child within and helping the children you love.

Isaacs, Susan and Wendy Ritchey. *I Think I Can, I Know I Can!* New York: St. Martin's Press, 1989. An invaluable guide! Offers a simple, five-step program teaching parents how to observe their children's inner dialogue and then show their children how to change the negative self-talk voices into positive ones. The authors offer specific advice on using self-talk to control anger, overcome fears, improve school performance, make and strengthen friendships, and handle stress.

Kaye, Kenneth. *Family Rules: Raising Responsible Children Without Yelling or Nagging.* New York: St. Martin's Press, 1984. A helpful guide explaining how you can custom-design a set of straightforward, consistently enforced family rules for discipline.

Lickona, Thomas. *Raising Good Children from Birth Through the Teenage Years.* New York: Bantam, 1983. Presents the predictable stages of moral development from birth to adulthood as well as down-to-earth advice hond guidance for each moral development stage.

Marston, Stephanie. *The Magic of Encouragement: Nurturing Your Child's Self-Esteem.* New York: William Morrow & Co., 1990. Invaluable guide to children's esteem enhancement; features simple-to-use activities as well as solid rationale for using them.

Mitchell, William and Charles Paul Conn. *The Power of Positive Parenting.* New York: Wynwood Press, 1989. Clear and reassuringly written, this book defines ways a caring parent can develop a child's self-confidence in both school and social situations, and in the process strengthen the parent-child relationship.

Nelsen, Jane. *Positive Discipline: Teaching Children Self-Discipline, Responsibility, Cooperation, and Problem Solving Skills.* Fair Oaks, CA: Sunrise, 1981. A straightforward, valuable guide to discipline with a positive approach.

Pappas, Michael G. *Prime Time for Families: Over 50 Activities, Games and Exercises for Personal and Family Growth.* Minneapolis: Winston Press, 1980. Easy-to-use ideas for family esteem building.

Phillips, Debora. *How to Give Your Child a Great Self-Image.* New York: Random House, 1989. Proven techniques for enhancing self-esteem in a highly-readable, simple framework. An invaluable guide for parents.

Popkin, Michael. *Active Parenting: Teaching Cooperation, Courage, and Responsibility.* New York: Harper & Row, 1987. Built on the theories of Adler and Dreikurs, this program offers a solid framework for enhancing basic parenting skills. Drawn from a successful video-based course, it has been used since 1980 by over 100,000 parents.

Reider, Barbara. *A Hooray Kind of Kid: A Child's Self-Esteem and How to Build It.* El Dorado Hills, CA: Sierra House,1988. A small manual packed with ideas and strategies to help every child become a "hooray kind of kid."

Youngs, Bettie B. *The 6 Vital Ingredients of Self-Esteem and How to Develop Them in Your Child.* New York: Rawson Associates, 1991. A practical and readable book teaching parents how to develop the building blocks of self-esteem. Dozens of theory-based ideas are presented to help parents improve their children's self-esteem.

Zimbardo, Philip B. and Shirley L. Radl. *The Shy Child: A Parent's Guide to Overcoming and Preventing Shyness from Infancy to Adulthood.* New York: Doubleday, 1982. Written by the expert on shyness, the manual presents not only research and theory on shyness but excellent strategies for intervention and prevention.

HOME ESTEEM BUILDERS

Notes

Notes

4

Home-School Communication

HOME ESTEEM BUILDERS

- Phone Communication
- Message Grams
- Weekly Progress Report
- Esteem Builder Grams
- Special Poems to Send Home to Parents

ACTIVITIES LIST

MISSION

COMPETENCE

Home Esteem Builders was developed on the premise that a home and school partnership is an integral element of effective esteem building. The material in this book provides educators with the resources to help parents enhance their children's self-esteem. Before distributing any of these materials to the students' homes, please make sure that they have been translated into the primary language of the parents.

4

Home-School Communication

Children can have no better inheritance than believing parents.

—NELS FERRE

One of the most frequently mentioned characteristics of a strong family-school relationship is effective communication. The type of home-school communication identified as most essential to the partnership school is one in which "communications with parents are frequent, clear, and two-way."[1] Such a process must be consistently planned for by the school staff, particularly since the image many parents have of school communication is largely negative. This negative concept has been repeatedly verified in a host of studies. Tangri and Leitch succinctly summed up this perception by saying, "Both parents and teachers recognized that most communication between them was negative teacher messages about poor student performance and parent complaints regarding events in school."[2]

The first step toward rebuilding an effective communication bridge between the home and the school is to disarm the connotation that information exchanged need always be negative. The second step is to work at creating a communication relationship based on trust. Individuals are much more prone to share ideas, open up toward one another, and work toward a common goal if the relationship is trusting. There are a number of ways the school can strengthen the home-school communication network. This chapter suggests ways to develop an esteem-building parent-school interchange that is "frequent, clear, and two-way." The rebuilding process must begin with the school.

In their work on the value of parent involvement with the school, Lyons, Robbins, and Smith (1982) identified the five major components of a comprehensive parent-community partnership program as:

1. Home-school communications
2. Parents as supporters
3. Parents as learners
4. Parents as teachers
5. Parents as advisors, advocates, and decision-makers[3]

Educational writer Janet Chrispeels pointed out how home-school communication is the one critical factor in the school's attaining the other components. "Without good communication, it

1. Henderson, Anne T., Carl L. Marburger, and Theodora Ooms. "Building a Family-School Relationship," article excerpted with permission from Beyond the Bake Sale: *An Educator's Guide to Working with Parents,* Columbia, MD: National Committee for Citizens in Education, 1986.

2. Tangri, S.S. and M.L. Leitch. *Barriers to Home-School Collaboration: Two Case Studies in Junior High Schools.* Final report submitted to The National Institute of Education. Washington, D.C.: The Urban Institute, May 1982.

3. Lyons, Peggy, Al Robbins, and Allen Smith. *Involving Parents: A Handbook for Participation in Schools.* Santa Monica, CA: Systems Development Corporation, 1982.

is unlikely that activities can be implemented and goals achieved in other components."[4] Effective communication between parents and schools is the foundation for all the other components. The school must actively work at keeping an ongoing dialogue between the staff and parents. The most effective communication is one which helps both school and family assist the child in learning.

PHONE COMMUNICATION

The telephone can be one of the school's most powerful allies. When used correctly, it can be a tool to strengthen communication between the parent and the school. Many schools recognize the hurried schedules of today's parents and have created strategies to enhance an effective dialogue between the school and home. Two very unique phone ideas were recently initiated by the Los Angeles Unified School District and Union School District in San Jose, California.

- **Telephone Homework Hotline.** The Los Angeles Unified School District instated a "telephone homework hotline." Each teacher records the homework assignments on a daily basis and describes any items of special interest that are occurring in their classroom. Parents can call a special phone number to find out what is happening in their child's classroom as well as make sure their child is completing the homework that was assigned.

- **Teacher Read-Aloud.** Another phone communication technique was developed by the Union School District in San Jose, California. The staff recognized educational research which reveals a direct correlation between students who are consistently read aloud to and their reading achievement. Each week teachers from various schools take turns recording children's literature selections such as *Where the Wild Things Are* by Maurice Sendak, *The Little Engine That Could* by Watty Piper or *Where the Sidewalk Ends* by Shel Silverstein. Students can call a special phone number each night to hear their teachers reading aloud to them.

These are just two possibilities schools have created to use the telephone system as a way to strengthen home and school communication. Another possibility is to have staff members take turns in the evenings manning a school "hotline" number. In this innovative technique, all school parents are given a phone number and are encouraged to call the number during certain hours to discuss with staff members their child's homework assignments or any school-related questions or concerns.

Positive Phone Messages

Here are some additional phone suggestions for teachers and principals to consider using to strengthen home-school communication.

- **Send Home Positive Messages.** A middle school in Riverside, California, makes it a school policy that for every negative phone call, the staff member must make two positive phone calls. The policy is written on masking tape and attached to each school phone. Remember that parents need reasons to praise their children. Each day try to make at least two positive phone calls to the parents of deserving students.

- **Sunshine Calls.** For younger students, place a plastic phone on a different student's desk each day. The teacher informs the students that their efforts are appreciated and that the teacher will be giving their parents a Sunshine Call during the day to let them know about their efforts.

- **On-the-Spot Call.** Many principals have found the phone to be an extremely powerful technique to recognize student behavior and achievements. The principal carries a cellular (portable phone) with him/her at all times. Whenever a student deserves recognition, the principal immediately calls the student's parents at home or office, and, in front of the student, lets the parent know about the student's success. A local business usually donates the phones, or the school holds a fundraising activity especially for this purpose.

---

4. Chrispeels, Janet A. "The Family as an Educational Resource." *Community Education Journal,* April 1987, p. 11.

- **A Call a Day.** Don Lowe, a teacher in Greeley, Colorado, has a particularly powerful parent communication policy. At the beginning of the school year, he informs every student's parent that they will hear from him by phone about their child's school progress at least once a week. He also tells them that no phone call will last more than five minutes. Every day after school, Lowe personally calls five to six of his students' parents. The process takes no more than twenty to thirty minutes a day, but what an effective use of time! By taking just a few minutes each night to communicate with parents, Lowe finds he minimizes (or eliminates) any major problems that may arise from misunderstandings or miscommunication. Furthermore, Lowe has created strong parent allies because they know he cares.

- **Phone Pass.** Distribute to each staff member a large quantity of official Phone Pass tickets (found on page 117). Explain to the staff that they may give a pass to any deserving student at any time during the day. Students can earn passes for academic achievement or behavior. The staff member who recognizes the student fills out the pass, explaining what the student "did well." The student then goes to the office and hands the pass to an office staff member. A large ledger book can be kept near the phone so that students may "sign in," noting they made a phone call home. The student then calls the parent to inform him/her about the achievement, reads the note the teacher has written on the Phone Pass, and then returns to class.

- **Back-to-School Introduction.** Setting a positive tone as a new school year begins is critical. Students as well as parents have "back-to-school" jitters and are concerned not only about who will be in their classroom but also "what will my teacher be like?" Teachers who take the time to personally call each student's parents send them a powerful message. That message is, "The teacher really cares."

The call need not be lengthy. No more than five minutes is necessary. The conversation could include a simple introduction, a few statements about the kinds of projects or goals the teacher has for the school year, and an invitation for the parent to stop by the classroom to visit or call the school at any time if there are concerns or questions. The teacher could then arrange to schedule a conference or make a phone call back to the parent. Always end the conversation with a personal comment or two about the child (how much you enjoy having the student in the class, or a strength or talent the teacher has observed about the student, or a concern about a particular behavior or academic area that needs immediate attention). The phone call is generally always appreciated and remembered.

- **School Phone Trees.** Parents can be involved in the process of calling other parents by operating Phone Trees. This technique allows parents to quickly find out information such as who can provide transportation for the field trip, who can furnish treats for the upcoming party, who will be in attendance at the next parent gathering, as well as help other parents with car-pooling problems or welcoming new families to the school's neighborhood.

- **Principal's Home Brighteners.** Duplicate a plentiful supply of the Principal's Home Brighteners form found on page 118. Distribute several copies to each staff member. The principal informs teachers that each week he/she would like to make at least two positive phone calls per class to parents telling them about their children's good deeds. Encourage teachers to fill out the form for deserving students in their classroom, being very specific as to exactly what the student did well. Each week set a goal as to a realistic number of home calls you can make, and then make them. (*Idea suggested by Dr. Steven Mahoney, principal at Landau Elementary School, Palm Springs, California.*)

- **Principal's Telephone Log.** Duplicate a plentiful supply of the Principal's Telephone Log form found on page 120 and store the forms in a folder near your phone. Use the forms to keep an ongoing record of conversations with parents. Taking the time to quickly jot down comments concerning each conversation will help recall students' names and personal information for future conversations. And parents appreciate the principal showing a personal interest in their children. Keeping a record of students' names and what was discussed as well as special points to remember for future conversations all help to create a stronger working relationship with parents.

- **Phone Log.** Teachers should be encouraged to keep ongoing records of their phone conversations with parents. Duplicate the Phone Log form found on page 119 in plentiful supply. Suggest that teachers keep copies of the forms in a convenient location or in their lesson plan books. Use the form to record any phone contacts with parents.

- **Parent Communication Record.** The record sheet found on page 121 is used by the teacher or principal to keep track of ongoing communication between the school and individual parents. Often such ongoing contact is needed in order to provide assistance for a particular student. Each contact should be noted for its effectiveness in communication.

WEEKLY PROGRESS REPORTS

Parents want to know how to help their children become more efficient learners. Regular communication between the home and school regarding students' academic progress is one of the most effective ways to build home support for the school. Such communication clearly helps parents stay informed on how their children are doing in school. One of the most effective ways to do this is through weekly progress reports. Reports sent home on a regular basis provide parents with immediate feedback regarding their children's school work and behavior, and help them track their school performance. For weeks prior to the report card, parents will have been receiving ongoing reports of their children's work habits as well as grades. Therefore, grades on the quarter report card will not be surprising to

the parents. If the report indicates children are experiencing difficulties in behavior, a subject, or in completing assignments, parents can immediately request a meeting with the school to work together on finding a solution.

Sending school progress reports home on a regular basis is well worth the effort. The most effective progress reports generally have a number of characteristics in common. Teachers should keep in mind the following guidelines:

- **Individual.** Progress reports should always be individual. A different form must be filled out for each student.

- **Regular.** Progress reports are much more effective if they are completed on a regular basis. Inform parents how often the reports will be sent home and then make sure to follow through. The most effective progress reports are sent home on a weekly basis.

- **Explained to Parents.** If parents are to effectively use the reports, they will need to understand the purpose of the reports, how often they will be sent, and when they are to be returned. A letter describing the program is included. Duplicate the form and send one to each parent.

- **Signature Required.** If parents are required to sign the form, there is a greater chance that they will receive it. Include a line on the form for parents to sign verifying that they read the progress report. Spaces for the teacher's signature as well as the student's signature are also desirable.

- **Returned.** Require the forms to be signed by the parents as well as returned the following school day. Keep students' progress reports in individual folders. They can become valuable record-keeping devices of students' school progress.

Preparing Progress Reports

Six sample progress reports are included for use by educators. Each report is slightly different in design. Choose the form that is most appropriate for a specific grade level or adapt one to meet unique needs. Duplicate the form so that each student has a copy. A letter explaining the program to parents is also included. Duplicate the letter form also. At the end of each week, quickly fill out a form for each student. Remind students you expect to see the form returned and signed the following school day. Send the completed form and the duplicated letter home with each student.

Weekly Folder

In cases where students bring home corrected work on a weekly basis, it may be desirable to attach the report to a folder or envelope. Students' work can then be stored inside the folder for parents to easily find. To make each folder: fold an 12" x 18" piece of construction paper in half so the folder is now 9" x 12". Now take another 12" x 18" paper and fold it in half the long way. It is now 6' x 18". Slip the long piece along the bottom of the folder so the folded edge is along the bottom edge. Staple the two pages together along the edges. The progress report is now stapled to the outside of the folder. The inside of the folder will have two stapled pockets. One pocket can be designated for "work to be finished" and the other pocket can be used to store "completed work."

Envelope

Another way to send completed student work home is to use a 9" x 12" manila envelope. Duplicate the progress report entitled "Weekly Folder" for each student. Glue the form on the front of individual envelopes. School work may be placed inside the

envelopes. The same envelopes may be used over and over until all the spaces are filled on the progress reports. New progress reports will then need to be attached to the envelope.

ESTEEM BUILDER GRAMS

One of the most effective home-school communication techniques is the school newsletter. Principals use them to send home information about a variety of subjects: schedules, conferences, cafeteria menus, school happenings and recognition of special students, to name a few. Newsletters can also be a tool for enhancing parent awareness in esteem building. Provided in this section are a series of Esteem Builder Grams (found on pages 143-168). Each Esteem Builder Gram is a complete, ready-to-duplicate page containing an important message for parents on self-esteem building. The news grams may be used in a variety of ways, including:

- **By principals:** Esteem Builder Grams can be included as part of the regular school newsletter.

- **By teachers:** Educators can periodically send home an Esteem Builder Gram as part of their ongoing parent-communication process.

- **By district administrators:** Esteem Builder Grams can be included as part of the districtwide newsletter sent home to parents.

- **As community news releases:** Grams can

be submitted to the local newspaper to be printed periodically as part of an Esteem Building Community Awareness Program.

Time Frame. There are thirteen Esteem Builder Grams. One gram may be sent home about every three weeks of a nine-month school year. The Esteem Builder Grams could also be used in conjunction with Home Esteem Builder Activities. A strong suggestion is to always send the news gram home on the same day of the week at regularly scheduled intervals. Parents are then expecting and even looking forward to receiving the information.

Gram Contents. Each gram focuses on a particular component of self-esteem (Security, Selfhood, Affiliation, Mission and Competence) and emphasizes a particular building block of the component that parents can enhance at home. Each news gram is numbered at the top so that they can be sent home in chronological order. All thirteen news grams also include practical, easy-to-use suggestions for parents to enhance their children's self-esteem.

Description of Grams

1. *Introduction to Self-Esteem: The Five Feelings of Self-Esteem* explains the five components of self-esteem and the purpose of the Esteem Builder Grams.

2. *Security: Esteem-Building Environments* describes Stanley Coopersmith's research on the three critical elements common to homes of individuals with high self-esteem.

3. *Security: Setting Limits* provides guidelines for establishing rules and limits.

4. *Security: Increasing Positivism* encourages the building of an environment conducive to esteem enhancement.

5. *Selfhood: Developing Individuality* explains how to enhance a sense of uniqueness and feeling of specialness.

6. *Selfhood: Exploring Significant Events* analyzes the important experiences in our

lives that help us acquire our sense of self-hood.

7. *Selfhood: Effective Encouragements* explores ways to praise that are most enhancing to self-esteem.

8. *Affiliation: Tracing Our Roots* describes how to develop a greater sense of affiliation by building a stronger sense of family ancestry.

9. *Affiliation: Awareness of Friendly Deeds* offers ways to enhance affiliation by increasing an awareness of specific friendly deeds.

10. *Mission: Coping With Mistakes* tells how to deal with mistakes by erasing the fear of mistakes.

11. *Mission: Goal Setting* explains how to set realistic and achievable goals to boost self-esteem.

12. *Competence: Strength Awareness* provides tools for building an awareness of talents, strengths, and assets to enhance the feeling of competency.

13. *Competence: Charting Improvement* helps family members recognize growth in competency.

Home Esteem Builder Activities

Esteem Builder Grams are designed to be used in conjunction with Home Esteem Builder Activities. There are forty Home Esteem Builder Activities. One activity was developed for each week of the school year. A chart listing the titles of the Esteem Builder Grams as well as the corresponding Home Esteem Builder Activities can be found on page 139. Titles of the Esteem Builder Grams appear on the chart in the order that they should be sent home to the parent, as the information in each gram builds on the one before. The Home Esteem Builder Activities are also listed in the order they should be sent home. Oftentimes, a Home Esteem Builder Activity enhances the same concepts mentioned in the Esteem Builder Gram. Because the activity reinforces the concept in the news gram, it is recommended that the Home Esteem Builder Activity and the accompanying Esteem Builder Gram be sent home the same week.

For each of the five components, eight different Home Esteem Builder Activities are provided to send home to students' families. A different activity is designed to be sent home each week. Suppose that Selfhood was the component the school or classroom was planning to focus on for two months. The chart on page 139 reveals that there are three Esteem Builder Grams available for home communication newsletters under this component. The chart also shows the order in which the grams and activities are to be correlated. The *Developing Individuality* Esteem Builder Gram should be sent home the same week as the Family-Name Shields Home Esteem Builder Activity. The next week, the news gram, *Exploring Significant Selfhood Events*, may be sent home in conjunction with the Home Esteem Builder Activity entitled Timeline. The third week in Selfhood enhancing cites an activity called History, but no news gram is described. For the fourth week in Selfhood the Home Esteem Builder Activity Me Collages is described. Again, no Esteem Builder Gram is needed to send home. The fifth week, though, both kinds of items are listed: *Effective Encouragement* is the news gram to send home, and Self-Praise is the reinforcing home activity.

Notes

Chapter 4 Activities

This official Phone Pass is hereby awarded for exemplary achievements:

To: _____

From: _____

Date: _____ Time: _____

Please take this pass and go to the office and call a parent. When you reach them, say: "Hi! I'm calling home because my school wanted you to know I did something special today. I... _____

_____

_____

_____

_____

_____

_____ "

_____

Esteem Builders' Complete Program
Jalmar Press, Rolling Hills Estates, CA

PRINCIPAL'S HOME BRIGHTENERS

Teacher ——————————— Date ———————————

Student ——————————— Parent's Name ———————————

Phone No. ——————————— Good Time to Call ———————————

One or two things student is doing well ———————————

——————————————————————
——————————————————————
——————————————————————
——————————————————————
——————————————————————
——————————————————————
——————————————————————

Teacher ——————————— Date ———————————

Student ——————————— Parent's Name ———————————

Phone No. ——————————— Good Time to Call ———————————

One or two things student is doing well ———————————

——————————————————————
——————————————————————
——————————————————————
——————————————————————
——————————————————————
——————————————————————
——————————————————————

PHONE LOG

Dear Teacher,

An excellent way to develop a rapport with parents of students in your classroom is through ongoing communication. Try to make it a practice to making at least one positive phone call for every negative call. As often as you can, take the time to make a personal contact with parents of those students needing extra assistance. Use this form to help you keep a record of your calls. Thank you!

Date	Parent	Comments About the Call

Esteem Builders' Complete Program
Jalmar Press, Rolling Hills Estates, CA

HOME ESTEEM BUILDERS

PRINCIPAL'S TELEPHONE LOG

DATE	PARENT	PHONE NO.	STUDENT	TEACHER	NOTES

Esteem Builders' Complete Program
Jalmar Press, Rolling Hills Estates, CA

HOME ESTEEM BUILDERS

PARENT
COMMUNICATION RECORD

Parent ———————————————————————————

Convenient Times to Call ——————————————————

Student ——————————————— Phone Number ——————————————

DATE	CONTACT	NOTES

Esteem Builders' Complete Program
Jalmar Press, Rolling Hills Estates, CA

"Esteem Building…the key to school and personal success….We can make a difference."

Dear Parents,

Attached to this letter to you find your child's weekly progress report. I feel it's extremely important for you to be continually informed on your child's school progress and so I have taken the time to complete the form regarding your child's work during this week. Every week you will be receiving a similar form. The progress report will let you know the quality of your child's work and behavior during that school week. Please take the time to discuss each report with your child. Then sign the report on the line indicating "parent signature" and return the form with your child on the following school day.

If at any time you would like to discuss your child's work, please contact the school and leave a message with your name and phone number or send a note to school with your child. I will then get back to you to arrange a time we can discuss your child's work.

Thank you for your time. I know that our working together is the most effective way to help your child become a successful learner.

Sincerely,

Esteem Builders' Complete Program
Jalmar Press, Rolling Hills Estates, CA

WEEKLY FOLDER

Dear Parent,

Each week your child will be bringing home this weekly folder with his or her work. Please take the time to review the work with your child. In order for me to see that you have gone over the assignments, sign the form on the space provided and return the folder empty the day after you receive it. Thank you!

Date	Signature	Comments

Esteem Builders' Complete Program
Jalmar Press, Rolling Hills Estates, CA

HEB Form25

HOME ESTEEM BUILDERS

WEEKLY PROGRESS REPORT

Student _____ Week of _____

Teacher _____

Please call me if you have any questions. Return this form signed on the next school day.

ASSIGNMENTS COMPLETED	ASSIGNMENTS NOT COMPLETED
Reading	
Written Language	
Spelling	
Social Studies	
Science	
Handwriting	
Math	

Attitude, Behavior and Study Habits:

Teacher and Parent Comments:

Esteem Builders' Complete Program
Jalmar Press, Rolling Hills Estates, CA

STUDENT PROGRESS REPORT

Student ————————————————   Date ——————————

PERIOD	SUBJECT	TEACHER COMMENTS

Student's Signature ——————————————————————

Parent's Signature ——————————————————————

Parent's Comments:

Please sign this form and have your child return it to school the following day. If you have any questions or would like a conference, please call the school.

WEEKLY STUDENT REPORT

Student _____   Date _____

Teacher _____

Subject _____

Number of Absences _____   Number of Tardies _____

Grades: + = satisfactory
        - = improvement needed
    NA = Not Appropriate

	Grade	Comments
Assignments Completed		
Homework Completed		
Quality of Work		
Respects Authority		
Work Effort		
Gets Along With Peers		
Class Participation		
Other		

Teacher Comments:

Parent Comments:

Parent Signature _____

Please return to class signed on the following school day.

Esteem Builders' Complete Program
Jalmar Press, Rolling Hills Estates, CA

PROGRESS REPORT

Student _____   Date _____

Teacher _____

Citizenship

Gets Along With Peers
Follows Rules
Assumes Responsibility
Respects Authority

Always	Usually	Sometimes	Seldom

Work Habits

Listens Attentively
Follows Directions
Completes Assignments
Uses Time Wisely
Works Independently

Always	Usually	Sometimes	Seldom

Academics

Reading
Math
Spelling
Written Language
Social Studies
Science

Excellent	Satisfactory	Unsatisfactory

Please sign and return to school on Monday.

Parent's Signature _____

Esteem Builders' Complete Program
Jalmar Press, Rolling Hills Estates, CA

WEEKLY SELF-EVALUATION

Name _____

Week _____

	MON	TUE	WED	THU	FRI
I was a good listener.					
I finished all my class work on time.					
I worked well by myself.					
I worked neatly and carefully.					
I finished all my homework on time.					
I contributed to class discussions.					
I followed all the class rules.					
I followed directions well.					
I was friendly and polite.					
I worked well with others.					

_____

Fill in your own comment.

Teacher Comments:

Parent's Signature _____

— 128 —

HOMEWORK RECORD

Student _____

Week of _____

Dear Parent,

    Homework assignments are an important part of your child's learning. It will be assigned Monday through Thursday and should take approximately _____ minutes per day. Please take the time each night to review your child's work with him or her. Parents need to then initial the square below which means you have looked over the work. If you have any comments or questions about the work, write a brief note in the space and I will get back to you as soon as possible. Thank you!

Monday	**Tuesday**
Signed _____	Signed _____
Wednesday	**Thursday**
Signed _____	Signed _____

Esteem Builders' Complete Program
Jalmar Press, Rolling Hills Estates, CA

A NOTE FROM SCHOOL

Dear Parent,

I just wanted to let you know that your child showed great improvement today in the following area: _____
_____
_____

Your child has been working very hard and should be congratulated!

Sincerely,

A MESSAGE FROM YOUR TEACHER

Dear Parent,

I wanted to let you know that your child is having difficulty in the following area _____.
You can help your child at home improve by doing the following:
_____
_____
_____.

Please let me know if you have any questions.

Thank you!

Esteem Builders' Complete Program
Jalmar Press, Rolling Hills Estates, CA

IT'S TIME TO SOUND OFF!

Dear Parent,

    It's a pleasure to let you know that your child has been working very hard in class and is doing much better!

    Thank you for your efforts at home.

        Sincerely,

SCHOOL MEMO

To: _____

From: _____

Re: Your child's school work.

Your child failed to complete the following assignment:

_____

_____

Please help your child finish the school work and return it as soon as possible.

Thank you!

Esteem Builders' Complete Program
Jalmar Press, Rolling Hills Estates, CA

A Great Week at School

Dear Parent,

I just wanted to let you know what a pleasure it was having your child in my class this week! One special reason for such a great week was because your child _____

_____

_____

_____

Sincerely,

_____

Gold Medal for Excellence

Is hereby awarded to _____

For _____

_____

It's a pleasure to be able to inform you that your child had an outstanding week!

Signed _____

Esteem Builders' Complete Program
Jalmar Press, Rolling Hills Estates, CA

A NOTE FROM YOUR CHILD

Date _____

Dear _____

    My teacher wanted me to write this note to you to let you know I did a great job in school. My teacher especially wanted to tell you that I _____

_____

_____

_____

_____

_____

_____

My teacher and I are pleased that I could bring this note home to you.

_____
Student's Signature

_____
Teacher's Signature

Esteem Builders' Complete Program
Jalmar Press, Rolling Hills Estates, CA

HEB Form35

GREAT DAY AWARD
GREAT WEEK AWARD

_____
STUDENT

WAS CAUGHT HAVING
A GREAT DAY! ASK YOUR
CHILD ABOUT IT!

_____
TEACHER

_____
STUDENT

WAS FOUND IN THE ACT
OF HAVING A GREAT SCHOOL WEEK
ASK YOUR CHILD ABOUT IT!

_____
TEACHER

Esteem Builders' Complete Program
Jalmar Press, Rolling Hills Estates, CA

GOOD NEWS REPORT

FROM:

_____

_____

_____

TO:

_____

_____

_____

_____

KEEP UP THE GOOD WORK! IT'S GREAT!

Esteem Builders' Complete Program
Jalmar Press, Rolling Hills Estates, CA

PROUD GRAM

Dear Parent,

Once again, you can be proud of your child's accomplish-ments in school.

This week _____ **accomplished** _____

_____

_____

Good work! Please congratulate your child again for me.
Sincerely yours,

_____

Date _____

SUPPORT GRAM

Dear Parent,

We have been working in the classroom on a variety of acade-mic areas. It would be most beneficial to your child's academic progress if you could assist at home in the following way:

_____

_____

Thank you for your support.
Sincerely yours,

_____

Date _____

Esteem Builders' Complete Program
Jalmar Press, Rolling Hills Estates, CA

_____

_____

_____

_____

_____

_____

_____

_____

_____

_____

_____

_____

_____

_____

_____

_____

Esteem Builders' Complete Program
Jalmar Press, Rolling Hills Estates, CA

SMILE-O-GRAMS

SMILE · ☺ · GRAM

TO: _____

I WOULD LIKE TO SHARE GOOD NEWS WITH YOU!!!

THANK YOU

_____

P.S. PLEASE CALL ME IF YOU WANT
ANY ADDITIONAL INFORMATION

SMILE · ☺ · GRAM

TO: _____

I WOULD LIKE TO SHARE GOOD NEWS WITH YOU!!!

THANK YOU

_____

P.S. PLEASE CALL ME IF YOU WANT
ANY ADDITIONAL INFORMATION

Esteem Builders' Complete Program
Jalmar Press, Rolling Hills Estates, CA

Notes

Notes

Chapter 4 Esteem-Builder Grams

ESTEEM BUILDER GRAM	HOME ESTEEM BUILDER ACTIVITY
SECURITY 1. The Five Feelings of Self-Esteem 2. Esteem-Building Environment 3. Setting Limits 4. Increasing Positivism	HEB1 Letter Home to Parents HEB2 Everybody Needs Praise HEB3 What Others Expect of Me HEB4 Rules…Rules…Rules HEB5 Changing Negative Messages HEB6 Finding Out About Each Other HEB7 Significant Others HEB8 Interview
SELFHOOD 5. Developing Individuality 6. Exploring Significant Events 7. Effective Encouragements	HEB9 Family-Name Shields HEB10 Time Line HEB11 History HEB12 Me Collages HEB13 Self Praise HEB14 Things I Like Collage HEB15 Special Qualities HEB16 The Inside Scoop
AFFILIATION 8. Tracing Our Roots 9. Awareness of Friendly Deeds	HEB17 My Family Shield HEB18 Family Tree HEB19 Family Books HEB20 Friendship Ingredients HEB21 My List of Friendly Deeds HEB22 Compliments HEB23 A Circle of Friends HEB24 Caring for Others
MISSION 10. Coping With Mistakes 11. Goal Setting	HEB25 Home Responsibilities HEB26 My Responsibilities from School HEB27 Goal-Setting HEB28 Making Self Changes HEB29 Targeting Success HEB30 Super Sleuth HEB31 Problem Pantomimes HEB32 Problem Report
COMPETENCE 12. Strength Awareness 13. Charting Improvement	HEB33 Work Folders HEB34 Our Family Strengths HEB35 I CAN HEB36 Journals HEB37 Overcoming Obstacles HEB38 Family Successes HEB39 Sharing Successes HEB40 Blue Ribbon

Esteem Builders' Complete Program
Jalmar Press, Rolling Hills Estates, CA

THE FIVE FEELINGS OF SELF-ESTEEM

No.1 Introduction to Self-Esteem

Selves are not born but made.
— ASHLEY MONTAGU

Self-esteem, the judgment or feeling we have of ourselves, plays an enormous role in your child's life. The perception your child has of himself/herself directly affects a number of areas including:

- choice of friends
- health and well-being
- ability to cope with trauma and obstacles
- job choice
- educational achievement
- behavior

As a child grows and has more experiences, his/her inner picture of self expands. This inner picture is made up of all the descriptions an individual attaches to himself/herself and is called "self-concept." We also know that individuals with high self-esteem generally have five important feelings. These five feelings that affect self-esteem are: Security, Selfhood, Affiliation, Mission, and Competence. Each feeling serves to mold the child's inner self-portrait. The stronger these feelings are, the stronger the child's overall picture of self. Strengths in these feelings often serve as armor to a lot of dragons in the world today: drugs, alcohol, sexual promiscuity, and teenage suicide to name a few. Positive self-esteem can be acquired with less than all five of the feelings intact; however, in general, the higher the number of feelings possessed, the higher the overall self-esteem.

THE FIVE FEELINGS

Security is the first feeling to be acquired. A child with a high level of security conveys a strong sense of assuredness and can handle changes or spontaneity without too much discomfort. This child feels safe, knowing there are people he/she can count on. He/she can trust.

Selfhood is the feeling acquired after Security is built. This is the answer to "Who am I?" When a good sense of self-knowledge is obtained, the child has an accurate and realistic description of his/her roles, attributes, interests, and physical characteristics. This child has a strong sense of individuality, and feels adequate and worthy of praise.

Affiliation refers to a sense of belonging and connectedness. Whenever a child is in relationship to another — be it family members, classmates, peers, or friends/acquaintances — there is potential for affiliation or belonging. A child who feels good about his/her social experiences generally feels accepted by and connected to others. This child not only seeks out others but is able to maintain friendships. He/she is able to cooperate and share as well as show compassion toward others.

• A Home Esteem Builder Newsletter From Your School •

Esteem Builders' Complete Program
Jalmar Press, Rolling Hills Estates, CA

Mission is the fourth component of self-esteem. A child with a strong sense of mission or purpose is not only able to set realistic and achievable goals but follows through on plans. This child takes initiative, feels responsible for his/her actions, seeks alternatives to problems, and evaluates his/her past performances.

 Competence is the fifth feeling of high self-esteem. The experience of success usually results in a child's feeling capable and, therefore, being willing to take risks as well as share opinions and ideas. However, the success must come from experiences that the individual sees as valuable and important to him/her. A child who feels competent is not only aware of his/her strengths but is also able to accept his/her weaknesses. Failure is generally not an issue; in fact, this child perceives mistakes as valuable learning tools.

This school recognizes how important your child's self-esteem is in the classroom. As a result, our staff has chosen the enhancement of student self-esteem as one of our essential goals. We also recognize we cannot do this alone. Parents are, of course, children's first teachers and most important significant others. We invite you to join us in our venture! You, too, can become an "esteem builder" by working with us in enhancing your child's self-esteem. To help you in this venture, a series of Esteem Builder Newsletters will be sent to you. Each newsletter contains an important self-esteem message and explores a different component of self-esteem. Each newsletter also provides you with suggestions of things you can do at home to build your child's self-esteem. We hope you find them valuable.

The greatest news about self-esteem is that it can be changed. Keep in mind that change takes place slowly, so don't expect dramatic results overnight. Your consistent attempts in self-esteem enhancement are crucial. Please let us know how best we can help you and your child. Together, we know we can make a difference.

THE BUILDING BLOCKS OF SELF-ESTEEM

• A Home Esteem Builder Newsletter From Your School •

Esteem Builders' Complete Program
Jalmar Press, Rolling Hills Estates, CA

── ESTEEM-BUILDING ENVIRONMENTS ──

No.2 Esteem Component: Security

If a child lives with approval, he learns to live with himself.
— DOROTHY NOLTE

Dr. Stanley Coopersmith, a child psychologist at the University of California at Davis, devoted his life's work to the study of self-image. His book, *The Antecedents of Self-Esteem*, has become a landmark in this area. One of Coopersmith's research goals was to try and find out what family conditions help to promote high self-esteem. His research team studied over 1,700 boys and their families and found that these boys' self-attitudes were formed either by how their parents or significant others saw them or by how they thought they were seen by parents and/or significant others. Coopersmith's study also discovered three very important elements common to children with high self-esteem, namely:

1. They came from backgrounds where they experienced the kind of love that expresses respect, concern, and acceptance. As children they were accepted for their strengths and capacities as well as for their limitations and weaknesses. It was clearly "love with no strings attached."

2. Their parents were significantly less permissive than were parents of children with lower self-esteem. Within the household, there were clearly defined rules, standards, and expectations and, as a result, children felt secure.

3. Their families displayed a high degree of democracy. The children were encouraged to present their own ideas and opinions for discussion (even ones that deviated from those of their parents).

We can change children's self-esteem. However, to do this we must create the kind of environment that builds esteem. Coopersmith's work clearly shows us that home environments that are most effective in enhancing self-esteem are those in which children:

- feel a sense of warmth and love
- are offered a degree of security that allows them to grow and to try new things without being overly concerned about failing
- are encouraged to have ideas and opinions
- recognize that there are clear and definite limits within the environment
- are given rules and standards that are reasonably and consistently enforced
- have a chance to succeed at their own levels
- are accepted "with no strings attached"

Coopersmith's findings provide important information as to the kind of environment to create that will truly enhance self-esteem. The following suggests ways you can apply Coopersmith's research to your own family:

- **Set Rules.** With your family, create a list of family rules and expectations following Coopersmith's criteria. Post these on the refrigerator.

• A Home Esteem Builder Newsletter From Your School •

Esteem Builders' Complete Program
Jalmar Press, Rolling Hills Estates, CA

ESTEEM BUILDER GRAM

- **Together Time.** Set aside private, uninterrupted "together" time with your child. Schedule the time on the calendar and then strictly adhere to the "conference" (phone off the hook and "do not disturb" sign on the door).

- **Love Notes.** Leave a note under your child's pillow affirming your special love for him/her.

- **Who We Are.** Teach your child the difference between who they ARE and what they DO. Children must learn that we love them because of who they are, not because of the things they DO.

- **Be Clear.** Make it clear to your child what he/she needs to do. Define your limits and rules clearly, and enforce them. Do allow your child some leeway within these limits.

- **Review Rules.** Regularly review your house rules as a family. Are they in need of updating?

- **Listen.** Take time to listen—really listen—to your child every day. Try not to add your judgment or evaluation to your child's opinion. Always judging your child prevents communication.

- **Show You Care.** Hug, love, and affirm. Tell your child how terrific he/she is and that you love him/her.

Self-esteem is closely tied to family and environment. When your child feels appreciated, listened to, genuinely cared for, and knows what you expect, his/her self-esteem is high. There is much you as a parent can do to build your child's self-esteem.

Esteem Builders' Complete Program
Jalmar Press, Rolling Hills Estates, CA

SETTING LIMITS

No.3 Esteem Component: Security

*People have a way of becoming what you
encourage them to be, not what you nag them to be.*
— SCUDDER N. PARKER

In his intensive investigation of what kinds of home environments enhance self-esteem, researcher Dr. Stanley Coopersmith found that clearly defined and enforced limits and standards are essential to well-being and security. Setting limits and realistic standards creates a security blanket for children. When they know what to expect and what to do in order to succeed, they feel safe and emotionally secure. In order to be most effective, parents, as their children's primary esteem builders, must consistently enforce the limits they set.

Coopersmith's research offers the following guidelines for establishing limits within a home that offers an esteem-building environment:

1. Make certain that rules are reasonable and realistic.
2. Set a small number of rules at a time. They can then be followed and enforced more easily without becoming a burden.
3. Regulate boundaries with consistency and firmness.
4. Establish clear consequences when rules are broken and follow through on them. Since children inevitably test the rules, continue to clarify and explain them.
5. Only enforce rules non-physically, and never threaten your child with loss of acceptance.

6. In order for rules to make sense to the child, they must first be meaningful to the parent. As an esteem builder you must genuinely believe and expect that the rules set will be observed.

7. Praise the child when he/she follows the rules.

When rules are consistently and fairly enforced, your child's esteem can be enhanced. The following suggestions are offered to help you nurture an environment in which reasonable limits and rules are set:

- **Design Rules and Limits.** Oftentimes, children get into trouble because they really didn't understand our rules and limits. Don't assume your child knows yours. Gather all family members together at a meeting and come to an agreement as to what the "house rules" are. Discuss all rules one at a time so that everyone understands what they mean. Finally, write the rules on paper and ask each family member to sign the list. Post the rules so all members can see them.

- **Establish Consequences.** Once rules are set, family members must then understand what will happen when a rule is broken. This is when consistency becomes critical. Once you set a limit and establish a consequence, you must follow

Esteem Builders' Complete Program
Jalmar Press, Rolling Hills Estates, CA

through on your word. Establish a realistic consequence for each rule that is broken. If the rule states, "Curfew is at 9 PM," the consequence for arriving later could be, "Home one hour earlier the following night" or "Grounded from the next activity." Try and make the consequence fit the misbehavior.

- **Periodically Review Rules.** Rules are not necessarily unchangeable. As children become older or new situations arise, calling a session to revise the rules may be in order. Take the time as a family to rethink the rules and consequences and, if needed, create a new list.

- **Stay Calm.** If your child has broken a rule, stay calm! Following misbehavior, it may be helpful to remove your child from the situation and from yourself until everyone "cools off." You can then deal with the issue more rationally at a later time. One of the benefits of setting clear consequences to any misbehavior is that the results are already spelled out to the child. Your job becomes the "enforcer" to carry out the consequence.

- **Model Rules.** Young children often have a difficult time applying the "rule written on the paper" to an actual situation. Sometimes role playing together what the rules looks like in real life can be helpful.

- **Behavior Is the Problem...Not the Child.** Emphasize to your child following any breaking of the rules that your frustration is with your child's behavior and not with him/her.

- **Private Signal.** Develop a private signal between you and your child to signal inappropriate behavior at a public event. Such a signal clues the child that his/her behavior is inappropriate and at the same time preserves their dignity.

- **Discipline Privately.** Always discipline your child privately and quietly. Reprimanding your child in front of others is humiliating and diminishes self-esteem.

- **Acknowledge and Celebrate Appropriate Behavior.** If you're not careful, you can overlook all the countless good things your child does. Purposely look for your child's good behavior and acknowledge it. Every once in a while plan a celebration event together, such as an ice cream cone, a movie, a picnic at the park, or a visit to a variety store to purchase an inexpensive toy. Celebrations need not be elaborate and expensive. When you acknowledge your child's good behavior by celebrating, there's a greater chance the behavior will be repeated. *Happy Enhancing!*

Esteem Builders' Complete Program
Jalmar Press, Rolling Hills Estates, CA

INCREASING POSITIVISM

No.4 Esteem Component: Security

If you think in positive terms, you will achieve positive results.
— **NORMAN VINCENT PEALE**

A sense of security is built in a positive environment. In this kind of atmosphere children immediately perceive they are welcomed and appreciated. In order to grow, children must perceive a sense of physical and emotional safety. They must feel they can trust those around them. And they must feel safe enough to share their own thoughts and opinions. A home environment can be destroyed by negativity. In a very short time, parents can not only bring themselves down but they can also bring down those around them. An inescapable truth about negativism is that it can be "caught." In no time at all, others begin to speak with the same derogatory tone as those around them. The good news is that "positivism" can also be caught, as well as taught. By building a more positive environment, parents can improve the family atmosphere and enhance their child's self-esteem.

There is another important reason to build a positive home environment. One of the ways children maintain their ideas about themselves is through "self-referent speech," that is, the way they talk to themselves about themselves. Negative statements are particularly detrimental to self-esteem. Rarely do parents stop to think about their child's inner language because it is largely automatic and internal; nonetheless, it is powerful. Continuous negative self-statements, such as "I can't do anything right" or "I'm ugly" do little to promote a positive sense of self.

How can a negative atmosphere be turned around into a more positive one? How can you help your child make positive self-statements? As you examine your own esteem building atmosphere, keep in mind the following ideas:

- **Model Positive Self-Statements.** You can't expect your child to catch something you don't have. Ask yourself, "How often am I modeling positivism?" Try to tune in to your ongoing dialogue with your child so you can listen to yourself, and then make the necessary adjustments in your speech.

- **5:1 Ratio.** Most research states that it takes at least five positive statements to combat one negative statement. Use the 5:1 ratio as a guideline for how many positive statements members in your family should aim for each day.

- **Family Rule: Positives Only.** Make it a family rule to try and say only positive statements. You can refer to these statements with terms such as "Builder-Uppers," "Sparkles," "Compliments" or "Fuzzies." Perhaps your family can come up with a term of your own.

- **Create Lists of Positive Terms.** Oftentimes children are hesitant to say positive statements because they're unaware of the words, phrases, or statements they could be saying. As a family, create an ongoing list of "Builder-Uppers." Keep the list visible and continue adding to it.

BUILDER UPPERS

Wow!
Great!
Super!
Awesome!
Wonderful!
I Like You!
Thank You!
Congratulations!

- **Label Put-Downs.** Statements that are not "Builder-Uppers" are often called "Put-Downs." You could also call them "Zingers," "Ouch!" or "Killers." As a family, you can develop a term of your own to label put-down kinds of statements. Or simply encourage family members to label any put-down statements from another family member by saying, "That's a put-down." Sometimes family members say so many negative statements to one another that they're unaware of how much these words have become part of their vocabulary. Pointing out put-downs

as they are said helps build an awareness of this habit, which is the first step toward breaking it.

- **1 Negative = 1 Positive.** As your family becomes more aware of what put-downs and put-ups (or builder-uppers) are, you can start a family rule: "For every negative statement you say, you must give me a positive statement back." These can be called "Turn-Arounds." If any member of the family says a put-down to someone else (or to himself/herself), he/she must then come up with one put-up statement.

- **Count Negatives.** If you're aware that negativism is rampant in your home, begin an active "attack" policy. Help each family member keep track of his/her own negatives on a chart or index card every day for a week. Younger children can use concrete objects, such as marbles or bottle caps, placing one object into a container every time they say a put-down.

- **Celebrate Positivism.** If you're not careful, you can overlook the good your child does. If you notice your child's positive behavior, be sure to point it out and celebrate it. Remember, oftentimes negative behavior has become a habit. You do it so many times that you become unaware of doing it. As a family, tune in to your negatives and pledge to focus more on the positives.

Esteem Builders' Complete Program
Jalmar Press, Rolling Hills Estates, CA

DEVELOPING INDIVIDUALITY

No.5 Esteem Component: Selfhood

All that we are is a result of what we have thought.
— **BUDDHA**

Before children can relate positively to one another and value each other in a way that promotes self-esteem, they must learn to value themselves. Every once in a while parents should hire a blimp to fly low over houses, parks, and playgrounds so that their child can read a banner that says, "You are special...be proud of it!" All children need to feel unique and to know that others appreciate and respect their special qualities. This is how children develop self-worth, a feeling essential to the attainment of high self-esteem. Such a feeling is not inherited; it is learned.

The development of individuality is a gradual process that begins with clarifying self-descriptions as well as understanding differences. This is the second critical feeling of self-esteem called Selfhood—it is the all-important answer to "Who am I?" As a child gains an awareness of his/her interests, attitudes, and roles, he/she also begins to recognize that not everyone is alike. The realization sets in that "my self-descriptions may not be the same as another person's." For positive self-esteem to evolve, a child must not only develop the feeling of being different but of being comfortable with that difference. "I recognize I have unique qualities and, as a result, I like myself even more."

There are three steps you can take to help your child acknowledge and respect his/her uniqueness. These steps are:

1. **Accept the child for his/her unique and distinct differences.**
2. **Build an awareness of interests, roles, and attributes that may influence self-descriptions.**
3. **Suggest new ways to expand your child's self-descriptions.**

The following suggestions can help you take these steps with your child.

- **"Who Am I?" Game.** Around the dinner table one evening, emphasize that each person, even though members of the same family, has special qualities that make his/her different from the others. Begin to model the "Who Am I" game. Explain that each person says one true and positive statement about himself/herself starting with "I am" and then turns to the person on his/her right. The game continues for several rounds until individuals run out of "I am" statements ("I am a painter," "I am a reader," "I am five feet tall," "I am creative," etc.) and family

— 151 —

members must help supply information about each other.

- **Different and Alike.** Each family member picks a partner. Give each person a piece of paper and fold it in half. On one half write "different" and on the other half write "alike." Tell each pair to think of eight ways they are alike and eight ways they are different. Answers could be written or drawn. In a larger family, have each two-some report their findings back to the rest of the family.

- **People Recipe.** Emphasize to your child that just as recipes differ, so do people. Many ingredients make up a recipe just as many personal characteristics make a child unique and special. Ask your child, "What are you made of?" Help him/her write down his/her answers as a recipe on a "recipe card." Save the card and duplicate it on bright-colored paper. Paste your child's picture on the back. The card makes a wonderful present to give relatives.

- **Time Capsule.** On a long strip of paper (white shelf paper or adding machine tape are possibilities), help your child create a time capsule. Use words or pictures drawn or cut out of magazines to depict your child's life. A few of the items that could be included are a handprint; a footprint; pictures of favorite foods, movies, and books; pictures of family/friends; and news clippings. Finally, roll the finished product in an empty paper towel tube and save it. Remember to open it next year, and in five and ten years time.

- **Selfhood Placement.** Using a 12" x 18" piece of construction paper or tagboard, help your child cover the paper with self-descriptive words or pictures. Photographs of your child could also be used. If desired, cover the placemat with clear contact paper available at variety stores to make it more durable. Placemats make great presents to give relatives. *Happy Enhancing!*

Recipe for Nancy

2 tbsp. niceness	*dash of smiles*
1 tsp. naughtiness	*a few hugs*

Mix the niceness and naughtiness. Add a dash of smiles and a few hugs. Bake well in the love and care of friends and family.

Esteem Builders' Complete Program
Jalmar Press, Rolling Hills Estates, CA

EXPLORING SIGNIFICANT EVENTS

No.6 Esteem Component: Selfhood

If you want to be respected, you must respect yourself.
— **SPANISH PROVERB**

A large part of a child's inner picture evolves as a result of his/her experiences with significant people and events in his/her life. Some are positive; others, negative. How your child perceives each experience is the most important factor in how this event will affect his/her self-esteem. Your child evaluates experience internally as either a success or a failure, enjoyable or unenjoyable, positive or negative, and he/she stockpiles each evaluation for future reference. This perception, of course, may or may not be accurate or realistic, but it has been logged and may be retrieved many years later.

Since significant experiences with events and people play such a large role in the formation of self-opinions, increasing your child's awareness of them can build his/her self-esteem. Activities that provide opportunities for your child to reflect upon significant experiences, and in the process help shift the existing self-image, are particularly beneficial for a child low in self-esteem. Commonly, he/she has a self-pitying attitude that "no one has as many bad things happen to them as I do." Important learning takes place when the child with low self-esteem discovers that negative experiences need not always be perceived that way. Your child doesn't need to dwell on the past; instead, he/she can actually turn a negative experience around by reflecting on it positively and finding out what he/she can learn in so-called "mistakes."

The following activities are designed to help your child explore the formation of his/her selfhood. All of them are more fun if every family member participates.

- **Your Life.** Begin by discussing your own life with your child. Point out what it was like to grow up in a different era. Mention how growing up in this period was alike as well as unlike today's world. Talk about the fun times as well as the sad times. In a few minutes, you can give your child a powerful overview of the main parts of your life.

- **Family Autobiographies.** At a family gathering one evening, take time to relate family autobiographies. Each family member takes a turn describing main events in his/her life that he/she thinks are significant. Other members can help with "add-ons" that the speaker may have forgotten. If each autobiography becomes particularly long, plan to do an autobiography on a different family member each evening.

- **Photo Albums.** Spend time together looking through your family photo albums. They are excellent tools for discussing key events that you may have forgotten. If you have photos of your own childhood, bring them out to explore

Esteem Builders' Complete Program
Jalmar Press, Rolling Hills Estates, CA

together. If your child does not have his/her own personal photo album, now might be the time to start one.

- **Time Lines.** This activity can be done using adding machine tape, plain white shelf paper, or butcher paper cut into a 12" x 48" (or longer) length. Begin by asking your child to think about the life events he/she feels are most significant to him/her. Make a list of these events as your child describes them. Now begin to list the events in chronological order on a long strip of paper. Along the margin write the year the event took place. Then help your child draw or write the actual life event.

- **Me Puzzle.** On a large piece of tagboard paper, ask your child to depict events in his/her life that he/she considers significant. These events may either be drawn or written using words, phrases, or sentences. Emphasize that the events depicted should be large enough to cover the paper, like in a large poster. Also emphasize that about two inches of space should be left around all sides of each event before drawing or writing the next experience. When the poster is completed, help your child make a puzzle with the poster. Cut out each event in the shape of a puzzle so that the pieces can all be reconnected. You may wish to cover the finished pieces in clear contact paper to create a keepsake.

- **Books.** There are many children's books whose themes lend themselves wonderfully to a parent/child discussion. Use these stories to get your child talking about the significant events in his/her life. A few suggestions include:

Higher on the Door by James Stevenson. Greenwillow Books, New York, 1987. The author remembers what it was like growing up in a village and waiting to get older. (Ages 4 to 9)

The Hundred Penny Box by Sharon Bell Mathis, Puffin Books, New York, 1975. A Newbery Honor medal winner of a touching account of a young boy's great-great-aunt Dew who is a hundred years old. Dew keeps an old box filled with pennies, one for each birthday, and recalls all the years of her life. (Ages 7 to 12)

The Keeping Quilt by Patricia Polacco. Simon & Schuster, New York, 1988. A homemade quilt ties together the lives of four generations of an immigrant Jewish family, remaining a symbol of their enduring love and faith. (Ages 5 to 10)

The Summer of the Swans by Betsy Byars. New York: Puffin Books, 1970. A teen-age girl gains new insight into herself and her family when her mentally handicapped brother gets lost. (Ages 8 to 12)

Remember, some of the most significant life events are yet to come. Be sure to point out these positive, wonderful events to your child as they happen. You could say, "There's another great event in your life. Be sure to remember it. It's a part of you forever!" *Happy Enhancing!*

Esteem Builders' Complete Program
Jalmar Press, Rolling Hills Estates, CA

EFFECTIVE ENCOURAGEMENTS

No.7 Esteem Component: Selfhood

*I now perceive one immense omission in my psychology — the deepest
principle of human nature is the craving to be appreciated.*
— WILLIAM JAMES

Every human being needs strokes and "pats on the back" letting that person know their efforts are appreciated. Children are obviously no exception. A parent's encouragement is powerful. In proper dosages, it can spur your child on to new heights. To make your praise more enhancing to your child's self-esteem, keep in mind the following points:

- **Earned and Deserved.** Children are quite perceptive and know if they really earned the praise they received. Be sure that the praise you give is deserved, or your statements will seem insincere.

- **Immediate.** The best time to give praise is on the spot, as soon as you observe the good behavior. Keep in mind that the longer you delay your praise, the less effective your comment is.

- **Specific.** The most effective praise lets your child know exactly what was done well. When you observe good behavior, don't say "good job"; instead, word your message specifically like this: "Ryan, you did a great job on this writing paper today because you remembered to use margins," or "Kelly, you were so cooperative today because you shared your toys with Billy."

- **Individual.** Effective praise is given directly to the deserving individual.

- **Repeated.** To help your child internalize a new image, praise must be repeated. Choose a strength or asset your child already possesses but may not be aware of (artistic, creative, thoughtful, kind, athletic, musical, etc.). Every time your child demonstrates the skill specifically praise the behavior. "I noticed how artistic you are. Look at the colors you chose!" or "You are very friendly. Your smile made your friend smile." Giving praise one or two times is not enough for a child with low self-esteem. Their internal image is so ingrained that you will need to repeat the praise for the same behavior, ideally four to six times a day for twenty-one days to see maximum growth.

• A Home Esteem Builder Newsletter From Your School •

Esteem Builders' Complete Program
Jalmar Press, Rolling Hills Estates, CA

ESTEEM BUILDER GRAM

BRIGHT IDEAS

1. Find the positives. Often parents over-look the good things their child does and focus on the negatives instead.

2. Avoid subtle encouragement of com-petition between siblings. This usually leads to rivalry and jealousy.

3. Focus on what is good about your child.

4. Let your child know his/her worth. Recognize improvement and effort, not just accomplishment.

5. Have faith in your child so he/she can have faith in himself/herself.

WAYS TO SAY HOORAY

- I knew you could do it!
- That's better than ever.
- That's a great idea.
- A couple more times and you'll have it.
- You're on the right track now.
- You're doing that much better today.
- You really have been working hard.
- That's coming along nicely.
- You have just about mastered that.
- You outdid yourself today.
- You're getting better every day.
- You haven't missed a thing.
- You must have been practicing to get so good.
- I'm happy to see you work like that.
- You're doing a great job.
- It's fun to work with you when you work so hard.
- You did some first-class work today.
- That's a good observation.
- Now you've figured it out.
- You must be proud of yourself.

Excellent! Super! Great! The Best! Magnificent! Awesome! Hooray! Superior! Spectacular perfor-mance! You have it! You're really thinking! Keep it up! Good thinking! Good going! That's it! Tremendous! That's good! Fantastic! You've got it! Nice job! Wow! Congratulations! Beautiful! Impressive! Very creative! You made it look easy! Much better! Sensational!

• A Home Esteem Builder Newsletter From Your School •

Esteem Builders' Complete Program
Jalmar Press, Rolling Hills Estates, CA

TRACING OUR ROOTS

No.8 Esteem Component: Affiliation

To forget one's ancestors is to be a brook
without a source, a tree without a root.
— **CHINESE PROVERB**

Affiliation is a feeling of belonging or of being connected to people who are important to one's self. This feeling is essential to self-esteem because how a person perceives himself/herself is related to the recognition he/she receives in relationship to others. The importance of interpersonal relationships in your child's life cannot be overstated. Your child needs to feel a sense of connectedness to other human beings—particularly individuals he/she feels are significant to him/her. When your child feels connected to the people he/she considers important, and in return receives their respect and approval, he/she gains a sense of affiliation. The first place this feeling of affiliation is felt is in the family.

A child's self-esteem grows roots when he/she develops ancestral pride. Learning about the family background helps your child connect with his/her past, and develop appreciation and respect for the national and ethnic backgrounds of his/her classmates. The following activities are designed to help your child connect with his/her ancestral history and in the process develop a stronger sense of belonging to the present. If you do these activities as a family, you'll find you are also enhancing a sense of family belonging that will last for a lifetime.

- **Ethnic Dinner or Luncheon.** As a family, discuss your heritage. Research foods that are native to your family's heritage. Plan a menu together. Each family member can be responsible for one special dish for the meal. One evening sit down and celebrate your heritage together.

- **Ancestry Cookbook.** Compile special recipes from relatives as a holiday keepsake. Write a letter explaining your intention of creating a family keepsake of favorite recipes. Ask each relative to write his/her favorite recipe on a postcard and send it to you. Now compile the recipes in a cookbook entitled "Ancestors' Recipes," or a title of your family's choosing. Your child can be responsible for decorating the cover. Duplicate the recipes and give each family an autographed copy.

- **Map Study.** On a large world map, together locate all the countries associated with your family's heritage and discuss the findings. Each family member can be responsible for making a small 1" x 2" flag of each country and gluing it to a pin or toothpick. Also discuss how relatives came to the United States and the hardships they faced.

- **Family Flags.** As a family, make a large flag. The flag should be a replica of your family's

• A Home Esteem Builder Newsletter From Your School •

Esteem Builders' Complete Program
Jalmar Press, Rolling Hills Estates, CA

country of origin. Possibilities include drawing the flag with marking pens or fabric crayons on a white sheet, or gluing felt pieces on a larger piece of felt. Hang it up on special family holidays or celebrations.

- **Family Shields.** This activity enhances your family members' awareness of the origin of their last name. You may need to do some library research on the origin and meaning of your last name. Now as a family cut a large shield from a 12" x 18" piece of construction paper or tagboard. Write your last name in large letters in the middle of the shield, then add a pictorial and/or written explanation of the name's derivation and meaning. Use colored marking pens, paint, or crayons to brighten up the shield. You may want to cover your finished product with clear contact paper to protect it. Remember to bring out the finished product on family holidays.

- **Family Trees.** There are dozens of ready-made family tree charts or books available at book or stationery stores that you may wish to copy or purchase. As a family, spend time discussing the names of your ancestors and the connections between all these people. Begin with your immediate family and see how far back you can go.

- **Ancestry Research.** With your family, research information concerning your family's country of origin. Visit the library together and look up books pertaining to the country. Find out information such as population, size, location, language, special customs, native food, natural resources, and past and present leaders. You may wish to start a family journal of your discoveries.

Finding out about your family's ancestry is a lifelong search. You may discover it's well worth the effort. Fond memories and shared traditions as a family may well be the outcome. *Happy Enhancing!*

Esteem Builders' Complete Program
Jalmar Press, Rolling Hills Estates, CA

AWARENESS OF FRIENDLY DEEDS

No.9 Esteem Component: Affiliation

One of the factors that erodes self-concept is the inability of some children to make and keep friends.
— **JAMES DOBSON**

Friends have an enormous influence on children's feelings of self; thus, affiliation is a crucial building block toward positive self-esteem. In a struggle for social recognition, peers can provide important avenues for the development of children's social skills and a sense of affiliation that adults and family experiences alone cannot fulfill.

Peer interactions also provide valuable lessons that shape children's self-perception or identity. Remarks such as "You sure are a good jumper, Billy" and "I like to be with you" are especially significant when students hear them from their peers.

By contrasting what they can and cannot do with the actions of their peers, students are able to make decisions about their selfhood and formulate opinions about their strengths and weaknesses. "Am I really good at spelling?" "Do others like my ideas?" "Am I too short?" These are the kinds of evaluations students frequently make as they interact with one another. As they win some acceptance and experience a few rejections, students arrive at significant verdicts about themselves.

Friends play an enormous part in children's feelings of self. In addition, unless they clearly understand how friends act toward one another, it is next to impossible for children to do friendly deeds for others.

The starting place for enhancing your child's affiliation with peers is to provide him/her with the opportunity to analyze characteristics so that, in turn, he/she can demonstrate them to others. The following suggestions are designed to help your child build a greater awareness of the power of friendship as well as specific things good friends do for others.

- **Friendly Deeds List.** As a family create a list of friendly deeds on a large chart. Begin by asking, "What are things you could do for someone else to make them feel happy?" Emphasize that friendly deeds do not have to be materialistic. The best deeds come from the heart.

- **Track Kind Deeds.** Have your family keep track of their kind deeds for a month. You could chart the friendly deeds on a blank monthly calendar. At dinner time each day, ask family members to name the friendly, kind things they did for others. Make a small mark for each deed on the calendar for that day.

- **Reinforce Friendly Behavior.** Praise your child each time you observe their friendly behavior. Label the behavior, "That was being friendly," and then specifically tell them what they did that was friendly (for example, "because you helped Pat pick up the forms").

• A Home Esteem Builder Newsletter From Your School •

Esteem Builders' Complete Program
Jalmar Press, Rolling Hills Estates, CA

- **Pillow Notes.** Leave a note under your child's pillow reinforcing his/her friendly behavior. "I noticed how friendly you were today when you...." Tell your child exactly what he/she did well.

- **Watch for Friendship.** Watch a family sitcom on the TV together. Purposely look for characters demonstrating friendly behaviors. Discuss what those behaviors are.

- **Do Friendly Deeds.** As a family do a friendly deed for someone who may be lonely. Discuss what kinds of things you could do and make a list (send a friend a letter, visit them, make a homemade present, pick flowers, etc.), then choose one and do it.

- **Dinner Table Discussion.** At the dinner table or other family gathering reinforce friendly deeds. Ask, "Who's had someone do something friendly for them today? What did this person do and how did it make you feel?" Extend the discussion.

- **Books On Friendship.** Go to the library together and ask the children's librarian to suggest a few selections of children's literature dealing with the concept of friendship. Read the book together and identify the friendly deeds of the character. A few suggestions are:

Rosie and Michael by Judith Viorst. New York: Atheneum, 1974. A delightful tale about two real friends, Rosie and Michael. The friends tell what they like about each other—they even tell about the bad things. (Ages 5 to 9)

Friends by Helme Heini. New York: Atheneum, 1985. A beautifully illustrated book for young children about the meaning of friendship. (Ages 4 to 8)

Sign of the Beaver by Elizabeth George Speare. New York: Dell, 1983. Twelve-year-old Matt must try to survive on his own in the wilderness. He is rescued by an Indian chief and his grandson, Attean. As the boys come to know each other, a beautiful friendship evolves. (Ages 9 to 13)

Bridge to Terabithia by Katherine Paterson. New York: Avon, 1977. A touching story of a special friendship between a boy and a girl. Jesse's friendship with Leslie and the worlds of imagination and learning that she opens up to him change him forever, and enable him to cope with the unexpected tragedy of her death. (Ages 10 to 14)

Keep in mind that one of the most powerful ways your child acquires the skills of friendship-making is by observing others who do it well. When you point out friendly deeds to your child, changes will take place. The changes you see will be gradual ones, so keep recognizing and reinforcing any of your child's friendly efforts. Finally, remember to model such deeds yourself. Good luck!

Esteem Builders' Complete Program
Jalmar Press, Rolling Hills Estates, CA

COPING WITH MISTAKES

No.10 Esteem Component: Mission

There is nothing final about a mistake, except its being taken as final.
— PHYLLIS BOTTOME

One of the inevitable facts of life is that everyone makes mistakes. Granted, some mistakes are more significant than others and harder to get over, but they are a part of life. How individuals deal with those mistakes is significant to their self-esteem.

Children with high self-esteem appear much better at coping with their errors. Watching children with positive self-perceptions deal with an error is always a magnificent sight. These children literally stand up, brush off their knees, and say, "Well, I blew it. What should I do differently next time?" They recognize that a mistake was made and admit the error. Most importantly, these children also develop a strategy to change the mistake and not do the same thing again. What they do, in reality, is learn from their errors.

The process of making and learning from mistakes is an extremely valuable life skill because learning involves risking. Every time children risk, they will not always be right. But, because they've tried something new, there's always the chance they will succeed. Each new success enhances self-esteem. Each esteem-enhancing experience refuels their desire to try again...and again...and again.

Children with low self-esteem deal with making a mistake quite differently. More often than not, these children use the experience to devalue themselves. "See, I told you I couldn't do anything right!" is the way children with low self-esteem respond. Instead of looking at the error as an opportunity to learn, these children interpret the experience as a reason to quit and "never do that again." The experience certainly was not self-enhancing; instead, it was self-devaluing.

The tragedy is that these children could have learned from their experience. If these children had known, "It's OK to make mistakes...mistakes are how you learn," the experience would have been seen in a different way. You can help your child cope with mistakes by offering him/her strategies to turn mistakes into learning opportunities. In the process, you can provide your child with an opportunity to enhance his/her self-esteem.

There are many ways parents can help erase the idea that "mistakes are bad." Keep in mind that changing behavior takes time and consistency. Finally, remember that your own way of dealing with mistakes is the most important lesson your child can ever learn on the subject. What follows are some suggestions to help your child erase the fear of making mistakes:

- **Tell Your Child, "It's OK to make a mistake."** Too many children are suffering from perfectionism. They try to be perfect. When a mistake happens (as it's bound to from time to time) the child is devastated and interprets this as mean-

• A Home Esteem Builder Newsletter From Your School •

Esteem Builders' Complete Program
Jalmar Press, Rolling Hills Estates, CA

ing he/she is "unworthy." Every now and then, tell your child, "It's OK to make mistakes. It happens to all of us."

- **Admit Your Own Mistakes.** It is important for parents to admit they do make mistakes. Children see you as "all powerful and all knowing." Obviously, parents do make mistakes, but, oftentimes, they keep them to themselves. Tell your child a mistake you've made recently. Discuss a mistake you remember making as a child.

- **Model Turning Your Mistake Around.** Yes, parents make mistakes, but high-achieving individuals learn from their errors. As you admit your mistake, remember to tell your child what you will do differently the next time. You could say, "I made the mistake of...and this is what I'll do instead...."

- **Share Mistakes of Famous Individuals.** Anytime the opportunity arises, point out a mistake made by a famous individual so that your child recognizes mistakes happen to everyone. Books are rich with sources. Newspapers always have fresh ideas. Here are a few examples you could use:

  Abraham Lincoln: Defeated for public office eight times before being elected President of the United States.

  Wright Brothers: Took seventy times to get the Kitty Hawk off the ground.

  Louisa May Alcott: Told by countless publishers that no one would ever read *Little Women.*

  Babe Ruth: The year he hit the most home runs he had the most strike-outs.

- **Help Your Child Learn Positive Self-Talk.** If you notice your child is very tense and concerned about making mistakes, help him/her learn to say inside his/her head a positive, affirming statement such as "I am calm and in control" or "I will try my best." The more your child says the statement, the more he/she will begin to believe it.

- **Help Your Child Label the Mistake as the Problem, Not Himself/Herself.** Often, the most self-devaluing part of making mistakes is not the mistake, but how the child chooses to interpret the error. Help your child admit he/she made a mistake ("I got this one wrong") and then help him/her label the mistake as the problem and not himself/herself ("I forgot the the capital of Nevada").

- **Plan a Strategy for Next Time.** After your child can admit the mistake and relabels the mistake as the error (not himself/herself), the final step is to develop a plan for next time: "This is what I'll do differently next time. I'll study the capitals ten minutes a night for the next two weeks."

Esteem Builders' Complete Program
Jalmar Press, Rolling Hills Estates, CA

GOAL SETTING

No.11 Esteem Component: Mission

The most important thing about goals is having one.
— GOEFFREY F. ALBERT

Self-motivated individuals generally have a clear idea of where they are headed. They have a sense of direction and a purpose in life. Generally, such individuals are successful in school and in life. Goals are what help them know where they want to be. Reflecting on the direction they wish to take provides the impetus to achieve that aim, and the establishment of goals helps to carry those individuals along the road to success.

The use of goals by individuals with high self-esteem has been well documented. One researcher stated that these individuals tend to use goals as a means of reinforcing their present level of self-esteem. Another study found that students who were successful in school tended to set personal goals that were both realistic and reasonable. And a twenty-one-year study of "peak performers" in sports, science, and entertainment found that one trait they all shared in common was setting goals for themselves—and then not stopping until they achieved them.

Goal-setting is a powerful tool for esteem building. It is also a tool that you can teach your child. The following strategies can help your child become more goal-oriented. Good luck in your attempts! Stop by the school and let us know how things are going with your esteem-building efforts. We'd love to hear from you!

- **Define Goal-Setting.** Many children find goal-setting a difficult task because they are not familiar with how the goal-setting process works in real life. Start by defining to your child what goal-setting means. You may find it helpful to equate the concept of goals with how sports are played. Explain that goals are what we "shoot for." In football and soccer, players try to get the ball across the goal line to score points. In life, an individual tries to improve something about himself/herself; a goal is something he/she is trying to achieve.

- **Talk About Personal Goals.** In order for children to feel comfortable talking about goals, parents need to share their own. At a convenient time, discuss with your child a goal you're trying to reach. Goals, at the beginning stage, are often called "wishes": "I really want to get better at my cooking," "I wish I was better at baking," or "Tennis seems like such a fun sport. I wish I were better at it." Take turns at making "wishes."

- **Set Family Goals.** To help your child set goals that are specific, ask each family member to think of one goal he/she wishes to achieve, acquire, or improve in. Remind each person that

Esteem Builders' Complete Program
Jalmar Press, Rolling Hills Estates, CA

the goal must be one he/she has control or power over. If anyone states a goal that he/she has no control over (i.e. "I want to grow five inches" or "I want to get rid of my freckles"), simply ask him/her, "Do you have power over that? A goal must be something you can control."

- **Write Down Goals.** Research states that individuals are much more likely to achieve their goals if they write them down. Ask each family member to write down on paper the goal he/she wishes to achieve and to follow these rules: Write the goal in the present tense beginning with "I am." Now briefly say what it is he/she wants to achieve and then state when he/she wants to achieve it by. Be brief, for example, "I am one pound lighter by Friday than I am now."

- **Draw Success.** Studies reveal that individuals can increase the possibility of achieving their goals by seeing images of themselves succeeding. Ask your child to draw a picture of himself/herself on paper as if he/she has already achieved the goal.

- **Be a Resource.** Oftentimes goals are not achieved because individuals do not know or have all the resources needed to achieve their goals. Ask your child, "What do you need and who do you need to help you make your goal?" Now talk through the resources needed for this goal and help your child acquire them.

- **Begin With Short-Term Goals.** First-time goal-setters need to see some immediate success. Have your child set a goal that can be achieved within two weeks. Some children need to set an even shorter goal (at the end of the hour, or day, or week). Set the length of the goal according to the time you think your child needs.

- **Monitor Goal-Setting.** Develop ways to monitor your child's progress as he/she works toward achieving a goal. Have frequent private conferences to evaluate his/her progress and see what kind of support is needed.

- **Celebrate Successful Goals.** As goals are achieved, celebrate them as a family! Then, help your child set the next goal and the next and the next.

• A Home Esteem Builder Newsletter From Your School •

Esteem Builders' Complete Program
Jalmar Press, Rolling Hills Estates, CA

—— STRENGTH AWARENESS ——

No.12 Esteem Component: Competence

In order to succeed, we must first believe we can.
— MICHAEL KORDA

All human beings need to feel successful and win approval from their peers. Your child is no exception. Society puts an enormous price tag on human worth, categorizing people into "have's" and "have not's." In the classroom it is those who get the gold stars versus those who don't. On the athletic field it is those who win the trophy or reach the goal versus those who don't. Attaching the label of a "success" onto some people means others will be labeled the opposite, as a "non-success" or a "failure."

Although every person is a mixture of strengths and weaknesses, children with high self-esteem tend to concentrate on their strong points. Positive experiences in the past have built in them a competent self-image and, as the saying goes, "Success begets success." With the taste of achievement still fresh on the palate, they feel free to take risks and to strive for still more success. Each additional success restimulates their efforts until these children are filled with positive reminders that allow them to see themselves as winners. They hold the philosophy, "I can do it!" and are willing to go the extra mile.

Students with low self-esteem are the opposite: they emphasize their weaknesses and failures. Because they have too few successes and frequent failures, these children end up with little incentive to try again. The attitude of "Why try, I'm just going to fail again" begins to form; once crystallized, it becomes a fixed part of the self-image and is hard to remold. These students feel incompetent because they believe their unsuccessful experiences are a sign of personal failure and inadequacy. The message they give to themselves is, "I am a loser."

All children need—and deserve—a chance to feel "success ringing in their ears." In order to have high self-esteem, students must feel successful. As a parent, you can help your child create a self-portrait that says, "I am a success." You do this by helping your child recognize his/her strengths and by continuing to provide him/her with the opportunity to build and demonstrate these areas of competence. To assist you in helping your child recognize his/her competencies, the following suggestions are provided:

• **Target a Strength.** Take time to think about your child's areas of competence. Many talents may already be apparent, some are just budding, and a few are waiting to be nurtured. Create a list of your child's possible strengths in areas such as music, art, social skills, gymnastics, athletics, communication, creativity, knowledge in a particular subject, animals…the list can be endless. Now target one or two that can be nurtured and developed over a period of time. Make a commitment to provide the resources to enhance these strengths.

• A Home Esteem Builder Newsletter From Your School •

Esteem Builders' Complete Program
Jalmar Press, Rolling Hills Estates, CA

- **Label the Strength.** Each time you see your child demonstrating the strength, point it out. "I noticed you are artistic." "You're displaying great athletic ability." "This shows again that you are creative." Remember to point out the strength only when your child deserves the praise. Praising just to praise has no validity; the praise must be earned.

- **Be Specific.** As you praise the strength, describe to your child exactly what he/she did to deserve your praise: "You're artistic because you used such details in your painting." "You are athletic because you displayed great skills in handling the ball." Praise your child for the strength and then add on a because.... The because lets your child know why you are praising him/her.

- **Strength Talks.** At bedtime, hold your child's hand in yours and say, "There are so many things you do well." Then name a different strength as you touch each finger. If you wish, you can write the strengths on his/her fingers with a watercolor pen.

- **Celebrate Strengths.** As a family, celebrate and acknowledge each other's strengths and accomplishments. One suggestion is to set out a unique placemat or plate for the individual to eat on. Because the placemat or plate is put out only for special occasions, everyone immediately knows there's something to celebrate.

- **Strength Lists.** Ask your child to name things he/she does well. Create a list and keep adding to it. To develop a new strength, it is best to focus on only one or two at a time. Each time your child demonstrates the strength, praise the competency specifically. New behaviors generally take twenty-one days to acquire. Don't give up; just keep providing the resources. Good luck to you!

• A Home Esteem Builder Newsletter From Your School •

CHARTING IMPROVEMENT

No.13 Esteem Component: Competence

Always remember that your own resolution to succeed is more improtant than anything else.
— **ABRAHAM LINCOLN**

As adults, we need to think we're improving, getting better at something, making progress! Knowing that we're doing well causes us to forge ahead and make continued efforts. An awareness that we're improving is like a "pat on the back" to keep trying. Children, like adults, need to see improvement, especially in school-related subjects where growth is constantly being measured.

For some students, a report card is all that is necessary as a reminder of individual progress. For other students, however, a report card is just another failure. Students with a low sense of competence continually come face to face with blocks to progress. The sad fact is that they may indeed be making noticeable growth in a difficult subject area, but the growth is never acknowledged. It's hard to feel competent if you measure your improvement in comparison to the progress of a top student. To enhance your child's competence, keep in mind the Bright Ideas found on the following page.

All students, whether they have high or low self-esteem, benefit from seeing their improvement in subject areas. This is fundamental to building and maintaining a self-image of competence and adequacy. One of the most powerful skills parents can teach

their children is to record their own progress. Students begin to recognize for themselves that they are actually improving!

- **Recording Progress.** Each week have your child record his/her progress in an academic area to "hear about" his/her abilities on tape. The recording need not be more than a minute or two per session. Try different areas, such as auditory memory (poetry, rhymes), or oral language (reading a passage from a book or original storytelling, or interviewing a friend, etc.).

- **Favorite Work Folder.** Purchase a large manila folder from a stationery store—the sturdier the better. Each week your child chooses the paper he/she is most proud of and places it inside the work folder. Be sure to look at previous work with your child to compare present progress with the past.

- **Bulletin Board.** Provide a bulletin board for your child to hang up work papers. Date each paper as it is completed and place it on the board in chronological order. Your child can instantly compare previous work to present. This idea is particularly effective if work is cho-

— 167 —

Esteem Builders' Complete Program
Jalmar Press, Rolling Hills Estates, CA

sen each time from the same academic area (i.e. all multiplication papers, all handwriting papers, etc.)

- **Paper Chains.** Provide an ample supply of light-colored construction paper cut into 1" x 5" lengths, a writing instrument, and glue or a stapler. Each time your child makes an accomplishment, write it on a paper strip, pass the strip through the next strip in the ring, and glue them together to form a chain. Continue adding new links and hang them around a room as tangible proof of accomplishments.

- **Accomplishment Journal.** Provide your child with a blank journal or composition notebook. Encourage your child to record his/her accomplishments and successes by filling out the form on a consistent basis.

Good luck in building your child's competence. Remember, building competence takes time and consistency. Your child needs to recognize he/she is getting better and does possess some special skills. When your child does show growth (however small), recognize and celebrate it! Then add, "I knew you could do it!" Let us know how you are doing!

BRIGHT IDEAS

1. In order to improve in a skill, children need to know exactly how they can turn their weaknesses into strengths.

2. Children should only compare their current work to their own previous work—never to the work of their classmates or siblings. Competition may be stimulating for children with high competence, but it is paralyzing to children with low competence.

3. For children who feel very low in competence, change will take time. It is most helpful to save samples of these children's work in a particular academic area or skill on a daily or weekly basis. Children can then compare their current papers with previous work. This is when they begin to recognize, "I'm getting better!"

4. Finally, students with low competence must be shown progress in highly concrete terms. They must have evidence they are improving. Just saying, "You're getting better!" will not be believed. Samples of actual work, tape recordings, or videotapes of the skill over a period of time is powerful. The student sees the growth.

Esteem Builders' Complete Program
Jalmar Press, Rolling Hills Estates, CA

Notes

Notes

Chapter 4 Poems

The Power of Expectations

Daddy expects me to be grown up.
If I prove to him that I am grown up,
he will love me.
But I feel frightened
because I am just a little kid.
And I feel terrified that he will
find out that I am frightened
and not grown up
and will not love me.
So I pretend not to be terrified
and he is proud of my being
what I am not.
Now he thinks that I am grown up
and I breathe a sign of relief.
But now that I am who I am not,
he expects me to be even more of who
I am not which terrifies me all the more
because I am now expected to be more of
someone I never was.
To complicate matters, he says I should never lie.
So if I tell him that I am not grown up,
he will be proud of my telling him the truth.
But I cannot tell the truth
about not telling the truth
because that is admitting to a lie.
Therefore, I must try harder
to be who I am not.

—AUTHOR UNKNOWN

97 Ways to Praise & Encourage a Child

• *Wow!* • *Way to go* • *Super* • *You're Special* • *Outstanding* • *Excellent* • *Great* • *Good* • *Neat* • *Well Done* • *Remarkable* • *I Knew You Could Do It* • *I'm Proud of You* • *Fantastic* • *Super Star* • *Nice Work* • *Looking Good* • *You're on Top of It* • *Beautiful* • *Now You're Flying* • *You're Catching On* • *Now You've Got It* • *You're Incredible* • *Bravo* • *You're Fantastic* • *Hooray for You* • *You're on Target* • *You're on Your Way* • *How Nice* • *You're Smart* • *Good Job* • *That's Incredible* • *Hot Dog* • *Dynamite* • *You're Beautiful* • *You're Unique* • *Nothing Can Stop You* • *Much Better* • *Good for You* • *I Like You* • *I Like What You Do* • *Beautiful Work* • *Spectacular* • *You're Precious* • *You're Darling* • *You're Terrific* • *Atta Boy* • *Atta Girl* • *Congratulations* • *You've Discovered the Secret* • *You Figured It Out* • *Hip, Hip, Hooray!* • *I Appreciate Your Help* • *You're Getting Better* • *Yeah!* • *Magnificent* • *Marvelous* • *Terrific* • *You're Important* • *Phenomenal* • *You're Sensational* • *Super Work* • *You're Very Creative* • *You're A Real Trooper* • *You Are Fun* • *You Did Good* • *What An Imagination* • *I Like the Way You Listen* • *I Like How You're Growing* • *I Enjoy You* • *You Tried Hard* • *You Care* • *You Are So Thoughtful* • *Beautiful Sharing* • *Outstanding Performance* • *You're a Good Friend* • *I Trust You* • *You're Important* • *You Mean a Lot to Me* • *That's Correct* • *You're a Joy* • *You're a Treasure* • *You're Wonderful* • *Awesome* • *A+ Job* • *You Did Your Best* • *You're A-Okay, My Buddy* • *You Made My Day* • *I'm Glad You're My Kid* • *Thanks for Being You* • *I Love You!*

Also: A Pat on the Back • *A Big Hug* • *A Kiss* • *A Thumbs Up Sign* • *A Warm Smile*

— DR. LOUISE HART. THE WINNING FAMILY: INCREASING SELF-ESTEEM IN YOUR CHILDREN AND YOURSELF. OAKLAND, CA: LIFE SKILLS PRESS, 1990.

Esteem Builders' Complete Program
Jalmar Press, Rolling Hills Estates, CA

Fifty Years From Now

*Fifty years from now
it will not matter
what kind of car you drove,
what kind of house you lived in,
how much you had in your bank account,
nor what your clothes looked like.*

*But the world may be
a little better because
you were important
in the life of a child.*

—ANONYMOUS

Esteem Builders' Complete Program
Jalmar Press, Rolling Hills Estates, CA

A Piece of Clay

I took a piece of living clay
And gently formed it day by day
And molded with my press and art
A young child's soft and yielding heart.

I came again when years were gone,
It was a man I looked upon.
He still that early impress wore,
And I could change it never more.

I took a piece of plastic clay
And idly fashioned it one day.
And as my fingers pressed it still,
It moved and yielded to my will.

I came again when days were past,
The feel of clay was hard at last.
The form I gave, it still bore;
But I could change that form no more.

—ANONYMOUS

Esteem Builders' Complete Program
Jalmar Press, Rolling Hills Estates, CA

Listen to the Children

*Take a moment to listen today
To what your children are trying to say.*

*Listen today, whatever you do,
Or they won't be there to listen to you.*

*Listen to their problems, listen for their needs.
Praise their smallest triumphs, praise their
smallest deeds.
Tolerate their chatter, amplify their laughter;
Find out what's the matter, find out what they're after.*

*But tell them that you love them every single night,
And though you scold them, make sure you hold them,
And tell them, "Everything's all right."*

*If we tell our children all the bad in them we see,
They'll grow up exactly how we hoped they'd never be.
But if we tell our children, we're so proud to
wear their name,
They'll grow up believing they're winners in the game.*

*Take a moment to listen today
To what your children are trying to say.
Listen today, whatever you do
And they will come back to listen to you!*

—ANONYMOUS

Esteem Builders' Complete Program
Jalmar Press, Rolling Hills Estates, CA

Guiding Hand

*I dreamt I stood in a studio
And watched two sculptors there.
The clay they used was a
young child's mind
And they fashioned it with care.
One was a teacher—the tools he used
Were books, music and art.
The other, a parent, worked with a
guiding hand,
And a gentle loving heart.
Day after day, the teacher toiled with touch
That was deft and sure.
While the parent labored by his side
And polished and smoothed it o'er.
And when at last, their task was done
They were proud of what they had wrought.
For the things they had molded into the child
Could neither be sold nor bought.
And each agreed they would have failed
If each had worked alone.
For behind the parent, stood the school
And behind the teacher the home.*

—AUTHOR UNKNOWN

Esteem Builders' Complete Program
Jalmar Press, Rolling Hills Estates, CA

To My Grown-Up Son

My hands were busy through the day,
I didn't have much time to play
The little games you asked me to.
I didn't have much time for you.

I'd wash your clothes; I'd sew and cook,
But when you'd bring your picture book
And ask me, please, to share your fun,
I'd say, "A little later, son."

I'd tuck you in all safe at night,
And hear your prayers, turn out the light,
Then tiptoe softly to the door,
I wish I'd stayed a minute more.

For life is short, and years rush past,
A little boy grows up so fast,
No longer is he at your side,
His precious secrets to confide.

The picture books are put away,
There are no children's games to play,
No goodnight kiss, no prayers to hear,
That all belongs to yesteryear.

My hands once busy, now lie still,
The days are long and hard to fill,
I wish I might go back and do,
The little things you asked me to.

—ALICE E. CHASE

Esteem Builders' Complete Program
Jalmar Press, Rolling Hills Estates, CA

ESTEEM BUILDERS
COMPLETE PROGRAM

5
_____

Home Esteem-Builder Activities

HOME ESTEEM BUILDERS

- Beginning the Home Esteem Builders Program
- Esteem Builder Planner
- Home Esteem Builder Activities

HOME ESTEEM-BUILDER ACTIVITIES

ACTIVITY LIST

AFFILIATION

MISSION

COMPETENCE

Home Esteem Builders was developed on the premise that a home and school partnership is an integral element of effective esteem building. The material in this book provides educators with the resources to help parents enhance their children's self-esteem. Before distributing any of these materials to the students' homes, please make sure that they have been translated into the primary language of the parents.

5

The Home Esteem-Builder Activities

Parents continue to be viewed as "significant others" long into the formal schooling years. It is logical to assume then that efforts directed at helping parents to improve their children's self-concepts should aid teachers in similar efforts in the classroom.

—DAVID SILVERNAIL

As their children's first teachers, parents are without a doubt the most important esteem builders in their children's lives. Most parents recognize their impact but have never been taught how to enhance self-esteem. The Home Esteem-Builder Activities in this chapter have been designed to help fill this void. The school alone cannot do the job of building children's esteem, but working as a team, the school and home can make powerful differences in the lives of today's students.

Weekly activity sheets are included for parents to use at home with their children to enhance self-esteem. There are forty worksheets in all—one for each week of a nine-month school year. Based on current research in esteem building, each activity is designed to enhance one of the five essential components of self-esteem (Security, Selfhood, Affiliation, Mission, and Competence). Here are some guidelines to help educators and parents in using the activities:

- **Develop Feelings Sequentially.** The activities are designed to be used in sequence. A chart of all forty Home Esteem Builder Activities is located on page 190-191. It is strongly recommended that educators send home the activity sheets in the order indicated on this table of contents. In general, esteem enhancement has been found to develop in a particular sequence; the sheets are numbered in this order. Security (a feeling of trust and safety) is

the first feeling to develop. Next comes a knowledge of Selfhood or identity. Around the same time Selfhood develops, a feeling of belonging, connectedness or Affiliation forms. Once these "foundation feelings" are laid, individuals can create a feeling of purpose, direction, responsibility, or Mission. As goals are reached, the final feeling of Competence (capableness and self-efficacy) is built. A more thorough explanation of this developmental process is provided in *Esteem Builders: A K-8 Self-Esteem Curriculum for Improving Student Achievement, Behavior and School Climate.*

- **Involve Both School and Home.** The Home Esteem-Builder Activities are meant to enhance the Esteem-Building Activities presented in the classroom. *They are by no means designed to be used as the only tool for self-esteem enhancement.* Educators are encouraged to schedule daily or weekly student esteem building activities as suggested in the "Esteem Builder Planner" (*Esteem Builders,* pages 22 to 41). At the end of the week, the Home Esteem Builder Activity corresponding to the feeling discussed in the classroom is sent home. The home is then reinforcing the same activities and feelings addressed at the school. This esteem-building team approach involving both school and home is when the most powerful results in esteem enhancement occur.

- **Do Activities Regularly.** The activity sheets are best used when they are sent home on a regular basis. This could be on a weekly or bimonthly basis. Parents should be told when to expect the sheets.

- **Respect Privacy**. Keep in mind that the Home Esteem-Builder Activities are meant to be done in the home between parents and children. To respect the privacy of families, *do not require that the completed activities be returned to school.* A form entitled "Family Gram" is included and may be used to communicate with parents about the activities. Parental comments or questions may be written on the "Family Gram" form and returned to school at the completion of each Home Esteem-Builder Activity. Also included in this section is a survey to send home to parents at the end of the program.

BEGINNING THE
HOME ESTEEM-BUILDERS PROGRAM

Implementing the Home Esteem-Builders Program is a simple process. Parents generally have four main questions regarding the program. The school should answer all four of these questions:

1. What is the purpose of the activities?

2. How often should I expect to receive an activity form?

3. How should I do these activities with my child?

4. What should I do with the completed forms?

Questions and concerns parents have about the program can be addressed in several ways. Here are some options:

- **Parent Letter.** A letter provided on pages 195-196 explains the Home Esteem-Builders Program to parents. Send a copy to parents to introduce them to the format of the program. A sample of the first Home Esteem Builder (HEB 2) may be included with the letter.

- **Parent In-Service.** The program may be explained to parents at an in-service or back-to-school night. Since one hundred percent attendance of parents is a rarity at school functions, this should not be the sole method of describing the program.

- **Parent Conferences.** Many schools choose to hand out the first Home Esteem-Builder Activity at parent-teacher conferences. At conferences, teachers can personally explain the program to parents and answer any questions or concerns. Parents who do not come to the conferences are mailed the parent explanation letter and the first activity sheet.

- **Principal Newsletters.** Principals can include reminders about the Home Esteem-Builder Activities in any newsletters they send home to parents. Newsletters could highlight an activity sheet a day or two before it is sent home. Parents are then aware that the form will be coming home sometime during the week.

Sending Home the First Activity

The first Home Esteem-Builder Activity can be sent home after the program has been explained to parents. The activities are designed to help parents reinforce the five components of self-esteem in their children. Because these components are learned in a developmental progression, the activities were ordered to correspond to this same developmental sequence. It is important, therefore, that the activities be sent home in the same sequence. A table of contents for all the Home Esteem-Building Activities and the order in which they should be used may be found on page 190-191. To prepare the first Home Esteem Builder Activity packet to be sent home to each household, include the following four items:

1. **Letter to Parents.** The first Home Esteem-Builder Activity listed on the table of contents is the *Letter Home to Parents.*

2. **Home Esteem-Builder Activity Log.** There is also a *Home Esteem Builder Activity Log* on page 193. Duplicate a form for each

household on light-colored construction paper or cardstock-weight material. Parents then mark off each Home Esteem-Builder Activity they complete with their children. The directions on the form tell parents to color in a house shape corresponding to the number of the activity they completed. The form reminds parents to complete the task each week and to expect 40 forms in all. Encourage parents to keep the form in a convenient location, such as on the refrigerator or on a family bulletin board. Explain that the form is to be used for the entire school year.

3. **Home Esteem-Builder Activity 2.** The first family activity is HEB2, entitled "Positive Reinforcement." Duplicate the form, found on page 197, for each family and attach it to the letter and the *Activity Log* form.

4. **Family Gram.** If educators wish to communicate with parents about the activities, they can send home the form entitled "Family Gram"—but use good judgment. Sometimes parents do not wish to comment on the activities. To have an open dialogue with parents about the home activities, duplicate a large quantity of the Family Grams and staple a Family Gram to the top of each activity. Use one color of paper for the Home Esteem-Builder Activity and another for the Family Gram.

5. **Activity Questionnaire.** An informal survey is also included. It is designed to be used at the conclusion of the program—after activity 38, 39, or 40. Parents are asked to assess the program by providing short answers to questions such as: "What did you enjoy most about the HEB program?" and "What suggestions do you have for future

Home Esteem-Builders Programs?" While probably only a handful of parents will return the form, these few responses may provide helpful insights for future planning.

For succeeding Home Esteem Builder Activities, follow the table of contents. Duplicate the activity for each family and attach a Family Gram if desired. One activity will be sent home in this manner each remaining week of the school year.

Reinforcing the Principles

The most effective way to teach parents home esteem-building principles and techniques is for educators to *always* teach the skills in conjunction with the same principles they are teaching in the classroom. The reason is obvious: the students receive double reinforcement. What is done in the classroom to enhance children's self-esteem is reinforced at home at the same time. There is another reason to teach the skills at home and at school simultaneously: if educators have done a good job teaching the principles in the classroom, students will teach the skills to their parents at home. When students see their families doing the same types of activities they did at school, they generally talk about the school activity and end up explaining the Home-Esteem Builder Activity to their parents.

Esteem-Builder Planner

One of the greatest benefits to the Home-Esteem Builder Activities is that each activity is designed to reinforce the esteem component presented in the students' classroom. A forty-week "Esteem-Builder Planner" describing how to integrate over 250 Esteem Builder Activities is provided in *Esteem Builders* on pages 22 to 41. Enhancing student self-esteem will obviously be much more effective if the same concepts can be reinforced simultaneously in the home and classroom.

Notes

Chapter 5 Activities

HOME ESTEEM BUILDER ACTIVITY CHART

CODE	ACTIVITY — FOR GRADE LEVELS K-8	SOCIAL STUDIES	SCIENCE	WRITING LANG.	ORAL LANG.	MATH	ART	LIT.	BEHAVIOR
HEB 1	LETTER HOME TO PARENTS			•	•				
HEB 2	EVERYBODY NEEDS PRAISE								•
HEB 3	WHAT OTHERS EXPECT OF ME			•	•				
HEB 4	RULES...RULES...RULES	•		•					•
HEB 5	CHANGING NEGATIVE MESSAGES				•				•
HEB 6	FINDING OUT ABOUT EACH OTHER			•	•				
HEB 7	SIGNIFICANT OTHERS	•		•	•				
HEB 8	QUESTIONNAIRE				•				
HEB 9	FAMILY NAME SHIELD	•		•	•	•	•	•	
HEB10	TIME LINE	•		•	•	•	•		
HEB11	HISTORY	•		•	•	•			
HEB12	ME TRACINGS			•	•		•		
HEB13	SELF PRAISE			•	•				
HEB14	ME COLLAGE			•	•		•		
HEB15	SPECIAL QUALITIES	•		•	•		•		•
HEB16	THE INSIDE SCOOP			•					
HEB17	MY FAMILY SHIELD	•		•	•		•		
HEB18	FAMILY TREE	•	•				•		
HEB19	FAMILY BOOKS				•			•	
HEB20	FRIENDSHIP RECIPE			•	•				

SUGGESTED SUBJECT CONTENT

Esteem Builders' Complete Program
Jalmar Press, Rolling Hills Estates, CA

HOME ESTEEM BUILDER ACTIVITY CHART

CODE	ACTIVITY FOR GRADE LEVELS K-8	SOCIAL STUDIES	SCIENCE	WRITING LANG.	ORAL LANG.	MATH	ART	LIT.	BEHAVIOR
HEB21	MY LIST OF FRIENDLY DEEDS			●	●				●
HEB22	COMPLIMENTS			●	●		●		●
HEB23	MY CIRCLE OF FRIENDS	●		●	●				
HEB24	CARING FOR OTHERS				●			●	
HEB25	HOME RESPONSIBILITIES	●		●		●			
HEB26	MY SCHOOL RESPONSIBILITIES	●		●		●			
HEB27	GOAL-SETTING	●		●	●				
HEB28	SELF CHANGES			●	●		●		
HEB29	MY TARGETING SUCCESS			●	●				
HEB30	SUPER SLEUTH				●				
HEB31	PROBLEM PANTOMIMES				●				
HEB32	PROBLEM REPORT			●	●				
HEB33	WORK FOLDERS						●		
HEB34	OUR FAMILY STRENGTHS	●		●	●				
HEB35	I CAN			●	●		●		
HEB36	JOURNALS	●		●	●		●		
HEB37	OVERCOMING OBSTACLES				●			●	
HEB38	SUCCESS				●				
HEB39	SUCCESS SHARING			●	●				
HEB40	BLUE RIBBON						●		

SUGGESTED SUBJECT CONTENT

Esteem Builders' Complete Program
Jalmar Press, Rolling Hills Estates, CA

HOME ESTEEM BUILDER ACTIVITY LOG

FAMILY _____

1	2	3	4	5	6
7	8	9	10	11	12
13	14	15	16	17	18
19	20	21	22	23	24
25	26	27	28	29	30
31	32	33	34	35	36
	37	38	39	40	

KEEP THIS FORM IN A CONVENIENT LOCATION TO REMIND YOUR FAMILY TO DO THE HOME ESTEEM BUILDER ACTIVITY. COLOR IN EACH SPACE AS THE CORRESPONDING ACTIVITY IS COMPLETED.

Esteem Builders' Complete Program
Jalmar Press, Rolling Hills Estates, CA

FAMILY GRAM

Please complete this form and return it with your child to school on the following school day. If you have questions or concerns please contact me and I'll get back to you.

TO: (Teacher) _____

FROM: (Family) _____

RE: The Home Esteem-Builder Activity

Comments:

PARENT GRAM

Please complete this form and return it with your child to school on the following school day. If you have questions or concerns please contact me and I'll get back to you.

TO: (Teacher) _____

FROM: (Family) _____

RE: The Home Esteem-Builder Activity

What my child enjoyed the most about the activity was:

What my child enjoyed the least about the activity was:

Esteem Builders' Complete Program
Jalmar Press, Rolling Hills Estates, CA

"Esteem Building…the key to school and personal success….We can make a difference."

Dear Parent,

Important educational research has found that self-esteem is one of the key ingredients to success and happiness. Studies have revealed that the attitude your child has about him or herself is closely tied to how successful he or she will be in school. The feeling of "I Can" is a powerful tool!

Since self-esteem is so crucial to academic achievement, motivation, and behavior, increasing student self-esteem has been chosen as a major school goal. The school cannot do this job alone since it is obvious that you play the most crucial role in the development of your child's self-perceptions. The enhancement of your child's self-esteem will be most effective if it is a joint collaborative effort between the school and the home.

To help you in your esteem-building efforts at home, each week your child's teacher will send home a "Home Esteem Builder." These activity sheets will contain a variety of different types of suggestions to enhance your child's self-perceptions. The Home Esteem Builders will suggest activities to build each of the five crucial components of self-esteem: (Security, Selfhood, Affiliation, Mission, and Competence) along with the rationale, that these components are important to your child's overall self-picture. These activity sheets are meant not only to serve as a guideline to you but also to be fun projects for you and your child.

You may wish to keep the following suggestions in mind as you do the Home Esteem Builders with your child:

Keep it Positive! Self-esteem is enhanced in environments that are warm and supportive. Be patient, be encouraging, and praise your child for his or her efforts. Everyone needs a pat on the back and it does wonders in building a positive atmosphere for learning!

Keep it Light! Learning time should be a fun time. Your own enthusiasm and pleasure will be reflected by your child as you work together to learn.

Bring in the family! Mom and Dad, brother and sister, Grandma and Grandpa can join in the fun of learning and sharing this meaningful family experience.

Refer to the principles again! Each of the Home Esteem-Builder activities is based on current research. The guidelines can be important principles you may wish to refer to again and again! Consider keeping the activity sheet in a convenient location (such as on the refrigerator) where all family members can visually be reminded of the topic of the week.

Esteem Builders' Complete Program
Jalmar Press, Rolling Hills Estates, CA

(HEB 1 continued)

The Home Esteem-Builder Activities are designed for you to use at home with your child. They do not need to be sent back to school as they are completed. You may wish to keep the completed forms from each week in a special folder. They are often fun to refer back to. You may even discover that your child wants to do the activity again at the future date.

A Family Gram will be attached to the front of each activity you receive. This form is meant as a way for us to communicate your progress with the Home Esteem-Builder activity. Please note any comments, concerns or questions you might have regarding the activity and return it to school with your child. If at any time you're like to meet with me personally or talk on the phone about your child's progress, please mention that on the form and we'll set up a time for a conference.

Finally, you will also find a "Home Esteem-Builder Activity Log." Please keep the form in a convenient location such as on your refrigerator, by your telephone or on a family bulletin board. Each time your family completes a Home Esteem-Builder Activity color in the space that corresponds to the activity number you did.

Your child's feelings about him or herself is a crucial component of learning. The attitude people hold about themselves affects, their level of motivation and determines, how and to what extent they will use the skills and abilities they possess. Let's work together to build your child's learning potential to the fullest. As always, if you have any questions or comments, please send a note.

Happy Enhancing!

POSITIVE REINFORCEMENT

Dear Parent,

 Everybody needs praise and positive reinforcement. "Catching someone doing something well" is a powerful way to change behavior. But, more often than not, we use negative reinforcement to make a point. Here are some suggestions to increase positive statements in the family.

Directions:
Below are different ways of telling family members that you are pleased with their efforts and are proud of them. Tack it on your refrigerator or another convenient location and keep track of how often positive statements are said to one another. Encourage family members to add other positive comments.

☐ Good for you!

☐ I'm proud of you!

☐ Terrific

☐ Thank you for working so hard.

☐ Thank you for bringing home this paper.

☐ Let's put this one on the bulletin board.

☐ Look how much better you're getting!

☐ I'm so pleased with you.

☐ You must be proud of yourself.

☐ You're very cooperative.

☐ _____

☐ _____

☐ That's great!

☐ Nice going!

☐ I like how you tried!

☐ Look how you improved!

☐ I like the way you did this!

☐ Nice job!

☐ You really outdid yourself today.

☐ Let's send this one to _____.

☐ Congratulations!

☐ I like your ideas.

☐ _____

☐ _____

Esteem Builders' Complete Program
Jalmar Press, Rolling Hills Estates, CA

WHAT OTHERS EXPECT OF ME

Dear Parent,

One of the most important feelings individuals with high self-esteem possess is a feeling of *security*. This is generally attained when the individual feels safe and knows what is expected of him or her. Psychologists say that parents play a critical role in building security by letting their children know clearly what is expected of them. The best expectations you can give are high but *achievable and realistic*. Then, the child has a chance to feel not only secure but also competent. *Happy Enhancing!*

Directions for student:

In the boxes below, write the name of each family member. In the remaining boxes write the names of people (grownups and peers) who are especially important to you. Now write below each person's name what you think they expect from you. What thing(s) do they want of you and expect you to provide?

Name: Expectation:	Name: Expectation:
Name: Expectation:	Name: Expectation:
Name: Expectation:	Name: Expectation:

Esteem Builders' Complete Program
Jalmar Press, Rolling Hills Estates, CA

RULES... RULES... RULES...

Dear Parent,

   Rules are a necessary part of our existence. An awareness of household rules (and what will happen if they are broken) helps build a feeling of security. Rules that are most beneficial for children are few but clearly stated and achievable. Also, they must be fully understood by all members of the family. This week's activity will help family members focus on your household rules. *Happy Enhancing!*

Directions for student:

List 5 rules you have in your home. Now rate the rule on how fair you think the rule is. Use the following numbers to indicate how fair you think the rule is:

> **1.** = Very Fair
>
> **2.** = Okay
>
> **3.** = Not fair

Finally, ask another family member to rate the rule. Have them sign their name and mark their rating.

HOME RULES		
Rules	**My Rating**	**Other's Rating**
Example: I have to take out the trash	3	1

Choose one rule that you dislike the most. How would you change the rule if you were the parent?

_____

_____

_____

_____

_____

Esteem Builders' Complete Program
Jalmar Press, Rolling Hills Estates, CA

CHANGING NEGATIVE MESSAGES

Dear Parent,

      Put-downs — or derogatory, negative messages — are destructive to self-esteem. This activity helps your child learn how to recognize the deadliness of put-downs, as well as helping him/her find ways to change negative messages to more positive builder-upper statements. When negative messages are minimized, the general result is a more secure, warm environment where self-esteem can grow. *Happy Enhancing*!

Instructions:

1. You'll need 10 or more strips of paper or small index cards.

2. Write a negative message on each paper strip. Use the suggestions below as a guide:

"Shut up!"	"Get out of here!"	"You're stupid!"
"You dummy!"	"Quit bugging me!"	"You're such a nerd!"
"Go away!"	"Quit copying me!"	"Leave me alone!"

3. Take a few moments to practice as a family how to change a put-down statement to a builder-upper. You may wish to write the rules on a card.

   • Start the message with an "I."
   • Tell the person how the message makes you feel. ("I'm angry...")
   • Add what the person did that made you feel that way. ("I'm angry because...")

"You're a dummy, Tommy!"

"I'm angry because you kicked me!"

4. Now place the put-down messages in a container (a bag or bowl will do). Take turns pulling a message from the container and reading it aloud. Pretend someone said it to you.

   How will you change the put-down statement to a builder-upper statement? (Other family members can also pull a card and take turns reading it to others in the group. The receiver must send back a message telling the sender they don't like what they heard.)

Esteem Builders' Complete Program
Jalmar Press, Rolling Hills Estates, CA

FINDING OUT ABOUT EACH OTHER

Dear Parent,

Children's interests (and adults') changes so frequently it is hard to keep in touch with where a person stands now. This activity helps family members find out more about each other. Choose one family member to be the leader; it will be his or her job to ask a series of questions to other members. A suggested list of questions appears below, but feel free as a family to come up with your own. The leader asks a series of questions until everyone has had a chance to answer each question. Feel free to read these to your non-reading child. Tape sessions. Keep a family journal. This is a family togetherness time to build each other up. You may wish to discuss what you learned about one another following the question period. *Happy Enhancing!*

SUGGESTED QUESTIONS
Choose ones appropriate to your family.

1. What is your favorite color?

2. Where is your favorite place to go?

3. Do you feel you get enough attention in your family?

4. What is your favorite family memory?

5. Where is your favorite vacation spot?

6. Who is your favorite friend?

7. What is your favorite TV show?

8. Who would you most like to see elected President of the United States?

9. What is your favorite all-time movie?

10. Where is your favorite place to eat?

11. What is your favorite meal?

12. What do you like most about this family?

13. Do you like your room?

14. What would you most like to change about this family?

15. What do you wish we would do more together? (Less)

16. What is your favorite book?

17. What is your favorite hobby?

18. What hobby (interest) do you wish we would do as a family?

19. When you are by yourself, what do you enjoy doing the most?

20. When you are with the family, what do you enjoy doing the most?

21. What is your favorite family tradition?

22. What is your least favorite family tradition?

SIGNIFICANT OTHERS

Dear Parent,

"Significant Others" are those individuals felt to be worthy, important or significant by your child. Experiences your child has had with these individuals (either positive or negative) have helped form his or her self-beliefs. As a family, you can help your child identify Significant Others and how they have played a role in his or her life. You may wish to discuss each person as he or she is named.

Directions:
Put your name in the center circle. In the stars surrounding your name, write the names of those people whom you consider to be the "most Significant Others" to you – those individuals who gave you direction, helped you see your strengths, or had the greatest impact on your life. Who are they?

Esteem Builders' Complete Program
Jalmar Press, Rolling Hills Estates, CA

INTERVIEW

Dear Parent,

   "Significant Others" (people whom a student considers important and significant to him or her) can play an enormous role in constructing his/her inner self-picture. They can help provide direction, guidance and feelings of worthiness. This activity gives students the opportunity to interview a Significant Other of their choosing and find out more about that person's school days.

Directions for student:
Interview an adult who is significant to you. Use the following information as a guide.

Full name: _____

Relationship to interviewer: _____

What was the hardest thing about growing up?

What is the hardest thing about now?

What subject did you enjoy the most?

What subject was the most difficult?

Who was your favorite teacher?

Why was this teacher such a favorite?

How was going to school then different from school now?

How is going to school now the same as going to school then?

What do you think a student has to do to become a good student?

Notes:

Esteem Builders' Complete Program
Jalmar Press, Rolling Hills Estates, CA

FAMILY NAME SHIELDS

Dear Parent,

An understanding of family heritage helps to provide an awareness of self-identity. You can help to enhance this awareness through family discussions about ancestry. You may wish to discuss such things as:

- The country of family origin (and information about the country: national character, exports, native dishes, customs, location);
- Special family customs or traditions derived from family ancestry;
- Origins about the family name.

Asking grandparents and relatives about family ancestry may provide important insights for all concerned. Regardless of the age, every child can benefit from finding out about his or her ancestry – both immediate (parents) and past (grandparents and great-grandparents). *Happy Enhancing!*

> To help your child discover the origin of his or her last name, consider making Family Name Shields. You may wish to enlist the help of grandparents or other family relatives to discover additional family trivia.

Materials Needed:

- Marking pens or crayons
- Scissors
- Light-colored paper (at least 12" x 18")

Procedure:

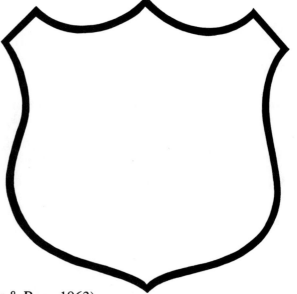

1. Fold the paper in half lengthwise. Lightly draw half a shield outline similar to the one shown here. Cut out the shape.

2. Write the family's last name in bold letters across the top of the shield.

3. Draw a pictorial explanation (or written explanation) of your family name's derivation and meaning.

4. Draw a flag someplace on the shield showing the name's country of orgin.

Suggested books for further family reading:

For younger children:
  The Sky Was Blue, Charlotte Zolotow (Harper & Row, 1963)
  Watch the Stars Come Out, Riki Levinson (E.P. Dutton, 1985)
For older children:
  Owls in the Family, Farly Mowat (Bantan, 1983)
  The Lucky Stone, Lucille Clifton (Delacorte, 1979)

TIME LINE

Dear Parent,

Not only do people play an important role in the formation of hour child's self-pictures, but events too are significant. This activity helps to expand your child's personal awareness of the significant events that have helped to shape his or her inner self-picture.

Materials Needed:

- Hole-punch
- Pencil or pens
- Rug yarn (at least 40")
- Index cards (cut into 1 1/2" x 5")

Procedure:

1. Ask your child to think about the many, many experiences in his or her life, explaining that these events helped to shape a self-picture. Help your child to think back and try to decide which events were the most important or significant. You may wish to pull out old photo albums or baby books to aid in this process.

Listed below are examples of significant events. As you read off each, ask your child to consider if the topic has an effect.

- Early moments (birth, walking, talking ... special events)
- Health (illness, operation, accident, handicap)
- Travel (special trips, outings, favorite places)
- Family events (birth of sibling, new job, move, etc.)
- Creative events (art, music lessons, dance, etc.)
- Physical events (sports, awards, hardships, etc.)
- Educational (school, special class, honors, hardships)
- Significant others (family, friendships, coaches, etc.)
- Traumatic events (death, divorce, accident)
- Other

2. Encourage your child to write each significant event on an index card strip with the approximate date of the event.

3. Punch a hold in the top of each strip with a hole-punch.

4. String the events as they occurred in your child's life along the strip.

5. Hang up the string for all to see and share. Encourage other family members to make a Time Line.

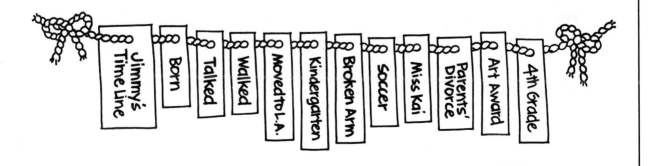

Esteem Builders' Complete Program
Jalmar Press, Rolling Hills Estates, CA

HISTORY

Dear Parent,

   This activity helps children reflect on their past and begin to understand the sequence of events in their lives. Please help your child complete this form, giving one significant event for each year of his or her life. Use the back of this sheet if you need more room to write. You may wish to take out old scrapbooks and baby books of your child's past to remember the events together.

My name: _____

My parents named me that because:

_____

_____

The date, time, and place of my birth is: _____

I weighed: _____ pounds, _____ ounces and was, _____ inches long.

_____ **year old, year:** _____ **Event:**

_____

_____

_____ **year old, year:** _____ **Event:**

_____

_____

_____ **year old, year:** _____ **Event:**

_____

_____

_____ **year old, year:** _____ **Event:**

_____

_____

_____ **year old, year:** _____ **Event:**

_____

_____

_____ **year old, year:** _____ **Event:**

_____

_____

_____ **year old, year:** _____ **Event:**

_____

_____

Esteem Builders' Complete Program
Jalmar Press, Rolling Hills Estates, CA

ME COLLAGE

Dear Parent,

     Self-concept is the inner picture each of us has of ourself. It is not a value judgment of self, only a series of thoughts based on our roles, experiences and perceptions. The description may or may not be accurate, but it plays a crucial role in the development of self-esteem (the evaluation each of us puts on yourself). The more accurate our self-picture is, therefore, the more accurate our self-esteem will be. You can play a key role in helping your child form an accurate self-concept by providing opportunities that sharpen or clarify the self-description content. This could include such things as pointing out personal interests, physical characteristics, strengths and unique qualities special to your child. *Happy Enhancing!*

Materials Needed:

- Wrapping paper, butcher paper or two pieces of poster board large enough for a full-sized outline of your child
- Marking pens, crayons or pen
- Scissors
- Old magazines or catalogs
- Paste or glue

Procedure:

1. Lay the paper full-length along the floor and ask your child to carefully lie on it. Trace around the body to form an outline.

2. Cut out, or have your child cut out the outline.

3. Explain that the outline is uniquely individual as are the characteristics, thoughts, and feelings your child possesses. Invite your child to think of things that make him of her unique. These could include: physical characteristics, interests, strengths, feelings, roles and attributes.

4. Ask your child to try and depict each of these unique qualities on the inside of the outline. These could be shown with words, drawings, magazine cut-outs, photographs and /or designs.

5. You may wish to consider having each family member make a "Me Collage" to hang up and discuss. They also make fun keepsakes.

Variation for older students:
Trace hand, foot; create a collage; make a self-portrait.

Esteem Builders' Complete Program
Jalmar Press, Rolling Hills Estates, CA

SELF-PRAISE

Dear Parent,

Research indicates that eighty-five percent of the time we talk we're not speaking to someone, we're speaking to ourselves. Self-talk is a powerful part of our lives and is also a critical part of our self-esteem, because we are either degrading ourselves or praising ourselves. This activity helps your child learn to praise himself/herself. Since our society teaches us to be modest, you and other family members can serve as models by keeping track of your own self-talk and letting your child occasionally hear it. *Happy Enhancing!*

This week, practice making positve comments about yourself.

Each Day:

1. Write down a positive self-comment next to the number 1. Start with "I ..." and tell yoursef something you like or are proud of about yourself. Keep the statement short.

2. Practice saying the statement you wrote about yourself all day.

3. Now find another family member to write a positive comment about you on line 2.

Example:

    1. I like my smile.   *Monday*
    2. I like the way you share.   Signed: *Dad*

POSITIVE COMMENTS

1. _____ *Monday*
2. _____ Signed: _____

1. _____ *Tuesday*
2. _____ Signed: _____

1. _____ *Wednesday*
2. _____ Signed: _____

1. _____ *Thursday*
2. _____ Signed: _____

1. _____ *Friday*
2. _____ Signed: _____

1. _____ *Saturday*
2. _____ Signed: _____

1. _____ *Sunday*
2. _____ Signed: _____

Esteem Builders' Complete Program
Jalmar Press, Rolling Hills Estates, CA

HOME ESTEEM BUILDERS

THINGS I LIKE COLLAGE

Dear Parent,

     This activity helps your child develop an awareness of the things he or she likes. Knowledge of interests and capabilities will help your child form a clearer self-concept. Other family members can make their own collages. At a "family together time" each family member can describe the things they most like to do and why. Hang them up for all to see!

Materials Needed:

- Scissors
- White glue or paste
- Heavy paper or cardboard
- Magazines

Procedure:

1. Ask your child to think about the things he or she likes.
2. Help your child look through magazines to find pictures of things he or she especially likes.
3. As your child finds each picture, help him or her cut them out.
4. Encourage your child to fill up the paper, but do not insist if he or she says they're finished.
5. Allow plenty of time for the glue to dry.

Discussion Starters:

1. Which things on your collage do you like the most? Why?
2. Can you find the thing you like the second best?
3. What things do you like that you couldn't find pictures of?
4. Can you think of things you really don't like?

A Collage of "Things I Like" by Mike

Esteem Builders' Complete Program
Jalmar Press, Rolling Hills Estates, CA

SPECIAL QUALITIES

Dear Parent,

Each of us needs to feel that we are special and unique in the eyes of others. The people we need to get attention from the most (those we love), however, are often too busy to show that they care. This activity provides a good excuse to turn that around. *Happy Enhancing!*

Materials Needed:

- 3" x 5" index cards (or paper cut into similar-size), at least 2-3 cards per each family member for each night.
- Crayons, colored ink pens, pencils, or marking pens.

Procedure:

1. Choose a different family member to focus on each night. You may wish to start with the youngest family member and work your way up the age scale or pull names from a hat.

2. After the member has been chosen, ask other family members to think about the person. Why is that person so special to this family? What things does he or she contribute that are special and unique? What strengths or qualities can be attributed to this person?

3. Pass out a few index cards to the family members. Explain that they are to write (draw or dictate) their thoughts about the starring family person. Each quality, contribution or special thought should be written on a separate card.

4. Members now take turns sharing their feelings about the person to the group (or individually).

5. Choose a new person on the following night until all family members have had the opportunity to star.

Follow-up Idea:

You may wish to consider providing each family member with an individual "scrapbook" (a few pieces of construction paper stapled along the edges) where they can put their quality thought cards. Some families like to collect all the cards and glue them into a larger "Family Scrapbook" to refer to again and again.

Esteem Builders' Complete Program
Jalmar Press, Rolling Hills Estates, CA

THE INSIDE SCOOP

Dear Parent,

Before we can evaluate ourselves realistically, we must have accurate self-descriptions. You can aid your child in these self-discoveries by helping him or her be more aware of distinct differences that create uniqueness. You could explain that characteristics are special qualities of ourselves that make us different. Each of us has different characteristics. Ask your child to list 10 characteristics that describe just him or her. You may need to suggest a few characteristics. Explain that some descriptions may be the same as another person's but no one has exactly the same combination. *Happy Enhancing!*

1. I am _____

2. I am _____

3. I am _____

4. I am _____

5. I am _____

6. I am _____

7. I am _____

8. I am _____

9. I am _____

10. I am _____

Put asterisks (*) by the characteristics that please you the most.

Circle the characteristic you wish you could change.

Esteem Builders' Complete Program
Jalmar Press, Rolling Hills Estates, CA

MY FAMILY SHIELD

Dear Parent,

   Research shows that families who share a close and accepting relationship are more likely to raise children who have higher self-esteem. Warm relationships form from quality time with one another. This activity helps your child reflect about your "together times." As your child colors pictures for each box, you may wish to add your own fond memories about the events. If you like, you can make a shield on a large piece of paper to allow for more descriptions.

DESCRIBE OR DRAW:

A word, picture or symbol to describe my family.	Something we enjoy doing together.
A special place we went together.	Our favorite holiday we spent together.
A situation where we solved a problem together.	A time we spent together.

Esteem Builders' Complete Program
Jalmar Press, Rolling Hills Estates, CA

FAMILY TREE

Dear Parent,

One facet of a child's self-concept is the appreciation and awareness of his or her physical characteristics. Explain to your child that physical characteristics are "givens" – we were born with them, and we look the way we do because of our genes. This activity helps your child study eye and hair color of immediate family members and helps increase an awareness of physical traits. If necessary, call grandparents and bring out the photo album so your child may get an accurate picture.

Directions:

Trace this tree pattern onto another piece of paper and cut it out. Use crayons to color the tree top green and the trunk brown (or use brown and green construction paper). Cut out several apple shapes. Each immediate family member receives an apple (parents, siblings, and grandparents).

Help your child write the eye and hair color of each family member on a separate apple. Print the member's role within the family (dad, brother, mom, sister) on the leaf. Then glue the apples onto the paper tree.

Esteem Builders' Complete Program
Jalmar Press, Rolling Hills Estates, CA

FAMILY BOOKS

Dear Parent,

The U.S. Commission on Reading has revealed that reading aloud is the single most important activity for building the knowledge required for eventual success in reading. Reading aloud is important not only to your child's reading achievement but also to self-attitude. Many children's books contain themes of selfhood, which can be used as a catalyst to wonderful family discussions that will help your child formulate a strong sense of identity. *Happy Enhancing!*

Directions:

The books below all deal with the theme of family relationships. Choose one (or a comparable book from another source) and read it aloud as a family. As you read it you may wish to begin a discussion by asking a few of the suggested discussion questions:

• Which character (if any) was most like you? Why?
• How is the book different (or the same) from what happens in our family?
• If this book was to be made into a movie who should play the main parts?
• If this story was about our family would the book have ended differently? How?
• Have you ever had any feelings that are similar to any of the characters? (If so, which character and what feelings?)

The books below, which are suitable for younger children, deal with characters who feel neglected and unloved by other family members. The problem is resolved in each case when the character comes to realize how important and loved he or she really is.

The Do Something Day, Joe Lasker (Scholastic, 1982)
Sam, Ann Herbert Scott (McGraw-Hill, 1967)
The Runaway Bunny, Margaret Wise Brown (Harper & Row, 1972)
The Quarreling Book, Charlotte Zolotow (Harper & Row, 1963)

These books are more suitable for older children and contain themes of family trials and tribulations. The characters make important solutions and reconciliations.

Owls in the Family, Farley Mowat (Little Brown, 1961)
Family Secrets: Five Very Important Stories, Norma Shreve (Knopf, 1979)
Brave Jimmy Stone, Elliot Aronald (Scholastic, 1975)

FAMILY ALBUM ACTIVITY

Materials Needed:

• Several pieces of colored construction paper
• Writing instruments
• Photographs (optional)

Bind together several sheets of construction paper (at least one page per family member). Each day select a different family member to write about. As a family, describe the member's interests, best qualities and physical characteristics. You may wish to include photos of the person or draw pictures of special memories other family members have of the individual.

FRIENDSHIP INGREDIENTS

Dear Parent,

      Individuals with high self-esteem generally possess a feeling of belonging. They know the qualities of friendship and instinctively act upon them when they're with others. As a family you can help each member improve their relations with others by focusing on what qualities a friend should have. Recognize and praise specific friendship qualities when you see your own child demonstrating them.

Procedure:

Place the recipe card below in a convenient and accessible location, such as on your refrigerator, and leave it there for at least a week. Throughout the week think about which qualities make a good friend. Each time you observe family members doing friendly acts, or displaying characteristics of friendship, write down next to their name what the family member did. At the end of the week read the list. What did you learn from each other? Write a recipe based on what you learned.

Recipe for a Friend

Name   Friendship Ingredients

Recipe for a Friend from the file of the _____ Family.

_____

_____

_____

_____

_____

Esteem Builders' Complete Program
Jalmar Press, Rolling Hills Estates, CA

MY LIST OF FRIENDLY DEEDS

Dear Parent,

Whether we like to admit it or not, friends play an enormous role in the development of our children's self-esteem. It is important for them to learn how they can become better friends, since in order to have friends one must be a friend. This activity increases children's awareness of the friendly actions they perform for others. Help your child keep track of his or her friendly deeds by writing them in the space below. Each family member may wish to keep his or her own record for the week.

_____
_____
_____
_____
_____
_____
_____
_____
_____
_____
_____
_____
_____
_____
_____
_____
_____
_____
_____
_____
_____
_____
_____
_____
_____
_____
_____

Esteem Builders' Complete Program
Jalmar Press, Rolling Hills Estates, CA

COMPLIMENTS

Dear Parent,

Students who give compliments to others tend to be more popular among classmates and receive compliments in return. Since social recognition is a powerful building block to self-esteem, helping your child to both give and receive compliments can be most beneficial. This activity is designed so that all members of your family can practice the art of complimenting.

Materials Needed:

- Yarn
- Hole-punch
- Stapler and scissors
- Paper plates (2 per hanging)
- Crayons
- Index cards or paper strips, cut 3" x 5"

Procedure:

1. Cut across one paper plate 4" from the bottom. Place the two plates together with the cut plate in front of the whole plate. The cut plate should be turned over so that its back is facing up. This will create an open space between the plates.

2. Connect the plates by stapling along the lower edges where the two plates join.

3. Encourage your child to decorate the plate. Add features with crayons, paper scraps or marking pens: create hair with paper strips or yarn lengths of appropriate colors. The goal is for the final product to look like his or her face.

4. Punch a hole in the top of the plate and tie a 24" yarn length to the top. Hang the plate face in an accessible location.

5. Encourage family members to create similar hanging plates to depict themselves.

6. At least once a day, encourage family members to write or draw a compliment to your child (or to each other). Compliments can range from "I love you" to recognition of special deeds or achievements ("Congratulations on your spelling test!"). Place these notes in the person's plate.

7. Try to find a time when all family members are together to "read" the written or drawn statements.

Variations for older child:

Have your child decorate a tote bag with his/her features. Use fabric pens or sew on pieces of material.

Esteem Builders' Complete Program
Jalmar Press, Rolling Hills Estates, CA

A CIRCLE OF FRIENDS

Dear Parent,

Friends play an enormous part in a child's self-esteem. They help build a child's feeling of affiliation as well as serving as social models and sources of feedback. It is helpful for children to reflect upon who their friends are and why they chose the friends they did. This week's activity helps children consider their sources of friends. *Happy Enhancing!*

Instructions:

1. Write your name in the first box marked "Name."

2. Write the names of 3 family members in the spaces marked "Name" across the top boxes.

3. Read the types of friends listed in the left-hand column. Now write the name of the friend who fits each description in your box. Ask each family member to do the same by writing their choice of friends under their column.

Type of Friend	Name:	Name:	Name:	Name:
1. A person I enjoy playing outdoor games with.				
2. Someone I enjoy talking to.				
3. Someone I could tell my problems to.				
4. Someone I could trust to keep a secret.				
5. Someone I would like to go places with.				
6. Someone who could help me with my school work.				

Esteem Builders' Complete Program
Jalmar Press, Rolling Hills Estates, CA

CARING FOR OTHERS

Dear Parent,

The real goal of building self-esteem is not to create egocentric individuals. Rather, it is to help students recognize that through caring and compassionate gestures toward others, they contribute to the happiness of others but also to their own happiness. Individuals who are altruistic, caring and compassionate generally have high self-esteem. These attributes do not emerge overnight, but are formed after the child has a strong positive sense of self. You can help your child grow in altruistic tendencies by praising gestures as you see them and pointing them out in others. Remember, there is no better model for caring than you. *Happy Enhancing!*

Materials Needed:

Choose one of the following books to share as a read-aloud with your family. Each of these books deals with the themes of caring, devotion and compassion, and can serve as an excellent discussion guide for your family.

For Younger Children:
Alexander and the Wind-up Mouse, Leo Lionni (Pantheon, 1969)
Do You Know What I'll Do?, Charlotte Zolotow (Harper & Row, 1958)
Harlequin and the Gift of Many Colors, Remy Charlip and Burton Supree (Scholastic, 1973)
A Chair For My Mother, Vera B. Williams (Greenwillow Books, 1982)
A Special Trade, Sally Wittman (Harper & Row, 1978)
Now One Foot, Now the Other, Tomie DePaolo (Harcourt, 1981)

For Older Children:
Charlotte's Web, E.B. White (Harper, 1952)
Star Mother's Youngest Child, Louise Moeri (Houghton Mifflin, 1975)
Sadako and the Thousand Paper Cranes, Eleanor Coeer (Dell, 1977)
Stone Fox, John Reynolds Gardiner (Harper & Row, 1980)
Where the Red Fern Grows, Wilson Rawls (Bantam, 1985)
Tuck Everlasting, Natalie Babbit (Farrar, Straus & Giroux, 1975)

You may wish to use a few of the questions below to begin a family discussion based on the book:

1. What was the problem in the book?
2. How did the character solve the problem?
3. What did the character do that showed he/she cared?
4. What deeds have you seen other people do for each other that showed they cared?
5. What could we do as a family for each other to show we care?

Esteem Builders' Complete Program
Jalmar Press, Rolling Hills Estates, CA

HOME RESPONSIBILITIES

Dear Parent,

      Children who are given responsibilities and chores in the home develop a greater sense of purpose and competence, which are also qualities common to children with high self-esteem. The chart below may be helpful to your family in designating chores for each member. It may also help children realize a sense of accomplishment through assuming responsibilities. *Happy Enhancing!*

Procedure:

1. Write the names of each family member in the spaces of the left-hand column.

2. Ask your children to think about responsibilities they would like to share in helping the family function as a family.

3. Next to each name write a chore the member has suggested or one you think he or she can handle.

4. At the end of each day have all members evaluate how effectively they fulfilled their responsibility. This could be a happy or sad face, a yes or no word, or a check mark.

5. At the end of the week reevaluate the chores. Children can choose to keep the same one, rotate responsibilities or pick a new one. You may wish to duplicate the chart to use for the next week.

Our Home Responsibilities								
Name	Chore	S	M	T	W	TH	F	S

Esteem Builders' Complete Program
Jalmar Press, Rolling Hills Estates, CA

MY RESPONSIBILITIES FROM SCHOOL

Dear Parent,

Students need to feel they have influence and control over their own lives, which enhances their sense of purpose and motivation. We can help them achieve this by providing them with responsibilities, such as school work done at home, so that they can recognize they are in charge of their own actions.

This activity helps your child learn to organize and take charge of his/her own school assignments. You may wish to make additional sheets that can be used every week.

Procedure:

1. Write each school assignment for home in the correct daily space.

2. Check off each assignment as you accomplish it.

3. Indicate how responsible you were for completing the assignment by ranking it with the following numbers:

   1 = very responsible (I did it all myself)
   2 = good (I did most of it myself)
   3 = fair (I needed lots of reminders and help)
   4 = poor (I didn't do it, or, someone else did the assignment)

DAY	ASSIGNMENT	ACHIEVED	RANKING
MON			
TUE			
WED			
THUR			
FRI			

Esteem Builders' Complete Program
Jalmar Press, Rolling Hills Estates, CA

GOAL-SETTING

Dear Parent,

      One of the characteristics of students with high self-esteem is that they generally set goals for themselves. They have an idea of what they want to accomplish, and they more often than not achieve what they set out to do. Goal-setting is a powerful technique for self-esteem building, and it can be taught. This week help your child set a goal. Make sure that the goal is achievable (and not too high or too low). The goal-setting form below may help you in this process. Don't forget to encourage and support your child's efforts. *Happy Enhancing!*

Goal-setter's name: _____

Date: _____

My goal is:

_____

_____

_____

_____

To make my goal I'll have to:

    1. _____

    2. _____

    3. _____

I hope to make my goal by: _____

Signed: _____

Witness: _____

A picture of me making my goal.

Esteem Builders' Complete Program
Jalmar Press, Rolling Hills Estates, CA

MAKING SELF CHANGES

Dear Parent,

Before students can make constructive changes within themselves, they must first be aware of what things they'd like to change. This activity helps students focus on what they like about themselves and then what they'd like to change about themselves. To make this a fruitful activity, it is important that students first be guided to their positive attributes. Help your child recognize that changes he/she wants to make should be changes that can be made.

Materials Needed:
- One piece of light-colored paper, at least 8 1/2" x 11"
- Colored marking pens or other writing instrument

Procedure:
Fold the paper in half lengthwise. Along the left edge of the paper write the words: "Things I Like About Myself." Along the other side of the paper write the words: "Things I'd Like to Change About Myself."

1. Place the paper in a convenient, accessible location.

2. Each time you think of something you like about yourself, write it on the left-hand side of the page. Other family members should be invited to write positive statements also. Spend a few days gathering your own positive self-statements and self-statements of others.

3. On the third day, begin to think of things you'd like to change about yourself. Remember, you may only write down things you really could change — some things we have no control over. If you'd like to, you may fold this part back so that others can't see your statements.

4. On the fifth day, look at all the changes you'd like to make. Choose just one you'd really like to change about yourself and which is possible to do. On the back of your sheet, write a plan for how you will make the change. What will you do? How will you do it? When will you do it by? Have someone witness it.

Esteem Builders' Complete Program
Jalmar Press, Rolling Hills Estates, CA

TARGETING SUCCESS

Dear Parent,

Setting goals is an essential part of your child achieving a sense of purpose. Realizing the goal is even more critical. However, students often set goals that are not realistic and therefore not achievable. As a result, self-esteem is lowered.

This activity will help your child focus on goals he or she has attained. Encourage him/her to set a goal that can be achieved within the week. The goal should be worded in a simple, brief statement. Throughout the week help him/her recognize the goal accomplishments by coloring in the bullseyes.

This week I'm going to aim for:

_____

_____

_____

_____

Each time I make my mark I will color in the bullseye.

DAY 1   DAY 2   DAY 3   DAY 4

DAY 5   DAY 6   DAY 7

My score for this week is _____

Esteem Builders' Complete Program
Jalmar Press, Rolling Hills Estates, CA

SUPER SLEUTH

Dear Parent,

Children who are successful problem solvers usually possess high self-esteem as well. Helping your child learn how to identify and solve his/her own problems early in life fosters a coping skill for successfully moving through obstacles later in life.

Procedure:

Family members take turns as the "Super Sleuth." You may wish to move clockwise in a circle so that everyone is appointed. The sleuth's task is to read (or have someone read) a problem from the list below. Members can suggest their own problems. The Sleuth must then (1) identify the problem and (2) tell how he/she would solve it. When the problem is solved, other family members may add their own ideas. Older children could discuss the consequences to each solution.

Problems for Younger Children

• The kitten from across the street is stuck up in the tree and can't get down. What would you do?

• You're on a walk with your friend. Your walk takes you across a deserted field where no houses are around. Suddenly, your friend steps in a hole. Her foot is caught and there's no one else around.

• You are at school and you see your friend Mark put the teacher's set of pens in his desk. Later the teacher asks the class if anyone knows what might have happened to the pens. Mark doesn't answer.

• You and your friend are walking home and throwing rocks at cans along the walk. Suddenly the rock your friend throws lands right in the neighbor's window and breaks the glass. Your neighbor runs out and sees both of you.

• You promised a boy in your class that you'd go to the movies with him. Your best friend comes up to you and asks you to go to the circus. It's on the same night. You really want to go to the circus.

Problems for Older Children

• You're spending the night at a friend's house. The friend's parents leave. Your friend suggests you try the liquor in the liquor cabinet. There's no one around.

• You're in a drug store shopping with your friend. You leave together and notice your friend has something from the store under his coat. You don't think he paid for it.

• You're at school taking a test. You notice the boy next to you is copying your answers on his test. The boy is one of your best friends, and you are all being graded on a curve.

• You're at school. One of the older kids comes up to you and offers you some free dope.

• You have a test tomorrow, which will determine your whole grade. One of your classmates whom you've been dying to be friends with comes up and invites you to a party for that night. It's the best party of the school year.

Others: Make up a problem based on a situation that you have faced.

Esteem Builders' Complete Program
Jalmar Press, Rolling Hills Estates, CA

PROBLEM PANTOMIMES

Dear Parent,

This week's activity provides your child with further opportunities to practice problem-solving skills. At this stage, it is important to guide your child into creating a wide variety of problem solutions as a first step to problem solving. Later you can help him/her decide which would be the best solution. *Happy Enhancing!*

Procedure:

1. Try doing this activity in two small family groups like in the game Charades. Any size team is fine.

2. Teams can come up with a list of problems or use the suggestions that appear below. Write each problem on a paper strip and put it into a container.

3. Each team then takes turns pulling a strip from the container. As soon as one member thinks of a solution, he or she begins to pantomime the solution and the other members of the group join in. The only rule is: No talking.

4. As soon as the other team recognizes the solution, stop the pantomime. It is now the next team's turn to pantomime another solution to the same problem. Continue trading teams with the same problem until each group can no longer think of any more reasonable solutions.

5. It's now time to pull another problem card from the container.

Pantomime Problems
(Cut out each problem and place in the container)

You're in a rowboat with friends. You see a hole in the bottom of the boat. Water is coming into the boat fast.

You're in a large store with your mom and a friend. You stop to look at something. When you turn to look for your mom, she's not there. You're lost!

Your very good friend is showing you a new model she just finished making. You drop it accidentally and it breaks.

Some friends are sleeping over at your house. Your parents leave the house for a little while. All of a sudden the lights go out.

You and your friends walk home after school. You try to get in the front door and find it's locked. You don't have a key.

You're in an elevator going up to the fifth floor of a building. All of a sudden it stops between the fourth and fifth floors.

You're home alone with a friend. You think you smell smoke.

Esteem Builders' Complete Program
Jalmar Press, Rolling Hills Estates, CA

HEB 32

PROBLEM REPORT

Dear Parent,

     This activity helps your child practice the skills of problem solving learned previously. It goes one step further: your child also will be deciding which solution is the best. The activity is designed to help your child to solve a problem he/she is facing by using these techniques. You may wish to suggest a simple problem to begin with and guide your child through the steps. This will be one more step toward helping your child take responsibility for his/her own actions. *Happy Enhancing!*

Procedure:

1. Name a problem you're having.

2. Tell about the problem.
   - When does it usually happen?
   - Where are you when it happens?
   - Who are you with?

3. How could you solve your own problem? List a few ideas.

4. Choose the best solution. Which would work for you?

5. Make a plan to start it.
   - I will solve my problem by (list solution):
   - I will solve it by (date):
   - I will need these things or people to help me:

Signed: _____

Witness: _____

Date: _____

Esteem Builders' Complete Program
Jalmar Press, Rolling Hills Estates, CA

WORK FOLDERS

Dear Parent,

Students with high self-esteem also feel competent. This feeling develops after repeated successes. It is particularly important for students to feel adequate concerning their school work. This activity helps students keep track of their school progress and allows them to see their competence increase.

Materials Needed:

- Rug yarn (60"), scissors, white glue, marking pens, crayons, hole-punch
- 2 pieces of tagboard or construction paper (at least 12" x 18" each)
- Decorating items such as: photographs, stickers, paints, felt scraps, construction paper scraps, glitter, sequins

Procedure:

1. Help your child place the two paper pieces on top of each other. Holding the two papers together, punch holes along three of the four sides about 1/4" from the edge. Leave one of the long edges unpunched.

2. String the yarn through the first hole and tie a secure knot.

3. Your child then laces yarn through the remaining punched edges. Tie the left-over yarn length to the opposite side to form a handle.

4. Encourage your child to decorate the folder in whatever fashion he/she desires — stickers, felt scraps, ink pens, crayons, paper scraps, stamps and photographs.

5. Each time your child brings school work home, sit down during an uninterrupted time and browse through it together. Encourage your child to choose a page or two of which he/she is most proud. Talk about what parts of the paper are most deserving of praise and openly verbalize your support. Be specific in your feedback. Your child needs to know exactly what was done well and why.

6. Date the papers together and put them into a folder.

7. Periodically look back at the papers and compare them to your child's current work. Talk about your child's growth and point out how much progress has been made.

Esteem Builders' Complete Program
Jalmar Press, Rolling Hills Estates, CA

OUR FAMILY STRENGTHS

Dear Parent,

     Students with high self-esteem also have confidence in their competence. ("I feel confident because I've made many successful accomplishments. I know I have strengths.") As a family you can help your child identify his/her strengths. Write each family member's name (including your own) in the spaces provided. For the next week, each time family members recognize a strength in each other, write it under the member's name. Be sure to point it out to one another and praise accomplishments!

NAME:	NAME:	NAME:
NAME:	**NAME:**	**NAME:**

Esteem Builders' Complete Program
Jalmar Press, Rolling Hills Estates, CA

"I CAN..."

Dear Parent,

Every child needs to hear success ring in his/her ears because it is a great competence booster. Each success contributes to a positive self-image. This activity helps your child to see his/her accomplishments. Other family members may make their own "I Can." Be sure to have your child publicly share each accomplishment so that all family members can reinforce his/her new achievements with praise.

Materials Needed:

- Scissors, white glue, crayons or marking pens
- Large coffee or juice can
- Paper cut into 5" x 5" squares

Procedure:

1. Ask your child to think about all the things he/she can do (you may need to make suggestions). As your child states each accomplishment, ask him/her to jot them down on a piece of paper (or ask your child to dictate responses to you as you record the comments).

2. Show your child how long the list is. Emphasize the number of accomplishments made.

3. Choose a few accomplishments your child is particularly proud of. Each of these may be illustrated on a piece of paper.

4. Allow your child to glue each accomplishment onto the can.

5. Allow plenty of time for the glue to dry. The can now becomes your child's permanent bank of accomplishments.

6. Each time your child performs a new achievement, ask him/her to add it to the can by writing the accomplishment on a piece of paper.

Discussion Starters:

1. Which thing are you most proud of?
2. Which thing was the hardest to learn to do?
3. What do you want to learn to do next?

JOURNALS

Dear Parent,

Keeping track of daily thoughts, dreams and accomplishments helps your child gain perspective on himself/herself. Your child can record these ideas on a few sheets of stapled pages. If necessary, make suggestions to your child of special achievements or moments that could be written down. At the end of a week's time your child may want to continue the written journal. *Happy Enhancing!*

Materials Needed:

- Stapler, pen or pencil
- 7 pieces (or more) of writing paper (for younger children you may use plain drawing paper)
- Colored paper, wallpaper, gift wrap or contact
- Paper for the cover

Procedure:

1. Take the pieces of paper and put them in a neat pile.
2. Staple the pages together in 3 places near the edge of one of the long sides.
3. Cut a cover for your book from wallpaper, gift wrap, material or colored paper. Make the cover big enough so that you can wrap it around the stapled edge of your book to make both a front and a back cover.
4. Decorate your cover. You could use colored ink pens, scraps of colored paper glued on, or any idea of your choice.
5. Wrap the cover around the stapled edge of your book. Staple the cover in place, using 3 staples along the same edge that you stapled before.
6. Trim the cover so that it is the same size as your book.

Write or draw in your journal every day for a week. Show or tell about what you did that day, what you wished had happened, someone you were with, something you did, how you would have changed the day, what you plan to do tomorrow, or anything else you'd like to recall about the day. Remember to put the date on each page as you draw or write.

OVERCOMING OBSTACLES

Dear Parent,

History is full of examples of important figures who struggled to overcome obstacles, and these individuals serve as powerful models to children. Their message of "Try, try, and try again" is also one that individuals with high self-esteem frequently have received and told themselves. It is never too early to instill this message in your child; namely, that success is often achieved only after failure.

Did you know that numerous famous historical figures had major obstacles in their life? Many of them were handicapped or came from abusive or neglectful home environments; others received constant negative messages from those who were important to them. Yet they all persevered to become successful.

- Albert Einstein was four years old before he could speak and seven before he could read.
- Abraham Lincoln was defeated from public office eight times before he was finally elected.
- When Thomas Edison was a boy his teachers told him he was too stupid to learn.
- Winston Churchill failed the sixth grade.
- Louisa May Alcott was told by an editor that she could never write anything that had popular appeal.

Choose one of the following books to read aloud as a family. As you read it, discuss what obstacles the character faced and what he/she did to overcome them.

Helen Keller, Margaret Davidson (Scholastic Book Services, 1973). [Grades K-3]

Louis Braille: The Boy Who Invented Books for the Blind, Margaret Davidson (Scholastic Book Services, 1974). [Grades K-5]

Child of the Silent Night: The Story of Laura Bridgman, Edith F. Hunter (Houghton Mifflin Co., 1963). [Grades 2-5]

Unforgettable Characters, compiled by Reader's Digest (Reader's Digest, 1980). [Grades 6 and up]

A Special Kind of Courage: Profiles of Young Americans, Geraldo Rivera (Bantam, 1977). [Grades 6 and up]

The Value of Patience, The Story of the Wright Brothers, Spencer Johnson, M.D. The Valuetale Series (William Morrow and Company, Inc.) [Grades 5 and up]

The Value of Believing in Yourself, The Story of Louis Pasteur, Spencer Johnson, M.D. The Valuetale Series (William Morrow and Company, Inc.) [Grades 5 and up]

Meet Abraham Lincoln, Barbara Cary (Random House, 1965). [Grades 5 and up]

FAMILY SUCCESSES

Dear Parent,

Children as well as adults need to feel successful. This activity allows family members the opportunity to reflect upon their past successes and then verbalize them. Make sure everyone says out loud his/her successes.

Materials Needed:

- Strips of paper or 3 x 5 cards
- Pen or pencil

Procedure:

Jot down the open-ended statements you find below on separate strips of paper. Fold the papers in half and place them in a container, such as a bag or bowl. Family members take turns pulling out a card from the container and completing the statement. Other members may add on to or suggest other successes for each statement. Continue until everyone has had at least two turns.

SUCCESS STATEMENTS

Something I'm really proud of is _____.

This year I learned _____.

I thought it would be hard, but I figured out how to _____.

There was a time when I couldn't _____ but now I can.

I'm glad I was successful at _____.

My greatest success is _____.

I've accomplished a lot of this year, especially _____.

If I want to, I can _____.

Something I can do all by myself is _____.

I taught myself how to _____.

I'm learning how to _____.

Esteem Builders' Complete Program
Jalmar Press, Rolling Hills Estates, CA

SHARING SUCCESS

Dear Parent,

All of us need to be reminded of our achievements and successes. Since knowledge of our accomplishments is a critical component of self-esteem, provide frequent opportunities for your child to reflect upon his/her past and present successes.

Materials Needed:

- A pillow case or grocery bag for each family member.

Procedure:

1. Ask each family member to find an object around the house. The object should represent something that the member is proud of, a special success. Give family members a few days to think of what object they would like to choose. If it is not possible to find the exact object, they may draw a picture of it instead.

2. Members place their objects in individual pillow cases or grocery bags and should be encouraged to keep their decisions secret.

3. On the chosen evening, each member will take a turn sharing his/her object. At first, you may give clues about the object (limited to 3) to see if family members can guess your choice. The speaker then removes the object from the sack and explains why the object is special to him/her.

BLUE RIBBON

Dear Parent,

Recognizing our successes and the successes of others is an important avenue for esteem building. This activity gives your child the opportunity to award himself/herself for a highly valued accomplishment. Encourage family members to make similar badges for themselves as well as making them for other family members. You may wish to have a special celebration evening where everyone's accomplishments are recognized.

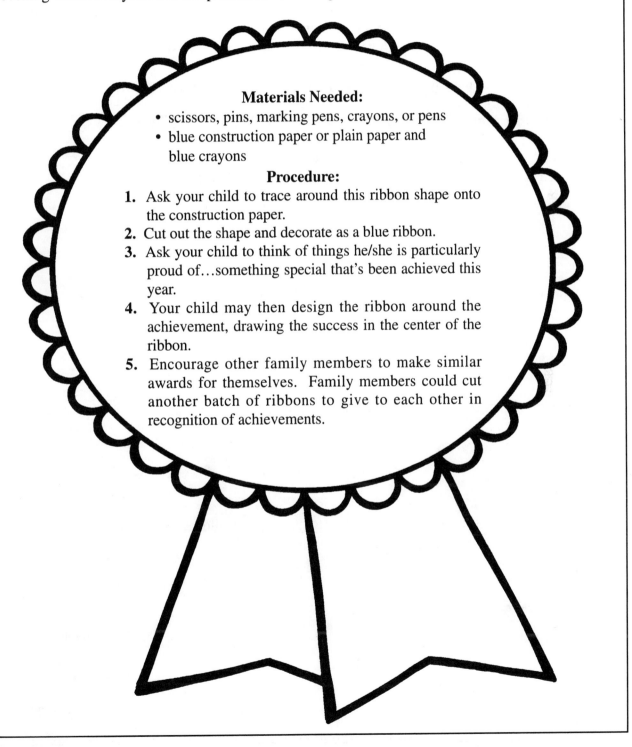

Materials Needed:

- scissors, pins, marking pens, crayons, or pens
- blue construction paper or plain paper and blue crayons

Procedure:

1. Ask your child to trace around this ribbon shape onto the construction paper.
2. Cut out the shape and decorate as a blue ribbon.
3. Ask your child to think of things he/she is particularly proud of…something special that's been achieved this year.
4. Your child may then design the ribbon around the achievement, drawing the success in the center of the ribbon.
5. Encourage other family members to make similar awards for themselves. Family members could cut another batch of ribbons to give to each other in recognition of achievements.

Esteem Builders' Complete Program
Jalmar Press, Rolling Hills Estates, CA

HOME ESTEEM-BUILDER ACTIVITY QUESTIONNAIRE

Dear Parent,

One of our school goals this year has been to enhance your child's self-esteem and help you learn how you can be instrumental in this process. We realize that your child's self-perceptions have a critical impact on achievement and behavior. We also recognize that you play one of the most significant roles in helping your child feel about him or herself. The Home Esteem-Builder Activities our school sent home weekly were one of the ways our staff has tried to involve you in this process. Please take a moment to answer the following questions and then send the survey back to school with your child. Thank you for your support!

1. How many of Home Esteem-Builder Activities did you do with your child?

   ☐ All   ☐ Almost All   ☐ Half   ☐ Almost Half   ☐ None

2. Which Home Esteem Builder-Activity did your child like best?

3. What things about the Home Esteem-Builder Program did you enjoy the most?

4. What things about the program did you (or your child) like the least?

5. What suggestions do you have for future Home Esteem-Building programs?

Parent Signature (optional)

Notes

6

Prescriptive Home Esteem Building

HOME ESTEEM BUILDERS

- Parent-Teacher Conferences
- Self-Concept Reframing
- Checklists for What to Look for in Your Child
- Home Esteem-Builder Tips

HOME ESTEEM BUILDER ACTIVITIES

ACTIVITIES LIST

SECURITY

SELFHOOD

AFFILIATION

MISSION

PAGE

COMPETENCE

PAGE

PAGE

Home Esteem Builders **was developed on the premise that a home and school partnership is an integral element of effective esteem building. The material in this book provides educators with the resources to help parents enhance their children's self-esteem. Before distributing any of these materials to the students' homes, please make sure that they have been translated into the primary language of the parents.**

6

Prescriptive Home-Esteem Building

What are the optimal conditions for a parent-teacher conference? A quiet corner, protection from interruptions and a teacher who listens. The words exchanged during the conference may be forgotten, but the mood of the meeting will linger on. It will decide the subsequent attitudes and actions of the parents.

—HAIM GINOTT

PARENT-TEACHER CONFERENCES

One of the greatest opportunities for strengthening the home-school connection is at parent-teacher conferences. In most schools, conferences are a required means of establishing contact and building rapport with parents. Educators find parent conferences can be enormously beneficial in eliciting parents' support for the school. Working as partners, teachers and parents can form concrete strategies for students who are experiencing difficulties.

Parent conferences can also be an ideal time for teachers and parents to work together in enhancing students' self-esteem. Here is an opportunity for teachers to educate parents in home esteem-building principles. During their time together, teachers and parents can discuss students' strengths and capabilities. Individual plans for students' improvement in achievement or behavior can be created. Specific strategies to enhance each of the five components of self-esteem can also be discussed.

Effective esteem-builder parent conferences must not be left to chance. They are always deliberately planned. Poorly planned or otherwise negative conferences can create friction between the home and school and intensify parental dissatisfaction. It is important to thoroughly prepare and organize conferences so that they can be as successful and positive as possible. When all persons involved are prepared, conferences will be more comfortable and productive.

Provided in this section are suggestions and materials to help make conferences as productive to student esteem enhancement as possible. Included are:

- **Student Self-Esteem Profile.** This is a quick parent survey to send home prior to holding conferences. The survey contains a series of descriptions characteristic of high and low self-esteem. Ask parents to read the list and rate their children in each characteristic on a scale of high to low. Then encourage parents to bring the form to conferences to serve as a discussion tool.

- **Student Self-Esteem Survey.** This is a simple self-esteem checklist of the five building blocks. It is strongly recommended that the form be sent home prior to the conference. Ask the student to fill it out at home and then the parents bring it to the conference to serve as a catalyst for discussion. *(Checklist designed by Campbell Elementary School.)*

- **What to Look for in Your Child.** These are checklists for each of the five components of self-esteem which describe behaviors and characteristics of children who are high or low in each of the feelings. Educators can use these forms during conferences to help parents understand each of the five feelings of high self-esteem and how such feelings may strengthen as well as limit learning and behavior. It is recommended that only one form be used per conference.

- **Home Esteem-Builder Tips.** These handouts on each of the five components describe home esteem-building tips parents can use to enhance the feelings in their children. Handouts could be distributed at the conclusion of conferences so parents can immediately begin the enhancement process at home. It is strongly recommended that the teacher hand out only one Esteem Builder Tip at a time.

- **Parent-Teacher Esteem-Builder Conference Form.** This form is created jointly by parents and teachers in an effort to discover children's strengths, interests, and assets. Teachers and parents then agree upon how these strengths will be reinforced in the home and school. A plan to improve one area impeding the student's school performance is also developed.

- **Self-Esteem Prescriptive Plan.** This is an ongoing form provided to organize and coordinate individual students' self-esteem enhancement. Duplicate one form for each student. Teachers and parents fill out the form together at conferences, identifying students' specific strengths and weaknesses in each of the five feelings. In addition, teachers and parents describe plans for specific strategies to help students grow in each of the five areas. The form can be duplicated so parents and teachers both have a copy. During any planning times, place a piece of carbon paper between the duplicated forms. Any written additions to the prescriptive plan will then be preserved. Teachers should keep one copy in each student's file throughout the school year. Parents should be encouraged to bring the form to conferences.

- **Parent-Student-Teacher Conference Form.** The purpose of this form is to create a dialogue between parents, students, and teachers that will help students improve. Make a copy of the form for students who might benefit from a three-way, parent-student-teacher conference. Arrange a time when all three parties are able to sit down together. The purpose of the discussion is not only to track students' progress but also to develop strategies for turn-ing weaknesses into strengths. During conferences, the teacher reviews the progress a student has made in a particular subject with both the student and parent and offers ways to improve. The student, in turn, makes his/her own statement about the work. Finally, the parent contributes his/her opinions and comments. In this way, students, teachers, and parents are in direct communication.

- **Before Conference Letter.** About a week before conferences are scheduled, educators might wish to send not only a reminder note but also a brief outline listing the conference agenda. An example of such a letter with a conference agenda is found on page 271.

SELF-CONCEPT REFRAMING

One of the most difficult questions teachers receive from parents of low self-esteem students is, "What can I do?" At conferences educators can teach parents a strategy that can make powerful differences in their children. Self-Concept Reframing© is a structure that is used most successfully with students who have very low selfhood. These students typically display an inability to receive praise. When someone does give them a compliment, they commonly deny or disregard the comment, or become a behavior problem in the classroom. The tragic aspect of their inability to accept compliments or praise is that they really don't feel worthy enough to accept this information; at the same time, they desperately need to have someone help them accept more accurate information about themselves. The new information educators give students is critical since it will serve as the starting point for rebuilding their self-esteem. Following are a few key points educators need to keep in mind for the classroom as well as to convey to parents at conferences:

- Change will happen for the child. The teacher or parent must be very committed to the concept and consistent with performing the steps involved in Self-Concept Reframing.

- Recognize that students with low selfhood are generally not risk takers. This means that the child generally does not volunteer to change his/her own behavior. The teacher or parent must be the agent for initiating change for the student.

• Honor the fact that the child is generally threatened by a change in his or her self-concept. Self-concept is an ingrained concept. The student's present self-concept may have been governing his or her behavior for quite a while. Do expect behavioral flare-ups. Respect the child's dignity by doing the reframing activity only in private…never in front of other students.

• Change is a gradual, evolutionary process. A rule of thumb is that it will take twenty-one days before a new behavior is acquired. Another rule of thumb is that the lower the student's feeling of selfhood, the longer the reframing process will take.

Beginning the Structure

The self-concept reframing structure is useful for teachers as well as for parents. It is strongly recommended that before beginning the structure, educators and parents do some homework regarding the child. Some questions adult esteem builders need to ask themselves include:

• "Do I have enough trust or rapport with this child to begin such a structure?" In order for the reframing structure to be successful, the child must see the teacher or parent involved in the process as a credible, trusting individual. It is much easier for the child to accept new information from someone he/she trusts. If trust has not been developed, the teacher or parent should take steps to build a stronger relationship with the child so that the process of restructuring self-concept can begin.

• "Do I have enough personal information about this child to attempt this structure? Do I know his/her interests, hobbies and strengths outside academic areas? Do I know personal likes and dislikes? Do I know what things this child really cares about?" If the answer to any of these questions is no, then consider the following suggestions:

1. A teacher can visit the child's home. Home visits can help build rapport with and add to an educator's knowledge of the child. A parent may need to spend more time with the child really listening to what he/she has to say.

2. Ask the child to fill out a survey of "personal interests and favorites." The survey may reveal facts about the child that the teacher or parent was not aware of.

3. Interview former teachers, coaches, counselors, or significant others who have been with the child. Capitalizing on other people's knowledge can prove valuable.

4. A teacher can ask a parent for help, and vice versa.

5. Sit down and talk to the child personally. Ask questions and encourage him/her to express himself/herself. Listen without judging what the child says.

Guidelines for Reframing

The following are general guidelines for using the reframing structure to change a child's self-concept. Teachers and parents involved in the process may wish to write down specific strategies they plan to use based on what they know about this particular child:

Reframing Steps:

1. Identify a child low in selfhood and with whom trust and rapport has been achieved.

2. Identify strengths, skills, or assets the child already possesses. Ideally, the skills should be ones that are in evidence when the teacher or parent is with the child; they also should be ones the child cares about.

3. Choose one (and no more than two) of the child's skills to target.

4. Choose the specific "label" (term or language) to identify the child's skills. The teacher or parent should use the same label every time the skill is targeted.

Targeting Steps:

1. Wait for the first moment the child demonstrates the skill. The skill should clearly be earned and deserved as a strength or talent. *Do not praise just to praise.*

2. Praise the child only in private. Keep in mind, one of the characteristics of a student low in selfhood is that he/she feels very threatened by public praise.

3. Praise the child's *behavior*; do not praise the "child."

4. When praising, be as *specific* as possible. The most effective praise tells the child exactly what he/she did well. This kind of praise lets the child know what behaviors to focus on in order to improve.

5. Be consistent in your attempts. Low selfhood children often do not perceive themselves worthy enough to receive your praise, do not give up.

6. Behavior change is a slow process. Behavior management theory tells us it generally takes 21 days days of repetition of the skill before a new behavior is acquired. You must do the same praise activity with the student every day for at least 21 days.

7. The lower the selfhood of the student the longer the reframing process will take. You may need to extend the "21 day" period.

8. Finally, think of other significant individuals the student may encounter during the week who could use the same process with you. The more the student hears the message the greater the likelihood they will receive the image and reframe their self-picture. Share the strategy with others. Together you can have even greater impact!

Notes

Notes

Chapter 6 Activities

SECURITY

When a child feels insecure and unsafe, he/she may indicate this with the following behaviors. It is normal to experience a few characteristics at home at one time or another. Have you noticed any of these behaviors lately with your own child? Are some characteristics more intense than others? Look for a pattern or an intensity of the characteristic. All of these behaviors greatly reduce the child's ability to learn.

_____ Avoids new situations; resistant to new challenges.

_____ Withdraws from close physical contact even with known persons.

_____ Distrusts others; hesitates or avoids forming close personal attachments.

_____ Exhibits symptoms of stress or anxiety (i.e. nail biting, hair twirling, thumb sucking, teeth grinding, shaking, crying without apparent reason).

_____ Challenges authority.

_____ Displays excessive and/or unfounded fears.

_____ Is uncomfortable with new experiences.

_____ Lacks knowledge of who can be counted on.

A child with a strong sense of security is likely to display the following behaviors:

_____ Knows who to count on and trust.

_____ Generally feels safe and secure; therefore, risks separating from trusted sources for brief periods.

_____ Displays few symptoms of stress and anxiety (see above).

_____ Has formed a trusting, personal relationship with a significant other.

_____ Is comfortable with close physical contact from known persons.

_____ Handles change and spontaneity with relative ease.

Security is a feeling of strong assuredness. Involves feeling comfortable and safe; knowing what is expected; being able to depend on individuals and situations; and comprehending rules and limits. A secure child feels emotionally and physically safe.

Esteem Builders' Complete Program
Jalmar Press, Rolling Hills Estates, CA

Home Esteem-Builder Tips
to Enhance Security

1. With your child, write down your family rules and expectations. Post these rules on the refrigerator. Make sure everyone clearly understands the rules. Finally, make sure the rules are ones that all members of the household are capable of following.

2. Parents that enhance self-esteem accept their children for their strengths as well as their shortcomings. This is called "unconditional love." Does your child perceive this acceptance?

3. When rules are broken, use natural consequences. Any punishment should be directly related to the offense. For example, if homework is not completed, TV and special activity privileges could be withdrawn; if coming home late is an issue, the curfew could be set back to an earlier time for future outings.

4. Set aside a private time each day to evaluate with your child his/her behavior. Begin on a positive note by pointing out one good behavior you noticed and then discuss one area that needs improvement. Talk about specific ways your child could improve.

5. Set aside a private, uninterrupted "together" time with your child. Schedule the time on the calendar and then strictly adhere to the "conference" (phone off the hook and "do not disturb" sign on the door). We all need time to strengthen and affirm our love.

6. Reaffirm your love and affection for your child during "Nighttime Affirmations." Each night spend a few private moments snuggling and affirming.

7. Do a self-check: How often are you modeling positive behavior and statements to your child? Remember, a large part of acquiring self-esteem is through modeling others and copying their behavior. Make sure you're projecting the image you want "caught."

8. Make it clear to your child what he or she needs to do.

9. Develop a checklist of duties your child needs to follow. Keep the rules simple and post them in an accessible location. Encourage your child to check off tasks as they are completed.

10. Emphasize to your child following any punishment that your frustration is with your child's behavior and not with him/her.

11. Stay calm during times your child is being punished. It may be helpful following a behavior infraction to remove your child from the situation and from you until everyone "cools off." You can then deal with the issue more rationally at a later time.

12. Model or role play applying home rules. This is particularly helpful with younger children.

13. Periodically review your home rules as a family. Are they in need of updating?

14. Take time to listen—really listen—to your child every day. Try not to add your judgment or evaluation to your child's opinion. Always judging your child stymies communication.

15. As you are talking with your child, practice "eye contact." Both of you can role play how to look into one another's eyes as you are talking.

Esteem Builders' Complete Program
Jalmar Press, Rolling Hills Estates, CA

Home Esteem-Builder Tips to Enhance Security (continued)

16. Help your child recognize how words can detonate other people's feelings. Discourage any words that put down others. Remind your child, "That's a put-down," as it is stated.

17. Avoid humiliating your child. Practice the rule, "Punish in private. Never in front of others."

18. Help your child become aware of individuals who are trustworthy. Talk about what makes them so.

19. When going to a new activity or event, discuss with your child beforehand what can be expected. Security means feeling safe. Help your child feel safer by role playing or discussing the parameters of the event (i.e. who will be there, how long the event will last, where it's located, what activities have been planned, what behaviors your child should have, and anything else that might be helpful).

20. Brand-new places and activities often heighten insecurity. Whenever possible, visit the location prior to the event with your child. Walk the premises and practice what you will do and say when the actual event happens.

21. Reinforce your child for any safe "risk taking" behavior (trying something new). Acknowledge to your child that trying new things is hard and that you admire the risk your child took.

22. Teach your child a few self-talk statements to "calm down" during insecure moments. Tell your child to say a few times inside his/her head prior to the insecure event a meaningful statement such as, "I am calm and in control" or "I can only do my best" or "I'll just try and give it my best shot." Your child may have a statement of his/her own to use.

23. Develop a quiet, secret signal between you and your child to indicate when his/her behavior at a public event is inappropriate. Such a signal preserves your child's dignity.

24. Describe to your child times when you didn't feel safe or secure as a child. Owning up to your feelings of insecurity often creates a "safe" atmosphere for your child to open up to you and describe his or her "unsafe feelings."

25. Reward your child with a special privilege when exemplary behavior (or noticeable improvement in behavior) has transpired.

26. Encourage your child to participate in different activities in order to have a variety of experiences. Begin with simple activities your child feels safer trying.

27. Be consistent with your discipline. Your child needs to know what to expect from you.

28. When you say you will do something be sure you do it. Your child needs to recognize that you follow through on your word.

29. If your child routinely arrives home before you, leave a "welcome home" message on a cassette, letter, or answering machine.

30. Remember to praise your child in front of others. Let your child hear you say how proud you are of him/her.

PARENT-TEACHER CONFERENCE
TO ENHANCE SECURITY

> *Security is a feeling of strong assuredness. Involves feeling comfortable and safe; knowing what is expected; being able to depend on individuals and situations; and comprehending rules and limits. A secure child feels emotionally and physically safe.*

Student: _____   Date: _____

1. Low **security** behavior characteristics the student is demonstrating: see page 251.

   •

   •

   •

2. **Security** strengths the child is demonstrating:
   Demonstrating at Home: Demonstrating at School:

3. Choose one technique from the Home Esteem Builder Tip to Enhance **Security**:
   Steps to Try at Home: Steps to Try at School:

4. The first thing we will do to make the plan happen:
   Home: Displayed at School:

Parent: _____

Teacher: _____

Esteem Builders' Complete Program
Jalmar Press, Rolling Hills Estates, CA

SELFHOOD

A child with a weak sense of selfhood may be identified by the following behavioral characteristics. It is normal to experience a few characteristics at one time or another. Have you noticed any of these behaviors lately with your own child? Are some characteristics more intense than others? Look for a pattern or an intensity of the characteristic.

_____ Frequently uses negative statements regarding self and others.

_____ Embarrasses easily; oversensitive to criticism.

_____ Lacks confidence in physical self or necessary physical skills; therefore, rarely engages in fine or gross motor activities.

_____ Is dependent on adults; anxious to please them.

_____ Is uncomfortable with praise; denies, undermines, disregards, or becomes embarrassed.

_____ Conforms or mimics others; is unwilling to express self in own way or risk being different.

_____ May seek acknowledgment for negative characteristics.

_____ Is misinformed regarding roles, attributes, or physical characteristics.

_____ Dresses in extremes, either to attract attention or to cover up the body.

_____ Can be hypercritical of self; uncomfortable with criticism.

A child with a strong sense of selfhood is likely to display the following behaviors:

_____ Expresses uniquenesses and individuality; risks being different.

_____ Has an accurate self-description in terms of physical characteristics, capabilities, roles, and attitudes.

_____ Generally makes positive statements about self and others.

_____ Identifies and expresses emotions appropriately.

_____ Is comfortable accepting praise and criticism.

Selfhood is a feeling of individuality. Acquiring self-knowledge, which includes an accurate and realistic self-description in terms of roles, attributes, and physical characteristics.

Esteem Builders' Complete Program
Jalmar Press, Rolling Hills Estates, CA

Home Esteem-Builder Tips
to Enhance Selfhood

1. Give your child positive feedback making sure that it is specific. Tell him/her exactly what you liked about his/her behavior and why.

2. Strive to say at least five positive statements to your child for every negative statement you say. We need at least five positives to counteract one negative statement.

3. Have your child write down what things he/she likes about himself/herself. This may be harder for your child than you think since we are taught to be modest. Volunteer ideas if your child can't think of any.

4. Teach your child to "disarm" derogatory/negative statements by replacing them with positive comments such as, "Maybe I am short but I'm also very smart."

5. To start a discussion starter, ask your child, "If you could change anything about yourself, what would you change and why?" Listen to your child's response. Do you need to help him/her build stronger self-acceptance?

6. To change a behavior, pinpoint one behavior your child has that he/she finds undesirable. Then help your child identify specific behaviors that could replace the undesirable behavior. Concentrate on only one behavior at a time.

7. Model positive self-statements in front of your child (i.e. "I'm really proud of the way I cooked this dinner" or "I think I look attractive when I wear my hair like this"). You may feel uncomfortable but you can't expect your child to say positive self-statements unless they hear you saying them, too.

8. Write down the qualities that make your child unique and hang the list in his/her room.

9. Get up extra early one day just so the two of you can go out to breakfast together (or dinner or "brown bag" it to school one day just to have lunch together).

10. Leave a note under your child's pillow affirming your love for him/her.

11. At least once a month let your child choose a day when just the two of you can be together. Write it on the calendar, plan for it and then do it.

12. Recognize your child for the special strengths he/she possesses. To help your child believe in the strength, center in on the same strength in your praise every day for at least three weeks.

13. Teach your child the difference between who they ARE and what they DO. Children must learn that we love them because of who they ARE, and not because of the things they DO.

14. Build in your child an awareness of his/her family ancestry. Develop a family tree together and discuss his/her identity.

15. Share your beliefs and values with your child.

16. Do a "Me Tracing" by having your child lie down on a long piece of butcher paper or brown wrapping paper. Trace around his/her body outline. Now, together fill in the outline with self-descriptions of your child. Use magazine pictures, photos, words, sentences, and/or self-drawn pictures.

Esteem Builders' Complete Program
Jalmar Press, Rolling Hills Estates, CA

Home Esteem Builder Tips to Enhance Selfhood (continued)

17. Make an "Identity Placemat" with your child. Use a 12" x 18" piece of construction paper or tagboard. Help your child cover the paper with self-descriptive words or pictures. Photographs of your child can also be used. Cover the placemat with clear contact paper to make it more durable. Placemats make great presents to give relatives.

18. Create a "Me Mobile" with your child. Construct the mobile from clothes hangers and cardboard tubes. Interests, skills, and physical characteristics can all be depicted on the mobile using photos, magazine pictures, written descriptions, actual objects, and self-drawn pictures. Have your child hang lengths of yarn from the mobile descriptions of himself/herself.

19. Show your child how to create a "Time Line" of his/her life. On a long piece of wrapping paper or adding machine paper, have your child list in chronological order the life events he/she feels are significant to him/her (i.e. "the time we moved," "when brother was born," "when I broke my leg"). Remember not to evaluate the opinions. Use the activity as a tool for discussion.

20. Encourage your child's originality and creativity. Stress that everyone is different and has their own uniquenesses.

21. Stress that it's not your "outer appearance" that is important—it's your "inner appearance."

22. Show respect for your child's uniqueness. Point out how your child is unique/different from other family members. Capitalize upon it!

23. Convey to your child a true acceptance of him/her. Let your face show your love.

24. Teach your child a "feeling vocabulary" to describe emotions. Use words such as frustrated, joyous, jealous, resentful, empathetic, hostile, etc. Being able to use appropriate words to express feelings is often a healthy alternative to physical violence.

25. Help your child understand how his/her appearance can be improved. Point out when he/she is most attractive.

26. Encourage each family member to develop a special talent. Hold a family talent show to share each person's unique talents.

27. Whenever appropriate discuss the emotions displayed by characters in movies, books, or TV shows. Expand your child's vocabulary of emotions by correctly identifying each character's emotions.

28. Respect the fact that your child is different from his/her siblings. Try never to compare children (especially never in front of each other).

Esteem Builders' Complete Program
Jalmar Press, Rolling Hills Estates, CA

PARENT-TEACHER CONFERENCE TO ENHANCE SELFHOOD

Selfhood is a feeling of individuality. Acquiring self-knowledge, which includes an accurate and realistic self-description in terms of roles, attributes, and physical characteristics.

Student: _____   Date: _____

1. Low **selfhood** behavior characteristics the student is demonstrating: see page 255.

    •

    •

    •

2. **Selfhood** strengths the child is demonstrating:
   Demonstrating at Home: Demonstrating at School:

3. Choose one technique from the Home Esteem Builder Tip to Enhance **Selfhood**:
   Steps to Try at Home: Steps to Try at School:

4. The first thing we will do to make the plan happen:
   Home: Displayed at School:

Parent: _____

Teacher: _____

Esteem Builders' Complete Program
Jalmar Press, Rolling Hills Estates, CA

AFFILIATION

When a child feels unaffiliated he/she may indicate this with the following behaviors. It is normal to experience a few characteristics at one time or another. Have you noticed any of these behaviors lately with your own child? Are some characteristics more intense than others? Look for a pattern or an intensity of the characteristic.

_____ Difficulty initiating and maintaining friendships.

_____ Sometimes connects with objects rather than with people.

_____ Is easily influenced by others.

_____ Isolates self from the group; appears to be lonely.

_____ Is uncomfortable working in group settings which may result in behavior such as withdrawal, reticence, bullying, showing off, being silly, monopolizing, being uncooperative.

_____ Ridicules or rejects others; is insensitive to their emotions and needs.

_____ Feels that others don't value him/her.

_____ Relies on adult companionship as sole source of affiliation.

_____ May be especially vulnerable to peer pressure.

A child with a strong sense of affiliation is likely to display the following behaviors:

_____ Understands the concept of friendship and initiates new relationships.

_____ Shows sensitivity and compassion toward others.

_____ Demonstrates ability to cooperate and share.

_____ Is comfortable in group settings.

_____ Easily achieves peer acceptance and is sought out by others.

_____ Demonstrates appropriate social skills.

_____ Feels valued by others.

Affiliation is a feeling of belonging, acceptance, or relatedness in relationships that are considered important. Feeling approved of, appreciated, and respected by others.

Esteem Builders' Complete Program
Jalmar Press, Rolling Hills Estates, CA

Home Esteem-Builder Tips to Enhance Enhance Affiliation

1. Rebuild a feeling of family belonging. Take time to do fun things together.

2. Have your child keep track of his/her deeds of kindness.

3. Create an ongoing list with your child of things you can do to be a friend.

4. Reinforce your child's courteous behavior. Make it a practice to model good manners to your child.

5. Together role play appropriate social skills such as making an introduction, greeting someone, or saying good-bye.

6. Ask your child, "Who is someone you know who people really like to be with?" Now discuss with your child the specific behaviors this individual does which make people want to be with him/her.

7. Develop with your child a list of phrases and statements that can be used in social situations (i.e. to introduce themselves or a friend, to extend a conversation, to close a conversation).

8. Post a month's calendar in a highly visible location. Have your child keep track of friendly deeds and thoughts by writing them on the calendar the day they occurred.

9. Help your child become aware of how powerful smiles are as a social builder. Together look for others demonstrating great smiles.

10. Strengthen a feeling of family belonging. Ask your child to help you plan a family outing.

11. Build in your child an awareness of how important a family is. Talk about your family background and create family traditions.

12. Show your child how to resolve conflicts amicably.

13. Teach your child to avoid verbal attacks and to send "I messages" instead. Start the message with an "I." Next, tell the person how you feel ("I'm angry"). Finally, tell the person what he did that made you feel that way ("I'm angry because you took my pencil"). Now practice sending "I messages" to one another until everyone is comfortable using them.

14. Recognize your child for any cooperative behavior. "I really appreciate your cooperative behavior when you...." Remember to point out exactly what your child did well.

15. Leave a note under your child's pillow reinforcing his/her friendly behavior. "I noticed how friendly you were today when you were with....You...." (Tell your child exactly what he/she did well.)

16. Set up a bulletin board and stock it with pins and blank paper so that family members can exchange compliments. Encourage family members to recognize one another's friendly behaviors. Family members can write or draw compliments to one another on note paper.

17. Demonstrate good sportsmanship for your child. Play board games together and every once in a while deliberately lose. Role play with your child how to lose "gracefully."

Esteem Builders' Complete Program
Jalmar Press, Rolling Hills Estates, CA

Home Esteem-Builder Tips to Enhance Affiliation (continued)

18. Teach your child a few playground games (i.e. kickball, basketball, four square, hopscotch) so your child can successfully play games with peers at recess.

19. Label positive social behavior. Compliment actions in specific terms such as, "Helping Ryan with the dishes tonight was so helpful" or "Sharing your toys with your sister was thoughtful."

20. Watch a TV sitcom as a family. Deliberately look for characters demonstrating friendly behaviors. Discuss what those behaviors are.

21. As a family, do kind deeds for someone who may be lonely. Write a letter, visit, make a special present, or pick some flowers for them.

22. Teach your child it's all right to say "no." Role play saying no assertively to a peer who wants your child to do something he/she doesn't feel comfortable doing.

23. Together, find a pen pal your child can write to. Show your child how to develop a friendship through the mail.

24. Check out from the library and read *The Shy Child* by Philip Zimbardo. The book has excellent suggestions for parents to use with isolated or shy children.

25. Encourage your child to develop a relationship with a child who has similar interests. Provide them with opportunities for fun and successful experiences together.

26. Provide each family member with a piece of rug yarn a yard long. Call it a "Care Rope." Ask everyone to keep track of their caring, friendly deeds. Each time one is performed, invite them to tie a knot in the rope.

27. At the dinner table or other family gathering, reinforce friendly deeds. Ask, "Who's had someone do something friendly for them today? What was it and how did it make you feel?" Extend the discussion.

28. Go to the library together and ask the children's librarian to suggest a few selections of children's literature dealing with the concept of friendship. There are many (i.e. *Charlotte's Web* by E.B. White, *Friends* by Helme Heine, *Rosie and Michael* by Judith Viorst). Read the book together and identify the characters' friendly deeds.

29. Practice courteous phone manners (answering the phone, taking a message, extending a conversation, saying good-bye).

30. Frame a photo of your family and provide a copy to your child to keep in his/her room.

31. Start a family journal of memories and traditions. Each family member can take turns writing special family memories in the book.

32. Show your affection for your child in physical contact. Develop a special set of "family hugs," just for your family.

Esteem Builders' Complete Program
Jalmar Press, Rolling Hills Estates, CA

━ **HOME ESTEEM BUILDERS** ━

PARENT-TEACHER CONFERENCE
TO ENHANCE AFFILIATION

> *Affiliation is a feeling of belonging, acceptance, or relatedness in relationships that are considered important. Feeling approved of, appreciated, and respected by others.*

Student: _____   Date: _____

1. Low **affiliation** behavior characteristics the student is demonstrating: see page 259.

    •

    •

    •

2. **Affiliation** strengths the child is demonstrating:
   Demonstrating at Home: Demonstrating at School:

3. Choose one technique from the Home Esteem Builder Tip to Enhance **Affiliation**:
   Steps to Try at Home: Steps to Try at School:

4. The first thing we will do to make the plan happen:
   Home: Displayed at School:

Parent: _____

Teacher: _____

Esteem Builders' Complete Program
Jalmar Press, Rolling Hills Estates, CA

MISSION

A child with a weak sense of mission may indicate this with the following behaviors. It is normal to experience a few characteristics at one time or another. Have you noticed any of these behaviors lately with your own child? Are some characteristics more intense than others? Look for a pattern or an intensity of the characteristic.

_____ Lacks motivation and initiative.

_____ Cannot see alternatives or solutions.

_____ Feels powerless; therefore, may exhibit attention-getting behaviors, such as whining or tattling, to gain control.

_____ Appears aimless, without direction.

_____ Rarely succeeds due to poor goal-setting (goals are either too high, too low or nonexistent).

_____ Is overly dependent on others and feels incapable of being in charge and influencing others.

_____ Avoids taking responsibility for his/her own actions; blames others, denies or inveigles others to do his/her work.

_____ Is indecisive and seeks to avoid making own decisions.

A child with a strong sense of mission is likely to display the following behaviors:

_____ Appears purposeful with a clear sense of mission.

_____ Is self-directed; shows initiative.

_____ Takes responsibility for his/her own actions and recognizes the consequences.

_____ Is decisive because he/she feels sufficiently empowered to have influence over the outcome of decisions.

_____ Seeks alternative solutions to problems.

_____ Sets achievable and realistic goals.

_____ Accurately assesses current capabilities and skills as well as past performances.

Mission is a feeling of purpose and motivation in life. Self-empowerment through setting achievable goals and being willing to take responsibility for the consequences of one's decisions.

Home Esteem-Builder Tips
to Enhance Enhance Mission

1. Teach your child how to set realistic goals.

2. Model your own goals and dreams with your child.

3. At least once a month sit down with your child and ask, "What's a goal you're working on?" or "What's something you're trying to get better at?" Discuss ways your child could then achieve the goal. Periodically ask your child about the goal: "How's it going? Is there anything I can do to help?"

4. Ask your child, "When you make a mistake how do you feel?" Stress that everyone makes mistakes and that no one is perfect.

5. Discuss with your child a mistake you made in the past. Describe how you corrected it or what you did differently the next time.

6. Assign meaningful duties to each family member to help them acquire a sense of responsibility. Set up a reasonable list of chores for each family member. Reward responsible behavior.

7. Don't continue making excuses for negligent behavior that was really your child's responsibility. The message the child receives is, "Someone will fix it. I don't have to be responsible."

8. Help your child set up a daily schedule. Show him/her how to block out specific hours for important obligations. Your child could then be responsible for deciding how much time to allot for various activities.

9. Ask your child's opinion on how to solve a problem you're confronted with (i.e. the newspaper wasn't delivered, you've misplaced a phone number, an appliance broke down). How you handle everyday problems can be a valuable lesson for your child.

10. Give your child opportunities to practice making decisions. Allow him/her to choose the dinner menu, family chores, TV viewing schedules, or family outings.

11. Show your child how to weigh the options and consider all the possible alternatives to a potential decision. Role play the decision-making process with your child.

12. Consider a problem with your child. Now teach him/her to brainstorm all the possible ways to solve the problem. Together list all the choices. Remind your child that all ideas count and not to judge any solution as you're brainstorming.

13. Help your child recognize that decisions have consequences. The choices we make can affect not only ourselves but others as well.

14. Have your child set a long-term goal of something he/she wants to purchase or a skill he/she wishes to obtain. A long-term goal should take at least three weeks to a month to obtain (much longer for older children). Ask your child to draw the goal or paste a magazine picture of it on a piece of paper. Hang the picture in a visible location so that everyone in the family can remember the goal. Help your child reach the goal.

Esteem Builders' Complete Program
Jalmar Press, Rolling Hills Estates, CA

Home Esteem-Builder Tips to Enhance Mission (continued)

15. Ask a children's librarian to suggest books at your child's reading level dealing with problems (*Swimmy* by Leo Lionni, *The Blanket That Had to Go* by Nancy Evans Cooney, *The Hatchet* by Gary Paulsen are just a few). Read the book together and stop before the character solves the problem. Brainstorm together things the character could do to solve the problem. Remember, everything counts! Now read the ending together.

16. Ask family members to share a goal they're dreaming of achieving. Now ask, "How can we make that dream become real?"

17. Together read in the newspaper an appropriate "Dear Abby" problem. Omit reading the printed solution. Now take turns pretending you are Dear Abby. What advice would you offer the letter writer? Now read the solution.

18. Develop ways to monitor your child's progress as he/she works toward achieving a goal. Have frequent private conferences to evaluate progress and see what kind of support is needed.

19. Ask your child to predict the amount of time a particular assignment will take. Note the time. At the completion of the task, ask him/her to compare the predicted time with the actual time required for completion.

20. Begin goal-setting with your child by setting a short-term goal (a goal that can be achieved within a day or two), then gradually help him/her set goals with longer time frames.

21. Practice problem solving as a family. Identify a problem (real or fictional). On different strips of cut-up notepaper, brainstorm ways to solve the problem. Write a different solution on each strip.

22. Obtain a copy of the children's magazine *Sports Illustrated for Kids*. Read the article "My Worst Moment and How I Overcame It," written each month by a famous sports figure. Point out how everyone has mistakes in their past but successful people learn from them.

23. Fold a piece of paper in half. On one side of the paper write, "What I Like," and on the other side write, "What I Want to Change." Explain there are some things we can change (i.e. haircut, dress style, study habits, and behavior) and other things that are "givens" (i.e. eye color, race, physical characteristics). Now help your child write words or phrases on each side of the folded halves answering the questions.

24. Talk about a problem you once had and how you dealt with it.

25. Teach your child to organize homework. Have him/her keep track of assignments in a small notebook by filling out the assignment for each subject and the date it is due. Finally, when the assignment is completed, encourage your child to check it off.

26. Encourage your child to keep track of their progress toward a goal for a month. Write the goal that he/she wishes to achieve for that month at the top of a calendar page. Remind your child each day to note his/her progress by making a plus or minus sign.

27. Remind your child that they are responsible for how they feel. Acknowledge behavior that demonstrates "maturity," such as admitting mistakes, acknowledging responsibility for actions, taking the blame for a problem instead of blaming others. These are all signs of maturity.

PARENT-TEACHER CONFERENCE
TO ENHANCE MISSION

Mission is a feeling of purpose and motivation in life. Self-empowerment through setting achievable goals and being willing to take responsibility for the consequences of one's decisions.

Student: _____   Date: _____

1. Low **mission** behavior characteristics the student is demonstrating: see page 263.

    •

    •

    •

2. **Mission** strengths the child is demonstrating:
   Demonstrating at Home: Demonstrating at School:

3. Choose one technique from the Home Esteem Builder Tip to Enhance **Mission**:
   Steps to Try at Home: Steps to Try at School:

4. The first thing we will do to make the plan happen:
   Home: Displayed at School:

Parent: _____

Teacher: _____

Esteem Builders' Complete Program
Jalmar Press, Rolling Hills Estates, CA

COMPETENCE

When a child feels incompetent he/she may indicate this with the following behaviors. It is normal to experience a few characteristics at one time or another. Have you noticed any of these behaviors lately with your own child? Are some characteristics more intense than others? Look for a pattern or an intensity of the characteristic.

_____ Is reluctant to contribute ideas or opinions.

_____ Is unwilling to take risks.

_____ Acts helpless; is dependent in areas where he/she can or should be competent.

_____ Acts out in areas where he/she feels incompetent by resisting, defying, daydreaming, cheating, or by displaying frustration, withdrawal, or lack of participation.

_____ Does not attempt many tasks because of overriding fear of failure or insecurity (displays "I can't" attitude and doesn't try).

_____ Is a poor loser; magnifies any loss or displays poor sportsmanship.

_____ Uses negative self-statements regarding accomplishments and may discount or discredit any achievement.

_____ Maximizes failures and minimizes successes.

A child with a strong sense of competence is likely to display the following behaviors:

_____ Doesn't easily give up in the face of obstacles.

_____ Seeks out challenges; takes risks.

_____ Accepts weaknesses and uses mistakes as learning tools.

_____ Is aware of strengths and positive characteristics.

_____ Generally feels successful at things deemed important.

_____ Eagerly shares opinions and ideas.

_____ Displays good sportsmanship; can handle defeat.

_____ Recognizes accomplishments and achievements, and may verbalize or internalize positive self-statements regarding them.

Competence is a feeling of capableness and self-efficacy in things regarded as important or valuable. Awareness of strengths and ability to accept weaknesses and effectively manage life's challenges.

Esteem Builders' Complete Program
Jalmar Press, Rolling Hills Estates, CA

Home Esteem-Builder Tips
to Enhance Enhance Competence

1. Help your child recognize and acknowledge when he/she does something well.

2. Ask your child to name things he/she does well. Help him/her add to the list.

3. At bedtime have a "Strength Talk." Hold your child's hand in yours and say, "There are so many things you do well. Then name a strength as you touch each finger. If you wish, you can write the strength on his/her fingers with a watercolor pen.

4. Be sure the task you want your child to learn is one that he/she is ready to learn. For instance, we don't push a two-wheeler on a child until he/she is developmentally ready. Is the task you've set one he/she really can achieve or should you start a step or two lower?

5. Capture special moments when your child demonstrates achievements. You could photograph, videotape, record, or write about them. Set aside a special box or folder for your child to store his/her accomplishments or achievements.

6. Celebrate family achievements that are special. How about a unique placemat or plate for the "achiever" to eat on? Everyone in the family instantly knows there's something to celebrate when the placemat or plate is put out.

7. Acknowledge your child for an accomplishment by saying, "I knew you could do it." This reinforces your child's confidence.

8. Set high but realistic standards.

9. Show your child how school assignments affect his/her life.

10. Set up a consistent homework schedule. Create a space as well as materials needed for successful study habits.

11. Ask questions to help your child evaluate himself/herself realistically. "Last week how well did you do?" or "How many did you get right?" or "How does your running time this week compare to last week's time?"

12. Teach your child to praise himself/herself for a job well done. After a success say, "Wow, you did a great job. Did you remember to tell yourself you did well?"

13. Ask your child to make a list of things he/she would like to learn. This could be a skill or a special area of interest. Encourage your child to develop the skill. Provide the materials your child may need to learn the skill or find out more about an area of interest.

14. Invite your child to spend the day with you at work. Discuss together the kinds of skills needed for the job as well as any special training or education.

15. If your child has expressed a desire for a particular future occupation, find an adult in this occupation and set up an opportunity for your child to meet him/her.

16. Have your child keep a journal or scrapbook of his/her accomplishments.

Esteem Builders' Complete Program
Jalmar Press, Rolling Hills Estates, CA

Home Esteem-Builder Tips to Enhance Competence (continued)

17. Each week discuss your child's homework papers with him/her. Together find at least one thing that demonstrates growth or improvement in a particular skill.

18. Provide your child with the opportunity to experience all forms of artistic expression—music, art, poetry, literature, etc.

19. Whenever you hear "I can't" from your child, remember that very often what he/she really means is, "I can't do it perfectly." Help your child begin by pointing out the first thing he/she could do to get started.

20. Clearly communicate to your child exactly what you expect from his/her performance. It's important that you have expectations but remember they should be reachable. When your child performs below his/her capabilities, have him/her redo the work to meet your expected standards.

21. Periodically reinforce hard work with a special treat or privilege.

22. Acknowledge special talents or skills your child possesses by saying, "I noticed how good you are at...because you...." Point out the talent but also identify exactly what your child does well.

23. Express confidence in your child's ability to succeed. Encourage your child to stretch to meet new challenges. Convey your belief in him/her.

24. Ask a children's librarian to suggest biographies written at your child's level about famous individuals who overcame obstacles. These might include Thomas Alva Edison, Helen Keller, or Abe Lincoln. Read the selection together and discuss the individual.

25. Rent a video such as *Hoosiers* or *The Miracle Worker*. View it as a family and discuss why some people are successful. Emphasize the qualities of perseverance and hard work.

26. Create an atmosphere that encourages family members to try and reach new heights of proficiency.

27. Have your child keep track of weekly grades in a particular subject for a long period of time. Point out improvement in a skill or create a specific plan as to how grades could be improved.

28. With your child, create a "Self-Collage" on a large piece of paper depicting his/her strengths and talents. Use personal drawings or magazine words or pictures. Ask family members to add to the list.

29. When you notice your child having problems at school or with homework, set up a conference with the teacher as soon as possible. Don't wait.

30. Increase your child's chances of experiencing success by means of planned activities. Achievements or accomplishments are self-esteem enhancers. Provide opportunities for your child to succeed.

31. Teach your child a new skill. Be sure you demonstrate the skill by modeling it. As you break down the skill step by step, simultaneously tell your child exactly what you are doing. The child learns through both words and example.

Esteem Builders' Complete Program
Jalmar Press, Rolling Hills Estates, CA

PARENT-TEACHER CONFERENCE
TO ENHANCE COMPETENCE

Competence is a feeling of capableness and self-efficacy in things regarded as important or valuable. Awareness of strengths and ability to accept weaknesses and effectively manage life's challenges.

Student: _____   Date: _____

1. Low **competence** behavior characteristics the student is demonstrating: see page 267.

    •

    •

    •

2. **Competence** strengths the child is demonstrating:
   Demonstrating at Home: Demonstrating at School:

3. Choose one technique from the Home Esteem Builder Tip to Enhance **Competence**:
   Steps to Try at Home: Steps to Try at School:

4. The first thing we will do to make the plan happen:
   Home: Displayed at School:

Parent: _____

Teacher: _____

Esteem Builders' Complete Program
Jalmar Press, Rolling Hills Estates, CA

BEFORE CONFERENCE LETTER

Dear _____

    I am looking forward to meeting with you at our scheduled conference on _____ *at* _____. *This is an excellent time for us to discuss your child's school progress and the academic and behavior goals we'd like to set for this year. To make our time together be as productive as possible, I have provided a list of the areas I'd like to talk about with you:*

- *Identify positive strengths and qualities about your child.*
- *Review your child's academic progress for this report period, including report card grades.*
- *Discuss your child's self-esteem and its impact on achievement and behavior.*
- *Answer your questions and concerns.*
- *Agree upon one area that needs improvement to help your child in school. Develop a plan together on what we will do to help your child improve.*

    If you have a special topic in mind that I have not included, please jot it down on the bottom of the form and send it back to school prior to our scheduled meeting.

Sincerely,

Esteem Builders' Complete Program
Jalmar Press, Rolling Hills Estates, CA

PARENT- STUDENT-TEACHER CONFERENCE

Student: _____

Teacher: _____

Parent: _____

Date: _____

SUBJECT	PROGRESS	WAYS TO IMPROVE

Esteem Builders' Complete Program
Jalmar Press, Rolling Hills Estates, CA

PARENT-TEACHER CONFERENCE

Student: _____

Date: _____

1. Strengths, interests or assets of the child:
   Displayed at Home: Displayed at School:

2. Choose one strength observable at home and school to reinforce and help the child become aware of:

3. Agree on one area needing improvement to help the child in school:

4. Plan to make this happen.
   Steps to Try at Home: Steps to Try at School:

5. How the parent and teacher will know the plan is working:

6. Ways we will celebrate the child's progress:

7. The first thing we will do to make the plan happen:
   Home: Displayed at School:

Parent: _____

Teacher: _____

Esteem Builders' Complete Program
Jalmar Press, Rolling Hills Estates, CA

HOME ESTEEM BUILDERS

SELF-ESTEEM PRESCRIPTIVE PLAN

Student: _____   Teacher: _____   Date: _____

	STRENGTHS	WEAKNESSES	STRATEGIES FOR GROWTH
Security			
Selfhood			
Affiliation			
Mission			
Competence			

Esteem Builders' Complete Program
Jalmar Press, Rolling Hills Estates, CA

STUDENT SELF-ESTEEM PROFILE

Student _____ Teacher _____ Date_____

Read the descriptive words below which are components of high and low self-esteem. Rate your child high if she/he demonstrates this behavior consistently and low if he/she does not demonstrate this behavior. Place an ✖ on the place on each line which you feel most adequately depicts your child's current behavior.

High ————————✖———————— Low

HIGH SELF-ESTEEM

• Self-confident	High ———————————	Low
• Secure with self	High ———————————	Low
• Face and manner project enjoyment of life	High ———————————	Low
• Flexible to situations and challenges	High ———————————	Low
• Open and receptive to new ideas	High ———————————	Low
• Makes friends easily	High ———————————	Low
• Assumes responsibility for self	High ———————————	Low
• Independent	High ———————————	Low
• Experiments with new materials	High ———————————	Low
• Speaks of accomplishments or short-comings with honesty	High ———————————	Low
• Open to criticism and comfortable about acknowledging mistakes	High ———————————	Low
• Defends self well against demeaning by others	High ———————————	Low
• Effective in coping with problems and demands	High ———————————	Low

LOW SELF-ESTEEM

• Difficulty making decisions	High ———————————	Low
• Seldom shows initiative	High ———————————	Low
• Withdraws from others	High ———————————	Low
• Does not resist social pressures	High ———————————	Low
• Dependent on others	High ———————————	Low
• Excessive timidity	High ———————————	Low
• Exhibits anxiety and anxiousness	High ———————————	Low
• Self-conscious when talking with others	High ———————————	Low
• Pessimistic and worries about future	High ———————————	Low
• Expects to fail	High ———————————	Low
• Lacks self-confidence	High ———————————	Low
• Puts down others and self	High ———————————	Low
• Fearful of new situations	High ———————————	Low
• Excessive bragging	High ———————————	Low
• Extreme need for encouragement and recognition	High ———————————	Low
• Reluctant to express ideas or opinions	High ———————————	Low
• Overly sensitive to criticism	High ———————————	Low

Esteem Builders' Complete Program
Jalmar Press, Rolling Hills Estates, CA

STUDENT SELF-ESTEEM SURVEY

Student: _____

Teacher: _____

Date: _____

	😊 Always	😐 Sometimes	😟 Never

SECURITY

	Always	Sometimes	Never
I trust a teacher at this school.	____	____	____
Changes in daily routine are easy for me.	____	____	____
This school is a safe and secure place to be.	____	____	____
I like new experiences.	____	____	____

SELFHOOD

	Always	Sometimes	Never
I like the way I look.	____	____	____
I like it when others praise me.	____	____	____
I'm comfortable with the way I dress.	____	____	____
It's easy for me to tell others how I feel.	____	____	____

AFFILIATION

	Always	Sometimes	Never
It's easy to make new friends.	____	____	____
I feel sorry when someone is hurt.	____	____	____
I like to cooperate and share in a group.	____	____	____
Other people like me.	____	____	____

MISSION

	Always	Sometimes	Never
I like to figure things out on my own.	____	____	____
I do my work without getting told.	____	____	____
I'm responsible for what I do.	____	____	____
I like to set goals.	____	____	____

COMPETENCE

	Always	Sometimes	Never
I like to share ideas in class.	____	____	____
I like to try new things.	____	____	____
I know what I'm good at.	____	____	____
I know my weaknesses.	____	____	____

* Permission for reuse approved by Cheryl Graves at Campbell Elementary, Arvada, CO.

Esteem Builders' Complete Program
Jalmar Press, Rolling Hills Estates, CA

Notes

Home Esteem Builders was developed on the premise that a home and school partnership is an integral element of effective esteem building. The material in this book provides educators with the resources to help parents enhance their children's self-esteem. Before distributing any of these materials to the students' homes, please make sure that they have been translated into the primary language of the parents.

Conclusion

*One must never lose time in vainly regretting the past
nor in complaining about the changes which cause us
discomfort, for change is the very essence of life.*

—ANATOLE FRANCE

There is an old superstition about the ocean that has been passed on from generation to generation. According to the story, every so often one wave comes along which is greater than any of the other waves that came before it. It's called the Ninth Wave, and the belief behind this myth is that there is no greater force. This wave is especially powerful because it derives its strength from the wind and sea working together in a special way. To catch the Ninth Wave at just the right moment requires perfect timing; the action must coincide precisely with the movement of the wave. Today there is such a powerful Ninth Wave within the reach of educators and to catch it could bring about significant educational change. To benefit from this wave, educators must prepare, recognizing how they can create this change so that when it's time to mount, they will be able to respond and ride the wave all the way to the top. The wave must be ridden full force, with no slipping backwards.

When educators catch that Ninth Wave, they cannot act alone: the ride they embark upon must be a collaborative venture in esteem building with the students' parents. As many hours as educators teach children and implement self-esteem enhancement techniques in the classroom, those children return nightly to the same environment that may or may not be conducive to esteem building. For educators to move forward in their effectiveness at enhancing student self-esteem, it is obvious that parents *must* be trained and involved in the esteem-building process. There is no denying that parents are an integral part of their children's school success. One of the greatest opportunities educators have to enhance the overall performance of their students is by teaching parents esteem-building principles that can be used at home.

Newspapers and the television media report constantly on the educational plight of today's youth. Economist Victor Fuchs and researcher Diane Reklis in a recent article published in the *Journal of Science* verified: "American children are in trouble....Both cultural and material changes have probably contributed to the problem." Researchers have pointed out several significant changes that have happened to American youth since 1960:

- Suicides and murders among teenagers have tripled;

- The percentage of girls under fifteen who have had sex has also tripled;

- Three in five children born today will live with a single parent by age eighteen;

- One student in six by ninth grade has tried marijuana, and one in three alcohol;

- Twenty-eight percent of students fail to complete high school;

- The percentage of children living in poverty in the United States has increased from one in twenty to one in five; and,

- SAT scores have dropped four percent in math and ten percent in verbal skills.[1]

The peril for students lies not only in a drop in test scores and a rise in behavioral problems but in another score that is, unfortunately, not such a large focus of the media. Young people's self-esteem is suffering as well. In fact, statistics point to a growing epidemic of low self-esteem. According to research conducted by The Gallup Organization, two out of three Americans suffer low self-esteem. LeRoy Foster, executive director of the National Council for Self-Esteem, points out these shattering facts regarding how students feel about themselves: "Four-fifths of children entering school feel good about themselves. By fifth grade, however, that figure drops to twenty percent, and by the twelfth grade it is only five percent. In another study involving 2,000 kids in 120 high schools the top two problems teenagers face were found to be loneliness and not liking themselves."[2] The latest studies released by the American Association of University Women provide additional confirmation regarding the low self-esteem epidemic plaguing our students. In a survey of over 3,000 girls in grades four through ten, researchers discovered a startling fact: "The longer American girls remain in our school systems, the lower their self-esteem becomes."[3]

The process of instituting an effective home-school esteem-building program involves a tremendous amount of time and energy. A legitimate question of the staff planners, therefore, should always be, "Can a school-initiated parent education program help parents affect the academic success of their children in a significant way?" In other words, "Is the program worth the time and energy and will students make educational gains?" One of the most hopeful research projects recently conducted on the impact parent education can have on students'

school achievement was described by Dr. T. Lee Burnham in *The Home & School Connection.* The home-school education project Burnham referred to involved three hundred students who had been identified by their teachers as being "classroom behavior problems." Researchers randomly divided the students into three groups. Each group received a different form of treatment for the same period of time. One third of the students were given counseling and tutoring. Another third received the same kind of counseling and tutoring as the first group; in addition, the students' parents and teachers were given special mentoring and training. The final group of students received no special help; they were completely left alone. Instead attention was focused specifically on their parents and teachers, who were given special training to help improve these children's achievement and behavior. Researchers found that the only group of students to show any significant behavior improvement was the last group.[4] This finding is significant for educators. It clearly tells us that educating parents and teachers as joint partners in techniques to enhance student behavior and achievement can have significant effects on improving students' educational performance.

Educators need to recognize that they do need help from students' parents. Too much valuable time is directed at finding fault or deciding where the blame lies for today's troubled educational system. Such exercises are inevitably futile and energy-draining. To achieve results in the lives of students, educators and parents must work together toward constructive and creative solutions. Schools may well need to change some of their thinking patterns and revamp some of their current policies regarding parent involvement in order to become more inviting toward the participation of parents in their children's education. Educators often voice the concern, "Parents just aren't involved anymore,"

1. "Survey: American Children Are in Trouble." *EDCAL.* Burlingame, CA: California School Administrators, vol. 23, no. 21, January 20, 1992, p. 4.

2. Foster, LeRoy. "Self-Esteem: The Core of Success and Happiness." *Adolescent Counselor.* Redmond, WA: A & D Publications Corp., vol. 4, no. 5, January 1992, p. 29.

3. "The AAUW Report: How Schools Shortchange Girls." Released by the American Association of University Women Educational Foundation, February 12, 1992 at the National Educational Summit on Girls, Washington, DC.

4. Burnham, T. Lee, Dr. *The Home & School Connection: How Your Home Life Affects Your Child's Success At School.* Utah: Shadow Mountain, 1986.

but, periodically, the school staff must consciously step back and pose a serious question to themselves, "What are we doing to encourage parents to work *with* us?" More specifically, the following issues need to be addressed:

- **Time Constraints.** Most businesses today offer flexible hours to accommodate the majority of families in which both parents work. Is the school offering such time flexibility? Could it be that parent involvement is low due to the times the programs are offered?

- **Relevance of Parent Programs.** Most parents want to help their children succeed. This is a basic premise of parenting. In other words, parents want to know how they can do a better job of raising their children. The school must always ask, "Are we offering the type of parent education programs that concern our parents?" or, even more importantly, "Do we know the needs of our parents? Have we taken the time to ask how we can help?"

- **Parental Constraints.** Yes, parent turnout for school events is typically on the low side these days. Before using the low turnout size as a reason to end school-sponsored parenting programs, the staff must seriously analyze all the conditions that may be contributing to low attendance. A few issues include:

1. *The Time and Dates.* Are there other scheduled events (work, sports, recreational, political, religious, cultural, etc.) that may be conflicting with the school-sponsored dates?

2. *Transportation Issues.* Do all parents have transportation to the activity?

3. *Child Care.* Are parents not coming because they are unable to find adequate child care during the parent programs? Is there a way the school can provide such services?

4. *Language Barriers.* Are the native languages of all the parents known? Are translators available for the activity?

5. *Inviting Atmosphere.* Many parents are actually threatened by the school. Repeated negative encounters with the staff regarding their children do not lend themselves to increased parent involvement. If parents have become discouraged and defeated, the school must empathize with parents to turn this scenario around. In too many cases, it's the parents who have dropped out of our system long before the students.

If the school seriously wishes to increase parent participation, it is essential to analyze all factors that could detract from it. Now, more than ever, educators must plan creative alternatives to accommodate the changes in today's American families.

A home-school collaboration committed to the educational enhancement of students does have positive effects on youth. Parents *can* and *do* significantly affect the self-esteem, achievement, and behavior of their children. *Home Esteem Builders* helps educators ensure that the parent-student impact is positive and that parents know how to create an environment which encourages the development of their children's self-esteem. While certainly not meant as a cure-all for home parenting, *Home Esteem Builders* is a first step toward a much needed delivery system of educating parents in the principles of esteem enhancement.

Building a home and school educational partnership that is truly collaborative is no easy task. Planners must never create a mind set that the process is one of ease and simplicity. Obstacles and frustrations are natural outcomes of any institutional change. I recognize that the task is enormous, but I also strongly believe that education is one of the best hopes this society has of changing the tide for today's students. The spirit that "we can create such a partnership" with parents so that children can succeed better, not only in school but also in life, must always be kept alive. After all, it was the good witch Glenda from the Wizard of Oz who countered Dorothy Gale's concern that she'd never get back to Kansas with, "Silly girl, you've always had the power, you just didn't *want* hard enough." Educators can use Glenda's advice in their quest to develop more effective parental enhancement of children's self-esteem. Never has there proven to be a time when youth are in such peril of emotional distress. Never has there been a time in the existence of public education when educators' concerns for their students' futures are more justified. Yet, never has there been a time when educators can have such an impact on the lives of generations of students. The reality is that the school may well be the last social agency that can create change for today's youth. I say to all educators, "If you *want hard enough,* you can open doors in your students' lives by inviting their parents to learn life-touching esteem-building principles along with you. You've always had the power. You need only commit yourselves as a force and do it. What an impact that wave will create when it smashes against the shore!"

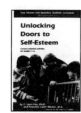

DISCOVER materials for positive self-esteem.
CREATE a positive environment in your classroom or home by opening a world of understanding.

Good Morning Class - I Love You (Staff)

Contains thought provoking quotes and questions about *teaching from the heart.* Helps love become an integral part of the learning that goes on in every classroom. Great for new teachers and for experienced teachers who sometimes become frustrated by the system. Use this book to begin and end your day. Greet your students every day with: *"Good morning class - I love you."*

0-915190-58-3, 80 pages, **JP-9058-3 $7.95**
5½ x 8½, paperback, illus./**Button $1.50**

Enhancing Educator's Self-Esteem: It's Criteria #1 (Staff)

For the educator, a *healthy self-esteem* is job criterion No. 1! When high, it empowers us and adds to the vitality of our lives; when low it saps energy, erodes our confidence, lowers productivity and blocks our initiative to care about self and others. Follow the *plan of action* in this great resource to develop your self-esteem.

0-915190-79-6, 144 pages, **JP-9079-6 $16.95**
8½ x 11, paperback

NEW

Enhancing The Educator's Self-Esteem It's Your Criteria #1

By Bettie B. Youngs, Ph.D.

Bettie B. Youngs, Ph.D.

NOT JUST AUTHORS BUT RESEARCHERS AND PRACTITIONERS.

I Am a Blade of Grass (Staff)

Create a school where all — students, teachers, administrators, and parents — see themselves as both learners and leaders *in partnership. Develop* a new *compact for learning* that focuses on results, that promotes *local initiative* and that *empowers* people at all levels of the system. How to in this *collaborative curriculum.* Great for self-esteem.

0-915190-54-0, 176 pages, **JP-9054-0 $14.95**
6 x 9, paperback, illustrations

Stress Management for Educators: A Guide to Manage Our Response to Stress (Staff)

Answers these significant questions for educators: *What is stress? What causes it? How do I cope with it? What can be done to manage stress to moderate its negative effects? Can stress be used to advantage? How can educators be stress-proofed* to help them remain at *peak performance? How do I keep going in spite of it?*

0-915190-77-X, 112 pages, **JP-9077-X $12.95**
8½ x 11, paperback, illus., charts

NEW

STRESS MANAGEMENT FOR EDUCATORS

A Guide to Manage Your Response to Stress
By Bettie B. Youngs, Ph.D.

Bettie B. Youngs, Ph.D.

NOT JUST WRITTEN BUT PROVEN EFFECTIVE.

He Hit Me Back First: Self-Esteem Through Self-Discipline (Gr. K-8)

By whose authority does a child choose right from wrong? Here are *activities* directed toward *developing* within the child an *awareness* of his own *inner authority* and ability to choose (will power) and the resulting sense of *responsibility, freedom* and *self-esteem.* 29 separate activities.

0-915190-64-8, 120 pages, **JP-9064-8 $12.95**
8½ x 11, paperback, appendix, biblio.

Let's Get Together! (Gr. K-6)

Making friends is *easy* with the activities in this thoroughly researched book. Students are paired, get to know about each other, produce a book about their new *friend,* and present it in class. Exciting activities help discover commonalities. Great *self-esteem* booster. Revised after 10 years of field testing. Over 150 activities in 18 lessons.

0-915190-75-3, 192 pages, **JP-9075-3 $19.95**
8½ x 11, paperback, illustrations, activities

NEW

Grades K - 6

LET'S GET TOGETHER!
Activities for Developing Friendship and Self-Esteem in the Elementary Grades
Affiliation/Belonging as Techniques that Work
C. Lynn Fox, Ph.D.

C. Lynn Fox, Ph.D.

100% TESTED — 100% PRACTICAL — 100% GUARANTEED.

Feel Better Now: 30 Ways to Handle Frustration in Three Minutes or Less (Staff/Personal)

Teaches people to *handle stress as it happens* rapidly and directly. This basic requirement for *emotional survival* and *physical health* can be learned with the methods in this book. Find your own recipe for relief. Foreword: Ken Keyes, Jr. *"A mine of practical help"* — says Rev. Robert Schuller.

0-915190-66-4, 180 pages, **JP-9066-4 $9.95**
6 x 9, paperback, appendix, bibliography

Peace in 100 Languages: A One-Word Multilingual Dictionary (Staff/Personal)

A candidate for the Guinness Book of World Records, it is the *largest/smallest dictionary ever published.* Envisioned, researched and developed by *Russian peace activists.* Ancient, national, local and special languages covered. A portion of purchase price will be donated to joint U.S./Russian peace project. **Peace Button $1.50**

0-915190-74-5, 48 pages, **JP-9074-5 $9.95**
5 x 10, glossy paperback, full color

NEW

ONE WORD MULTILINGUAL DICTIONARY

PEACE IN 100 LANGUAGES

By:
M. Kabattchenko,
V. Kochurov,
L. Koshanova,
E. Kononenko,
D. Kuznetsov,
A. Lapitsky,
V. Monakov.
L. Stoupin, and
A. Zagorsky

Shalom • Paz
PEACE! Paix • Vrede

ORDER NOW FOR 10% DISCOUNT ON 3 OR MORE TITLES.

The Learning Revolution (Adult)

A revolution is changing your life and your world. Here's a book that tells how this revolution is taking shape in America and how it can give us the world's best educational system by the year 2000. That revolution is gathering speed -- a revolution that can help us learn anything five times faster, better, and easier. A must reading for parents, teachers and business people.

Hardback, JP9634-3 $29.95
6 x 9, many quotes, biblio., 528 pages

Reading, Writing and Rage (Staff)

An autopsy of one profound *school failure,* disclosing the complex processes behind it and the *secret rage* that grew out of it. Developed from educational therapist's viewpoint. A must reading for anyone working with the *learning disabled, functional illiterates* or *juvenile delinquents.* Reads like fiction. Foreword by Bruce Jenner.

0-915190-42-7, 240 pages, **JP-9042-7 $16.95**
5½ x 8½, paperback, biblio., resources

Reading, Writing and RAGE

D. Ungerleider, M.A.

DISCOVER books on self-esteem for kids.
ENJOY great reading with Warm Fuzzies and Squib, the adventurous owl.

Larry Shles, M.A.

Moths & Mothers/Feathers & Fathers: The Story of Squib, The Owl, Begins (Ages 5-105)

Heartwarming story of a tiny owl who cannot fly or hoot as he learns to put words with his feelings. He faces frustration, grief, fear, guilt and loneliness in his life, just as we do. Struggling with these *feelings*, he searches, at least, for *understanding*. *Delightfully illustrated*. Ageless.

0-915190-57-5, 72 pages, **JP-9057-5** **$7.95**
8½ x 11, paperback, illustrations

Hoots & Toots & Hairy Brutes: The Continuing Adventures of Squib, The Owl (Ages 5-105)

Squib, who can only toot, sets out to learn how to give a mighty hoot. Even the *owl-odontist* can't help and he fails completely. Every reader who has struggled with *life's limitations* will recognize his own *struggles* and *triumphs* in the microcosm of Squib's forest world. A parable for all ages.

0-915190-56-7, 72 pages, **JP-9056-7** **$7.95**
8½ x 11, paperback, illustrations

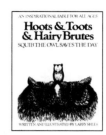

Larry Shles, M.A.

NOT JUST AUTHORS BUT RESEARCHERS AND PRACTITIONERS.

Larry Shles, M.A.

Hugs & Shrugs: The Continuing Saga of Squib, The Owl (Ages 5-105)

Squib feels *lonely, depressed* and *incomplete*. His reflection in the pond shows that he has lost a piece of himself. He thinks his missing piece fell out and he searches in vain outside of himself to find it. Only when he discovers that it fell in and not out does he *find inner-peace* and *become whole*. Delightfully illustrated. Ageless.

0-915190-47-8, 72 pages, **JP-9047-8** **$7.95**
8½ x 11, paperback, illustrations

Aliens in my Nest: Squib Meets the Teen Creature (Ages 5-105)

What does it feel like to face a snarly, surly, defiant and non-communicative older brother turned *adolescent*? Friends, dress code, temperament, entertainment, room decor, eating habits, authority, music, isolation, *internal and external conflict* and many other *areas of change* are *dealt with*. Explores how to handle every situation.

0-915190-49-4, 80 pages, **JP-9049-4** **$7.95**
8½ x 11, paperback, illustrations

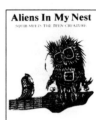

Larry Shles, M.A.

NOT JUST WRITTEN BUT PROVEN EFFECTIVE.

Larry Shles, M.A.

Do I Have to Go to School Today? Squib Measures Up! (Ages 5-105)

Squib *dreads* going to *school*. He day-dreams about all the reasons he has not to go: the school bus will swallow him, the older kids will be mean to him, numbers and letters confuse him, he is too small for sports, etc. But, in the end, he *goes because* his *teacher accepts him "just as he is."* Very esteeming. Great metaphor for all ages.

0-915190-62-1, 64 pages, **JP-9062-1** **$7.95**
8½ x 11, paperback, illustrations

Scooter's Tail of Terror
A Fable of Addiction and Hope (Ages 5-105)

Well-known author and illustrator, Larry Shles, introduces a new forest character — a squirrel named Scooter. He faces the challenge of addiction, but is offered a way to overcome it. As with the Squib books, the story is *simple*, yet the message is *dramatic*. The story touches the child within each reader and *presents the realities of addiction*.

0-915190-89-3, 80 pages, **JP-9089-3** **$9.95**
8½ x 11, paperback, illustrations

Larry Shles, M.A.

100% TESTED — 100% PRACTICAL — 100% GUARANTEED.

Alvyn Freed, Ph.D.

TA for Tots (and other prinzes) Revised (Gr. PreK-3)

Over 500,000 sold. New upright format. Book has helped thousands of young *children* and their *parents* to better *understand* and *relate to each other*. Helps youngsters realize their *intrinsic worth* as human beings; builds and strengthens their *self-esteem*. *Simple* to understand.
Coloring Book $1.95 / I'm OK Poster $3

0-915190-73-7, 144 pages, **JP-9073-7** **$14.95**
8½ x 11, paperback, delightful illustrations

TA for Kids (and grown-ups too) (Gr. 4-9)

Over 250,000 sold. An ideal book to help youngsters *develop self-esteem*, esteem of others, *personal and social responsibility*, critical thinking and independent judgment. Book recognizes that each person is a unique human being with the capacity to learn, grow and develop. Hurray for TA! Great for parents and other care givers.

0-915190-09-5, 112 pages, **JP-9009-5** **$9.95**
8½ x 11, paperback, illustrations

Alvyn Freed, Ph.D.
& Margaret Freed

ORDER NOW FOR 10% DISCOUNT ON 3 OR MORE TITLES.

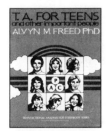

Alvyn Freed, Ph.D.

TA for Teens (and other important people) (Gr. 8-12)

Over 100,000 sold. The book that tells teenagers they're OK! Provides help in growing into adulthood in a mixed-up world. Contrasts freedom and irresponsibility with knowing that *youth need the skill, determination* and *inner strength* to reach *fulfillment* and *self-esteem*. No talking down to kids, here.

0-915190-03-6, 258 pages, **JP-9003-6** **$21.95**
8½ x 11, paperback, illustrations

The Original Warm Fuzzy Tale (Gr. Pre K-Adult)

Over 100,000 sold. The concept of Warm Fuzzies and Cold Pricklies originated in this delightful story. A *fairy tale* in every sense, *with* adventure, fantasy, heroes, villians and a *moral*. Children (and adults, too) will enjoy this beautifully illustrated book. **Warm Fuzzies, JP-9042 $0.99 each.**

0-915190-08-7, 48 pages, **JP-9008-7** **$8.95**
6 x 9, paperback, full color illustrations

Claude Steiner, Ph.D

OPEN your mind to wholebrain thinking and creative parenting.
GROW by leaps and bounds with our new ways to think and learn.

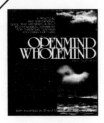

Openmind/Wholemind: Parenting and Teaching Tomorrow's Children Today (Staff/Personal)

Can we learn to *treat* the *brain/mind system* as *open* rather than closed? Can we learn to *use* all our *learning modalities, learning styles, creativities* and *intelligences* to create a product far greater than the sum of its parts? Yes! This primer for parents and teachers shows how.

Bob Samples, M.A.

0-915190-45-1, 272 pages, **JP-9045-1 $14.95**
7 x 10, paperback, 81 B/W photos, illust.

Unicorns Are Real: A Right-Brained Approach to Learning (Gr. K-Adult)

Over 100,000 sold. The *alternate methods* of *teaching/learning* developed by the author have helped literally thousands of children and adults with *learning difficulties*. A book of *simple ideas* and *activities* that are easy to use, yet dramatically effective. Video of techniques also available: **VHS, 1½ hrs., JP-9113-0 $149.95. Unicorn Poster $4.95.**

0-915190-35-4, 144 pages, **JP-9035-4 $12.95**
8½ x 11, paperback, illus., assessment

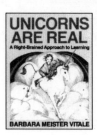

Barbara Meister Vitale, M.A.

NOT JUST AUTHORS BUT RESEARCHERS AND PRACTITIONERS.

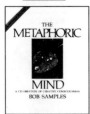

REVISED

Metaphoric Mind: A Celebration of Creative Consciousness (Revised) (Staff/Personal)

A plea for a balanced way of thinking and being in a culture that stands on the knife-edge between *catastrophe* and *transformation*. The metaphoric mind is *asking* again, quietly but insistently, *for equilibrium*. For, after all, equilibrium is the way of nature. A revised version of a classic.

Bob Samples, M.A.

0-915190-68-0, 208 pages, **JP-9068-0 $16.95**
7 x 9, paperback, B/W photos, illus.

Free Flight: Celebrating Your Right Brain (Staff/Personal)

Journey with Barbara Meister Vitale, from her uncertain childhood perceptions of being *"different"* to the acceptance and adult celebration of that difference. A how to *book for right-brained people in a left-brained world*. Foreword by Bob Samples- *"This book is born of the human soul."* Great gift item for your right-brained friends.

0-915190-44-3 , 128 pages, **JP-9044-3 $9.95**
5½ x 8½, paperback, illustrations

Barbara Meister Vitale, M.A.

NOT JUST WRITTEN BUT PROVEN EFFECTIVE.

NEW

Imagine That! Getting Smarter Through Imagery Practice (Gr. K-Adult)

Understand and *develop* your own *seven intelligences* in only minutes a day. Help children do the same. The results will amaze you. Clear, step-by-step ways show you how to create your own imagery exercises for any area of learning or life and how to *relate imagery* exercises *to curriculum content*.

Lane Longino Waas, Ph.D.

0-915190-71-0, 144 pages, **JP-9071-0 $12.95**
6 x 9, paperback, 42 B/W photos, biblio.

Becoming Whole (Learning) Through Games (Gr. K-Adult)

New ideas for old games. *Develop* your *child's brain power, motivation* and *self-esteem by playing*. An excellent parent/ teacher guide and skills checklist to 100 standard games. Included are auditory, visual, motor, directional, modality, attention, educational, social and memory skills. Great resource for care givers.

0-915190-70-2, 288 pages, **JP-9070-2 $16.95**
6 x 9, paperback, glossary, biblio.

NEW

Gwen Bailey Moore, Ph.D. & Todd Serby

100% TESTED — 100% PRACTICAL — 100% GUARANTEED.

Present Yourself: Great Presentation Skills (Staff/Personal)

Use *mind mapping* to become a presenter who is a dynamic part of the message. Learn about transforming fear, knowing your audience, setting the stage, making them remember and much more. *Essential reading* for anyone interested in *communication*. This book will become the standard work in its field. **Hardback, JP-9050-8 $16.95**

Michael J. Gelb, M.A.

0-915190-51-6, 128 pages, **JP-9051-6 $9.95**
6 x 9, paperback,illus., mind maps

The Two Minute Lover (Staff/Personal)

With wit, wisdom and compassion, "The Two-Minute Lovers" and their proteges guide you through the steps of *building* and *maintaining* an *effective relationship* in a *fast-paced world*. They offer encouragement, inspiration and practical techniques for living happily in a relationship, even when outside pressures are enormous. Done like the "One Minute Manager".

0-915190-52-4, 112 pages, **JP-9052-4 $9.95**
6 x 9, paperback, illustrations

Asa Sparks, Ph.D.

ORDER NOW FOR 10% DISCOUNT ON 3 OR MORE TITLES.

The Turbulent Teens: Understanding Helping, Surviving (Parents/Counselors)

Come to grips with the difficult issues of rules and the limits of parental tolerance, recognizing the necessity for *flexibility* that takes into consideration changes in the adolescent as well as the imperative *need for control*, agreed upon *expectations* and *accountability*. A must read! Useful in counseling situations.

James E. Gardner, Ph.D.

0-913091-01-4, 224 pages, **JP-9101-4 $8.95**
6 x 9, paperback, case histories

The Parent Book: Raising Emotionally Mature Children - Ages 3-15 (Parents)

Improve *positive bonding* with your child in five easy steps: *listen* to the feelings; *learn* the basic concern; *develop* an action plan; *confront* with support; *spend* 1 to 1 time. Ideas for helping in 4 *self-esteem* related areas: *awareness; relating; competence; integrity*. 69 sub-catagories. Learn what's missing and what to do about it.

0-915190-15-X, 208 pages, **JP-9015-X $9.95**
8½ x 11, paperback, illus., diag/Rx.

Harold Besell, Ph.D. & Thomas P. Kelly, Jr.

ORDER FROM: B.L. Winch & Associates/Jalmar Press, Skypark Business Center, 2675 Skypark Drive, Suite 204 , Torrance, CA 90505
CALL TOLL FREE — (800) 662-9662 • (310) 784-0016 • FAX (310) 784-1379 • Add 10% shipping; $3 minimum   1/94